Praise for
The Death of Inflation

"This highly readable book – Roger Bootle's economic thriller – is to be commended not only for its attempt to restore the balance of people's minds about the inflationary threat, but also as a vivid account of the state the world economy is now in."
William Keegan, New Statesman

"This is an interesting and timely book which constitutes a brilliant analysis of movements in inflation over the years and is clearly written in language which is comprehensible to the layman. Roger Bootle is to be congratulated upon having explained both the implications and advantages of living in a world of zero inflation, although he is careful to point out that the transition to that desirable state will engender considerable problems of adjustment and the final destination is likely to be something of a mixed blessing. However, it is in relation to financial assets that he conveys his direst warnings; since if inflation is truly dead but markets do not believe it, then the western world will be saddled with real interest rates high enough to threaten economic disaster. "
Nigel Forman MP

"Roger Bootle – economist, raconteur, wit and now book author – has written a thriller. A great read, formidably argued."
Bill Jamieson, The Sunday Telegraph

"Bootle's brisk, clearly written book provides a new slant on the economic terrain and spells out the implications of zero inflation for individuals, corporations, investors and governments, dispensing often unorthodox advice."
Publishers' Weekly

"I welcome this lively and lucid contribution to current economic debate by one of London's leading commentators, who has been among the first to perceive that inflation is yesterday's problem."
Peter Jay, BBC Economics Correspondent, former British Ambassador to the US

"Bootle's book is excellently written and thought-provoking. Even the tabular and graphic information is stimulating, with the historical data he provides particularly fascinating."
David Fairlamb, Institutional Investor

Also by Roger Bootle:

Theory of Money (with W.T. Newlyn), Oxford University Press

Index-linked Gilts: A Practical Investment Guide, Woodhead Faulkner

The Death of Inflation

Surviving and thriving in the zero era

Roger Bootle

NICHOLAS BREALEY
PUBLISHING

LONDON

This new edition first published in paperback by
Nicholas Brealey Publishing Limited in 1997

36 John Street
London
WC1A 2AT, UK
Tek: +44 (0)171 430 0224
Fax: +44 (0)171 404 8311

17470 Sonoma Highway
Sonoma
California 95476, USA
Tel: (707) 939 7570
Fax: (707) 938 3515

http://www.nbrealey-books.com

First published in hardback in 1996
Reprinted 1996 (three times)

ISBN 1-85788-148-6
Library of Congress Cataloging-in-Publication Data
Bootle, R. P.
    The death of inflation: surviving and thriving in the zero era/ Roger Bootle.
        p. cm.
    Includes bibliographical references and index.
    ISBN 1-85788-148-6
    1. Inflation (Finance) 2. Cost and standard of living. 3. Interest rates. 4. Finance,
    Personal. I Title.
    HG229.B595   1997   96-7874
    334.4'1 – – dc20   CIP

British Library Cataloguing in Publication Data
A catalogue record for this book is available from the British Library.

Printed in Finland by Werner Söderström Osakeyhtiö

Contents

Preface to the Second Edition

THIS BOOK IS PRIMARILY ADDRESSED, NOT TO MY FELLOW ECONO-
mists, but rather to that much-maligned character, the intelli-
gent general reader. Accordingly, I have tried to avoid jargon,
kept theoretical disputes as far as possible in the background, and reduced
notes and references to a minimum, confined to the end of the book.

The book is divided into three parts. Part I is devoted to the exposi-
tion of my thesis, while Part II discusses the consequences for individuals and businesses and for the worlds of property and investment.

In Part III, I discuss the historical evidence on inflation and interest
rates and the implications of my thesis for economic policy. I have not
neglected my fellow economists entirely, for I try to address some of the
theoretical issues raised by my ideas in Chapter 8, though again, I have
tried to make this accessible to the non-economist.

In this paperback edition I have greatly expanded the discussion of
policy issues in Chapter 9, including extended consideration of how
European Monetary Union may affect my thesis. I have also reviewed
how my thesis has stood up against the rush of events since the first edition was published. So far at least, I think I can say fairly well.

Perhaps this means that the hornets' nest of criticism which the first
edition stirred up will now be quieter. Somehow I doubt it. I knew that
the book was controversial so I expected controversy, but some of the
criticism was widely off beam. Some of it even suggested that the
authors had not read the book but simply imagined what might be in it.
In Chapter 9 I reply to my critics, both well read and ill read.

Chapter 8 caused me most difficulty because of the wide discrepancy of views about the current state of play in theoretical economics. I
am sure that it will not find favour in many quarters. Some economists
appear to believe that monetarism is dead and there is no need to kick
the corpse. But others still believe that analysing money supply trends

is all there is to understanding and forecasting inflation.

More importantly, as I have found at the various seminars where I have presented my ideas, even those who would not identify themselves as monetarists tend automatically to think in terms of the monetarist framework when considering the big issues regarding inflation which are the subject of this book. This is probably because without such a framework, in theoretical terms, inflation then seems indeterminate, a prey to assumptions about starting points, historical processes, expectations and institutions. This, though, is precisely my point. Accordingly, I have found it necessary to argue how and why money supply analysis is not the be all and end all of inflation, and how the various real forces which I adduce have their bearing.

Going on from historical interpretation to give a radical view of the future is a dangerous business. Despite my conviction that inflation is likely to stay very low, and may at some times even be negative, I have to face the possibility that I could be proved wrong by events. In particular, even if my general thesis is right, some unforeseeable event such as the outbreak of a major war could cause an upsurge of inflation. It would be so much safer to stick to discussion of the past! But as Keynes put it: 'Economists set themselves too easy, too useless a task if in tempestuous seasons they can only tell us that when the storm is long past the ocean is flat again.'[1]

The plain truth is that, whether we acknowledge it or not, we all of us have to live on the basis of some sort of assumption about the future. In the financial sphere, few assumptions are more important than those we make about inflation, and I firmly believe that the assumptions we should now make about inflation have fundamentally changed. Accordingly, I think I would be failing the reader if I produced merely a history of inflation which had nothing to say about how today's prevailing orthodoxy might be surprised by events over the years to come. But I can hardly hope to keep my views on this secret until the end of the book. The title has surely given the game away right at the beginning.

In the course of preparing the book, I have accumulated debts of gratitude to a large number of people. I must begin by acknowledging a longstanding intellectual debt to the late Professor Sir John Hicks who, when I was one of his graduate students, first introduced me to the striking history of inflation in Britain and instilled in me the idea that understanding its history is vital to understanding inflation itself.

I was extremely fortunate that many people read the typescript, either in whole or in part, or reviewed some of the work which preceded it, and gave me the benefit of their comments. In this respect I am grateful to Brian Blackshaw, David Burnett, Stephen Chilcott, Mark Cliffe, Adrian Coles, Michael Ferguson Davie, Peter Day, Vincent Duggleby, Joe Dwek, Professor Walter Eltis, Christopher Firminger, Lawrence Gooderham, Professor Sir Douglas Hague, Will Hutton, Bill Jamieson, Peter Jay, William Keegan, Tony Key, Tom Maddocks, Professor Patrick Minford, Christopher Morris, John Moxon, Piotr Poloniecki, Marian Read, Professor Colin Robinson, Terry Roydon, Christopher Smallwood, Don Smith, John Spiers, Robert Tomkinson, Frank Turley, Leslie Warman, Patrick Whittingdale, Jack Wigglesworth, Colin Wilde, Andrew Wilson and Andrew Withey.

I would also like to pay particular tribute to my colleagues at HSBC, especially Jonathan Loynes and Ian Shepherdson, who helped me enormously, diligently collecting data, preparing charts and reading drafts. I am also grateful to the participants at the various seminars at which I have presented my ideas for both their critical comments and helpful suggestions. I owe a special debt to my secretary, Marion Riley, who tirelessly worked on the book at the same time as keeping the normal work of the department going, and also to Walter Allan for encouraging me to write the book and for introducing me to my publisher, Nicholas Brealey, who has been a fount of ideas and inspiration.

I am especially grateful to my employers, the HSBC Group, for their generosity and understanding. Although most of the book has been written in my own time, they have allowed me respite from some of my usual responsibilities to be able to complete it. Nevertheless, the views here expressed are my own, and the HSBC Group (not to mention the individuals referred to above) are not necessarily in agreement with them.

Last, but not least, I am grateful to my wife for her patience and forbearance in putting up with evenings, weekends and holidays given over to 'the book'.

Despite both help and influence from many quarters, responsibility for any errors or omissions remains fully my own.

Roger Bootle
London, February 1997

Part I

The Death of
Inflation

1

The Zero Era

There is no subtler, no surer means of overturning the existing basis of society than to debauch the currency; the process engages all the hidden forces of economic law on the side of destruction and does it in a manner which not one man in a million can diagnose.

J.M. Keynes[1]

For a hundred years the world has been suffering from periodic changes in the level of prices, producing alternate crises and depressions of trade... It is not too much to say that the evils of a variable monetary standard are among the most serious economic evils with which civilisation has to deal.

Irving Fisher (1922)[2]

IMAGINE A WORLD WITHOUT PERPETUAL INFLATION: PRICES IN THE shops falling in some years, rising in others; pay rising by 2 or 3% in the good years, static or falling in the bad ones; house prices as likely to fall as to rise; interest rates fluctuating in the range 2–4%.

Is this a purely imaginary world? No. It is the way things were most of the time before the onset of perpetually rising prices in the years after the Second World War. And it is the world to which I believe the countries of the west are gradually returning.

Inflation is a process of continually rising prices, implying a continually falling value of money. Acceptance of this process is ingrained in our habits of thought and action. Anyone born in the last 60 years has known nothing else but prices continually rising, and it is natural for people to assume that the future is going to be similar to the recent past. Sometimes, though, this assumption can be dangerously off beam. It was wrong to think that the 1970s were going to be like the 1960s, just as it had been wrong to think that the years after the Second World

War would be like the 1930s. Sometimes history reaches a breakpoint. It is at a breakpoint now.

East and West

It is already plain that there has been a dramatic change in the inflationary environment. In Japan, it is painfully evident. In 1995, far from the threat of inflation, it was fear of *deflation* that kept the Japanese authorities awake at night. For many prices had already fallen. The Japanese have a marvellous expression for it: *kakadu hakai* or 'price destruction'.

The pricking of the so-called 'bubble economy' by the imposition of high interest rates in 1990–91 (later reinforced by the effects of a superstrong exchange rate for the yen) saw asset prices crumble. As Figure 1.1 shows, land prices fell continuously from 1991 to 1996, while the Tokyo stockmarket index fell from a high of nearly 40,000 in 1990 to a low of just under 15,000 in mid-1995, before recovering to stand at just over 18,000 in February 1997. In December 1996 wholesale prices were some 7% *lower* than they had been in 1990.

As Figure 1.2 shows, consumer price inflation also fell dramatically. Indeed, in 1995, despite an inefficient and price-sluggish distribution system, prices in the shops barely rose at all. In fact, in November 1995 the annual rate of inflation was *minus* ½%. It subsequently picked up – the rate for 1996 as a whole was 0.1%. But if the distribution system had passed on lower costs fully to the consumer, there is no doubt that we would already have witnessed sustained consumer price deflation in Japan. This is not another example of innate Japanese superiority, for in the 1960s and 1970s Japan suffered from high inflation as badly as did the countries of Europe and North America. It is only recently that Japan has been transformed from a high inflation economy into an economy hovering on the brink of deflation.

But far from bringing on the state of nirvana which the collapse of inflation is so often alleged to induce, this fall in inflation brought the Japanese economy close to disaster, with the financial system in desperate straits, the property market shell-shocked, the stockmarket hovering on the brink of meltdown, and the banking system held together on a wing and a prayer. Moreover, having cut interest rates to ½%, as

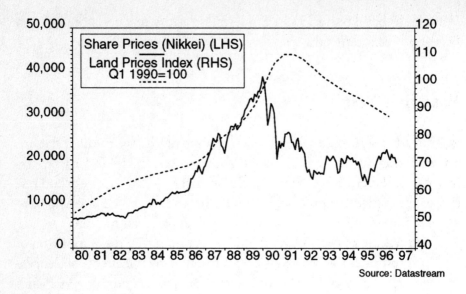

Figure 1.1   Japanese asset prices, 1980–97

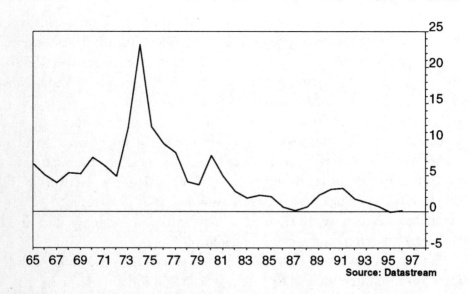

Figure 1.2   Japanese inflation, % year on year, 1965–96

far as traditional monetary policy is concerned, by the end of 1995 the authorities had more or less reached the end of the line.

To make matters worse, although they launched several substantial packages of increased spending and tax reductions to boost demand (the policy advocated by followers of the great economist John Maynard Keynes), the authorities were concerned about using this standard remedy on a very large scale. They were worried by Japan's adverse long-term fiscal prospects due to its rapidly ageing population. Indeed, in 1997, taxes were set to *rise*. At least by the beginning of 1997, the economy was growing again, but no one could be confident that the crisis was over.[3] Yet this is not a uniquely Japanese difficulty. Throughout the west, government debt levels pose a problem, even with very low inflation. If the economy tipped over into deflation, most western governments would probably feel constrained from adopting the Keynesian remedy.

Although we like to think that the economics of deflation are now so well understood that anything like a repeat of the 1930s is unthinkable, the Japanese experience is salutary. It shows that the dangers of deflation are very far from being over. In fact, in the world's seven leading economies, known as the Group of Seven or G7, inflation has collapsed, as Figure 1.3 shows. If it has not quite reached current Japanese levels, it has at least fallen to levels last seen on a sustained basis in the 1960s. In 1996, inflation was about 2% in France and well under 2% in Germany and Canada. True, it was a good deal higher in several countries which had suffered currency weakness – it was over 3% in Spain and in Italy it started the year at over 5% before falling below 3% by the end of the year. But these rates were low compared to those countries' inflationary history. And in one of the supposedly most inflationary countries, the UK, inflation was 2½%. Moreover, as I shall argue, not solely in Japan but in many countries there could be a *deflationary* danger ahead. Indeed, Sweden experienced deflation in 1996.

In fact, the countries of the west are closer to falling prices than published figures suggest. Official measures of inflation *overstate* true inflation. They consistently fail to take full account of quality improvements in what people buy, miss the emergence of new goods such as computers and mobile telephones (which tend to fall in price) and do not recognise the full effect of consumers switching to lower priced goods or sources of supply.[4]

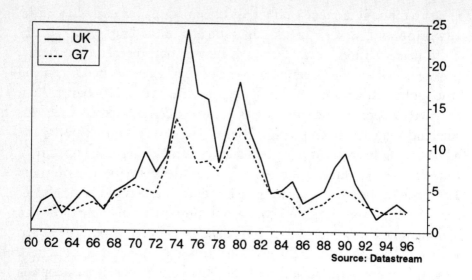

Figure 1.3   Inflation in the G7 and the UK, % year on year, 1960–96

Estimates vary as to how large this systematic overstatement of inflation is, but most economists reckon that it is in the range of ½–2%. At
the end of 1996, the Boskin Commission[5] reported that the US CPI
overstated inflation by 1.1%. A similar conclusion probably applies to
most western countries. This means that when, in 1994–5, the world's
monetary authorities and financial markets were obsessed with the dangers of inflation bounding up, across much of the western world there
was virtually no inflation at all. Not only was inflation negative in
Japan, but it was virtually zero in France and Canada, minimal in
Britain and the US and minuscule in Germany.

There are some parts of the world, however, where it is a very different story. In China, for example, inflation was over 20% in 1994, and
all the 'tiger' economies continue to have some sort of inflationary
problem. Moreover, high inflation persists in much of Latin America,
eastern Europe and the former Soviet Union. The reason for this contrast between the old established 'west' and the new dynamic 'east' will
emerge in Chapter 2. (Although it does some violence to geographical
reality, I shall refer to all of the dynamic countries as 'eastern', but I
include Japan with the 'west'.)

Nevertheless, outside Japan, both media commentators and financial markets are deeply reluctant to recognise the extent of the change in the inflationary environment. They are perennially inclined to focus on one or other problem areas which are supposedly set to cause inflation to flare up again – commodity prices, healthcare costs, the effect of falling unemployment on labour costs, or exchange rate weakness. Yet the facts repeatedly challenge their pessimism.

In December 1996, after a prolonged period of strong growth in employment, the US core Consumer Prices Index (CPI) stood at just 2.6% up over the year, *down* from the average of the previous two years. Moreover, 1996 was the fifth consecutive year that CPI inflation had been 3% or less, despite much higher food and energy prices. Meanwhile, from the beginning of the economic expansion more than five years earlier, producer prices had risen by not much more than 10% by the end of 1996, compared with nearly 20% on average in the previous four expansions. In 1996 even the inflation rate for consumer services (excluding energy but including healthcare) was below 3½%.

Against nearly all expectations and predictions, after sterling came out of the ERM in September 1992, British inflation continued to fall, averaging 2½% in 1994, despite undergoing sharp inflationary pressure from the much lower exchange rate. In 1995 it moved up again, but only slightly. Nor was low inflation bought at the expense of slow growth. On the contrary, after its exit from the ERM the UK was one of the faster growing economies in the OECD. Most strikingly, growth of average earnings edged lower at the same time that unemployment fell.[6]

This has been a common theme in several countries, stretching from North America to New Zealand. In the US, in 1996, average hourly earnings rose by just 3¼% despite unemployment running at under 5½% of the workforce. Under pressure from a variety of forces (which I discuss in Chapter 2) – changes in technology, weak unions, the more competitive climate and the changing shape of work itself – pay simply does not behave in the way that it used to. And without pay inflation you cannot have sustained price inflation. It is precisely the failure to recognise the extent and significance of these changes in the labour market which explains why so many forecasters have proved much too pessimistic about the inflationary environment. Pay inflation is the dog that didn't bark.

The implication is clear – the old regime of high inflation has collapsed. But no one is quite sure what has taken its place.

The Hope

What the policy-makers are all aiming at and hoping for is *minimal inflation*, that is to say, a regime where the price level continues to creep up a bit each year. Although the precise numbers differ from country to country, getting and keeping inflation somewhere in the range 0–3% is the explicit policy objective of the German Bundesbank, the Banque de France, the Bank of Canada, the Bank of England, the Reserve Bank of New Zealand, the Bank of Finland, the Bank of Spain and the Swedish Riksbank. The US Federal Reserve does not have an explicit inflation objective in the same way, but its implicit objective is clearly very similar.

Setting the objective of minimal rather than zero inflation is partly accounted for by the idea that 'a little bit of inflation does you good' and partly by the fact that, as pointed out above, official measures of inflation overstate true inflation. The idea is that if the authorities manage to get *measured* inflation in the 0–3% range, then in reality there will be very little inflation at all. The objective is similar to aiming for zero when inflation is properly measured.

Pursuit of minimal inflation has also become the established creed among academics and commentators. And for most businesses and con-sumers, it has a familiar ring to it. It may not be exactly reassuring, but at least it isn't downright threatening. It represents more of the same, only less so.

Cynics among us will be tempted to say that precisely because all these groups either expect, hope or plan for it, minimal inflation, that is to say, *comfortable* inflation, is unlikely to happen. The lesson of history is that something will come along to spoil these hopes. In the secret recesses of the central banker's mind, the leading candidate for that something is a resurgence of inflation, landing us back with the sharply rising prices, high interest rates and instability of the 1970s. In my view, however, if there is to be a big surprise, it is more likely to be the reemergence of *falling* prices, for the first time since the 1930s.

At the moment, price deflation is far from the intentions of policy-makers. But, of course, what they intend and aim for is one thing; what actually results may be quite another. The world's governments and central banks did not plan for, forecast or anticipate the depression of the 1930s, nor the inflationary explosion of the 1970s. Rather, their hopes, intentions and plans were overwhelmed by events. In today's conditions, by setting policy so as to achieve a regime in which prices hardly rise at all, they run a serious risk that they will end up, not with a return to high inflation, but rather with price *deflation*.

Precisely because this would be so unexpected and ill-prepared for, it could have extremely dangerous consequences. If minimal inflation is the hope for the future, then price deflation is the fear.

Fear of Falling

The very pain inflicted by the process of reducing inflation (*disinflation*) makes a tip-over into deflation more likely. If the economic system were completely adjusted to minimal inflation then the danger of falling prices might be remote. But it is not. Consumers have become heavily indebted, particularly in order to purchase property, on the assumption of continual inflation. Without it, they will find their debts more burdensome. Many companies are both heavily indebted and are substantial owners of real assets. Governments throughout the western world have massive liabilities predominantly in long-term, fixed-interest form. As inflation falls, the real value of their interest payments will be higher than they originally bargained for and their balance sheet position will deteriorate.[7]

The effect of all these factors is to constrain spending and to weaken confidence as inflation falls. In principle, there ought to be gainers to offset these losers, but two factors undermine the forces which might otherwise be brought to bear to offset the deflationary forces emanating from debtors. First, the very novelty of the economic environment I am describing unsettles confidence – falling prices for real assets such as property, very low interest rates, decreases in the general level of prices. Secondly, the rising real value of financial assets owned by creditors is of no benefit if it means that the debtors cannot pay.

The effects would be still more alarming if it came to be believed that, as substantial owners of non-performing assets, the *banks* were in trouble. For then the integrity of people's savings, and indeed the very monetary system itself, would seem to be imperilled. Once this stage is reached, we are beyond the rational models of economists and into the realms of mass psychology. We are dealing with the economics of fear.

Indeed, it is possible to imagine a vicious circle developing between falling asset prices, falling prices in the shops, rising real debt levels and downwardly spiralling expectations, reminiscent of what happened in the 1930s. If consumers expect prices to fall then they defer purchases, which puts more downward pressure on prices. Falling prices raise the real value of debt and force debtors to cut back on their spending. Some debtors inevitably go under, thereby endangering financial institutions and the banking system, which depresses confidence still further.

The behaviour of stockmarkets may play a key role in this process. They are vulnerable to massive changes in sentiment which undermine the existing basis of valuation, causing a collapse of asset values and a loss of confidence which can spread beyond the realms of finance into what economists call the *real* economy, that is to say, the world of production and jobs. Whether or not it is a stockmarket 'crash' which leads the move towards deflation, a crash could well occur as a result of a move originating elsewhere, or the two could develop symbiotically, as happened in Japan in 1994–5.

After the stockmarket crash of 1987 failed to bring serious adverse implications for world economic growth, never mind the financial collapse that some commentators feared, it has become fashionable to dismiss the relevance of stockmarket values to economic activity. This is foolhardy. In 1987 we were fortunate. Central banks took evasive action; Japan, which seemed the weakest link, avoided becoming seriously embroiled; because the markets had risen precipitously in the months beforehand, the elevated level of the market was not firmly believed in and the losses were easily absorbed; and the underlying growth momentum in the economy was sufficiently strong that the shock was absorbed.

These factors provide no grounds for complacency about the effects of any future sharp drop in stockmarkets. Indeed, the system has subsequently become more fragile. The growth of mutual funds is a particular worry. In 1980 there were only 458 equity, bond and income funds in the US with combined assets of just under $60 billion. But by 1994, the number was 4394, with assets of $1500 billion. And the number of individual mutual fund accounts rose from 7 million in 1980 to 89 million in 1994.[8] If individual holders of mutual funds panicked in a crisis they could cause a financial market crash.

Meanwhile, the world of 'sophisticated' institutional investors could be imperilled by the enormous growth of the market in *derivatives*, that is to say, financial instruments such as futures, options and swaps which are *derived* from the familiar, plain vanilla, financial assets such as deposits, loans, shares and bonds. Although there is nothing inherently wrong with derivatives, and indeed their appropriate use can greatly enhance the financial efficiency of business, they offer increased scope for speculation and, if badly used and managed, they carry enormous risks, as the world discovered when Barings bank collapsed in 1995 following speculation in the futures market by the trader Nick Leeson. Well-managed banks and savings institutions have these risks under control, but no one can be sure about the fringes of the financial system, nor about how the system as a whole would behave in a crisis.

Nightmares Made Real

For the last 50 years, price deflation has seemed beyond the realms of plausibility. Now it does not. It has not struck most economic thinkers as a serious prospect, partly because in the last 25 years inflation has been high, and partly because in the period before that, when inflation was low, in most countries price rises were continuous, with no break into deflation. Economists' thinking about the future implicitly envisages a return to the sort of inflation which ruled in the 25 years immediately after the Second World War. If then, why not now?

But the whole weight of history stands against this conclusion, as will be explained in Chapter 7. The price level rising year after year without fail is an aberration. It happened after the war for two interrelated reasons. First, demand was high and growth strong, buoyed up on a self-reinforcing wave of optimism. And, by a combination of luck and judgement, for the first 25 years there was no major demand shock to shatter this combination.

Secondly, because of the various inhibitions against lower prices and the restraints on competitive markets which I stress later in this chapter, prices, let alone pay, showed no tendency to fall even when demand was on the weak side. In those conditions, it would have taken a mammoth demand shock to bring on price deflation.

But neither of these conditions obtains today. We begin with generally modest growth and relatively high unemployment (except in the US and parts of the Far East). And confidence is fragile. Meanwhile, as I argue in Chapter 2, just about all the structural and institutional inhibitions to falling prices are crumbling. The result is that in today's conditions, a significant downturn in demand *would* produce falling prices.

Interest Rates Cannot Be Negative

The deflationary danger is increased by one oft-forgotten but extremely powerful fact – interest rates cannot be negative. The reason is simple. Currency (notes and coins) does not pay interest and its nominal value is fixed. It is precisely this which means that currency loses value from inflation. But it also means that it gains in real value if prices fall.

Accordingly, if banks, under leadership from the central bank, tried to impose negative interest rates on bank deposits, then people would withdraw money from the banks and hold hoards of cash on which no negative interest rate was incurred. (Because this would risk a banking collapse, the monetary authorities would have to increase the supply of notes to match the increased demand.) So the practical impossibility of negative interest rates is deep rooted in the nature of money itself. It is a problem of monetary economies.[9]

The implications are devastating. Once the interest rate has hit zero, the authorities have lost the power to boost aggregate demand by cuts in interest rates. They have used the last shot in the locker.[10]

The result is that if prices fall, real interest rates are bound to be positive. And if they fall at a faster rate, then real interest rates rise, even though the system is clamouring for lower or even negative real rates.

This characteristic makes systems with a very low inflation rate extremely dangerous. They are vulnerable to sharp downturns of demand which conventional monetary policy is powerless to resist.

A Different Policy Objective

So the danger of an accidental tip-over into deflation when the authorities are aiming at inflation in the 0–3% range is substantial. But quite apart from accidents, everyone should be aware of the chances of a more explicit embrace of falling prices *as a deliberate act of policy*.

For minimal inflation is questionable as an objective, even if much or all of it is illusory, in the sense that it represents overrecording of true inflation. It means that money still falls in real value. People will still be confused about the relationship of money values over time, and the living standards of people on fixed incomes may continue to be squeezed as time goes on.[11]

Moreover, as price and wage flexibility increases as a result of the competitive forces I describe in Chapter 2, it will be less useful to have a little bit of inflation to oil the wheels. They will work perfectly well without it. Accordingly, although inflation in the 0–3% range is what the authorities would currently like to see, this objective may yet change.

This should not be surprising: policy objectives are always in a state of flux. In the years immediately after the war, the idea that the attainment and maintenance of 0–3% inflation should be the main economic policy objective would have seemed madness itself. Employment was then the chief concern. After the inflationary crisis of the 1970s, policy-makers abandoned employment as the central objective and replaced it with the suppression of inflation. But the idea of attaining and maintaining inflation as low as 0–3% would then have seemed not madness, but pure fantasy.

Now that reaching this target will prove much easier, the authorities could readily adopt a more searching objective, for instance zero inflation. The intellectual trend already seems to be moving in this direction. As one central bank economist put it in late 1995, reviewing the outcome of an international conference of central bankers and economists:

it is quite difficult to mount a wholly convincing case for an 'optimal rate of inflation' very different from zero.[12]

There are even some voices being raised now in support of what economists call *long-run price stability*.[13] The idea of a stable price level sounds attractive but it is not exactly what is on offer, and economists who trumpet the virtues of stable prices are often guilty of misleading the public in a very dangerous way. For there will always be shocks to the system which push up the price level. If there is to be long-run price stability, however, these phases must be followed by periods when prices fall, so that phases of rising and falling prices offset each other. Thus the regime which economists call price stability most people would call price *instability*. And if the authorities were to embrace such a regime as an objective of policy, then there would have to be periods when they *aimed for* falling prices.

This is not to be dismissed as an idea from the lunatic fringe, however bizarre it seems in the context of the last 50 years. It is being actively discussed by serious economists today. Ideas which are denigrated in one age have a way of being lauded in the next.

Strangely enough, it is even possible, just about, to imagine the idea of *continually falling* prices being accepted as an objective of policy, in the same way that the orthodoxy of the post-war years has been to favour continually rising prices. It would have some support from history as a plausible objective. From its Napoleonic War peak in 1812 to 1896, the price level in Britain fell by a half. In the US, prices fell even more. Yet during that period there was persistent economic growth and a tremendous improvement in living standards.

And in the past the idea of continually falling prices has had plenty of heavyweight theoretical support. Indeed, a dispute raged among economists in the late nineteenth century, continuing up to the Second World War, about the desirability of a stable price level compared to a regime in which prices varied according to the level of productivity. On the latter view (known as 'the productivity norm') continually rising productivity would produce continually falling prices (although periods of falling productivity would produce rising prices). In such a system there would be general stability of wages and salaries, thereby obviating the need for the constant renegotiation of labour contracts. Whereas 'price stability' brings stability in *output* prices, the productivity norm brings stability in *input* prices.[14] More recently, Milton Friedman also argued that a regime of falling prices would be better than a regime of broadly stable prices.[15]

Isn't it strange that something which most people would find positively scary, namely falling prices, is made to sound quite cosy by some great economic thinkers? The reason is a sharp difference of perspective. Friedman's suggestion was envisaged as part of a world where people's expectations and the economic structure, including the level and type of debt, are adjusted to continually falling prices. In this way no distortions are created and no financial instability caused.

This sounds remarkably like the imaginary world of perfectly anticipated inflation so beloved by theoretical economists, only with the signs reversed. In fact, perfectly anticipated deflation is as impossible as perfectly anticipated inflation. Moreover, if prices fell continuously, this would lead to the same confusion about relative values over time that exists with persistent inflation.

Outright Deflation

I said above that one of the apparent advantages of a regime of steadily falling prices is that there could be greater stability of pay. In an *outright* deflation, however, pay rates are far from static. They fall along with prices. Indeed, the two chase each other downwards.

Nothing like this has been seen since before the Second World War, although there have been many occasions when workers have suffered substantial falls in their *real* incomes by accepting, or being forced to accept, increases in money earnings below the rate of inflation. Equally, in the conditions of high unemployment which became the norm in western industrial economies in the 1980s and 1990s, particular groups of workers sometimes accepted reductions in their pay even in money terms in order to try to preserve their jobs. But ever since the Second World War, the notion that the general level of earnings could fall has seemed like an idea out of the Ark.

In present conditions, when we have not even adjusted properly for low inflation, never mind a period of falling prices, a phase of falling incomes hardly bears thinking about. It could be catastrophic. Once the demon was let loose, it could be difficult to control the rate of fall and the state of expectations about the fall. With current levels of debt, outright deflation is a nightmare almost beyond imagining.

Even without falls in pay, though, the first onset of falling prices would be a shock after the continual upward movement of the last 60 years. It might well be regarded as apocalyptic by business. That is why even initially mild price deflation poses such a great danger. There is always a risk, particularly when financial structures and expectations are not geared to it, that a period of falling prices could whip up depression psychology and unleash a financial whirlwind of disaster.

Fluctuating Prices

Although it is possible that, having started to fall, prices could go on falling for a long time – just as they went on rising – in my view this is unlikely to happen in practice. For a start, the natural tendency of the economy to bounce back would operate against this, quite apart from the thrust of macroeconomic policy which would be set to resist it.

Over and above this, there would continue to be some resistance to falling prices in the institutional structure, especially to falling pay. The continuing power of labour market institutions, although now much attenuated, as well as state regulations on minimum wages and the like and the extensive system of state benefits, all of which are set in money terms, would all support the existing level of money incomes.[16] And without falls in pay, the rate of decline of prices would be constrained.

So the fall in prices would have a limit. But what happens after prices have stopped falling? They will rise again; yet that too will have a limit. When prices rise in the upswing, the caution and fear of people who have just seen prices fall, coupled with the continued tendency of the monetary authorities to stand against persistently rising prices lest this should lead to the reemergence of an inflationary problem, will ensure that there is a limit to how far prices can rise. So although in this world prices can rise and fall, they are limited in both directions. It is a regime of *bounded price instability*.

I think we may already be entering this regime. But of course, the 'up' phase of a fluctuating general price level is indistinguishable from the continuation of the regime of minimal inflation which central banks intend for us. It will be only be when prices start to fall that it will be clear that something radical has happened. Even then, it will not be clear exactly what that something is. For when the general price level initially falls, people may come to assume after a while that falling prices are now the order of the day, just as rising prices were once the norm – in other words that we could be heading for the deflationary nightmare.

Moreover, when prices rise again after the first period of falling prices, it would be natural for people to believe that the phase of falling prices was simply a one-off interlude. It may only be when the general level of prices starts to fall for the *second* time that it will become evident that this is really a completely new environment. It may well be long after this that it is possible, looking back, to perceive this as a period of what economists like to call long-run price stability, that is to say, a regime in which prices readily go up *and* down.

On this view, the future may consist of phases which correspond to both the hopes and fears discussed earlier. Over the long haul, in a regime of bounded price instability something like the same results may be attained as obtain under minimal inflation, but by averaging pluses and minuses. Accordingly, in order to avoid unnecessary duplication and repetition, in the succeeding chapters I shall analyse the consequences of *zero inflation*, meaning this to encompass both the world of minimal inflation where the price level creeps up, but ever so slowly, and the world of bounded price instability where it falls as readily as it rises.

But where appropriate, I shall give separate consideration to the phenomenon of falling prices. For if I am right in believing that bounded price instability will characterise the new order, it will be the phases of falling prices which will sharply mark out the new world from its predecessor, and which will pose the greatest dangers in the years ahead.

Where's the Beef?

Putting aside the dangers of falling prices, will the achievement of zero inflation make a big difference to our well-being? According to one view, inflation is a great economic evil, on a grand scale, capable of destroying economic and political systems, on a more prosaic level, capable of distortions which undermine efficiency and hinder economic growth. In extreme versions, just about every economic ill under the sun is attributed to inflation – unemployment, low growth, inequality, low real wages. One can imagine some anti-inflation stalwarts even going on to add rising crime, the state of the environment and the decline of the family.

Needless to say, for those who take this line, it has been worth reducing inflation, virtually at any cost. It is like an all-out war between society and an impersonal enemy. (In fact, the language of economists and policy-makers sometimes reflects exactly this state of mind. People do sometimes speak of the *war* against inflation.) Accordingly, the reduction of measured inflation to 0–3%, effectively amounting to its complete demise, should bring a cornucopia of benefits, including lower unemployment and faster growth.

This seems to be at least the official thinking of the British government. In September 1995, the British Chancellor, Kenneth Clarke, was still rating inflation as public enemy number one. Replying to the idea that inflation should be allowed to rise in order to achieve faster growth, he said:

> History should have taught everyone that such thinking is a dangerous nonsense. Inflation damages growth. Inflation harms investment. Inflation damages prosperity. Inflation destroys jobs.[17]

But it is possible to take another, quite different, view. There is a strong tradition in economics that inflation affects nothing *real*. In the inflationary process all money values are driven up, with the result that, although the price of everything rises when measured against money, any good is as cheap or expensive *compared to the alternatives* as it was before. It is just like changing the unit of account, shifting from marks to francs or redefining the coinage. There is no real effect whatever.

In that case, the end of inflation will not bring any real benefits either. It is largely irrelevant. We are then left wondering what all the fuss was about. Why the determination to get inflation down in the first place?

There is a wealth of empirical evidence which can be used to support this view. There is no startlingly clear connection between high growth and low inflation. Indeed, a number of countries, such as Brazil and China, have experienced both high growth and high inflation. Evidently, high inflation does not preclude rapid economic growth even if it does not encourage it.

There is even a train of thought, both in theoretical economics and in popular thinking, that regards inflation not only as not too bad but actually as decidedly healthy and positive – provided that it is not *too* fast. After all, the argument runs, inflation eases the real burden of debt and thereby acts to the advantage of debtors and the disadvantage of creditors. That is supposedly socially desirable because the debtors are more likely to be the poor (i.e. good) and creditors the rich (i.e. bad). Over and above that, it should help to boost investment and hence raise economic growth because investment is financed on borrowed money, or if it is not, it is at least judged against the returns available on money, returns which are eaten away by inflation.

This favourable effect on investment is also encouraged by the boost which inflation supposedly gives to feelings of optimism. Money values are always rising – product prices, share prices, land values, savings, wealth values. Everyone *feels* so much better off, even if they aren't. But the mere feeling takes on economic significance because it has the effect of increasing optimism about the future, hence boosting investment and consumption and raising economic growth, thereby making the optimism self-fulfilling.

In addition, inflation enables relativities to be changed without anyone having to undergo a painful and difficult fall in the nominal price of their product, or in their nominal income level, or in the value of their house, or of their pension. Such changes are achieved gently, almost imperceptibly, by the continual rise in all prices, except yours – your product, your wage, house or pension. Inflation provides a mechanism for adjustment by stealth.

Needless to say, if you were to believe that this view fairly captures the role of inflation, then you would believe that the end of inflation, far from enhancing our economic well-being, could actually make us worse off, perhaps even disastrously so.

The Importance of Keeping in Step

What are we to make of all this? The correct assessment is more complex than a black and white answer.[18] For a start, since the late 1970s inflation has been demonised. Typically, people think that the rise in price of the goods or services they buy is because of inflation, but the rise in price of the goods or services which they *sell* (including, of course, their labour) is something quite different: a legitimate result of 'improved quality' or 'scarcity' perhaps? Accordingly, people have thought that if only *inflation* stopped, while allowing their incomes or house prices to rise as normal, then of course they would be better off!

Equally, many of the ills created by inflation through disturbed relativities are caused by governments' refusal to alter quickly enough prices which are under their control, because 'that would be giving in to inflation'. Governments have tried this trick with exchange rates, public sector wages and public sector charges. In each case, the attempt to hold on to one particular price or group of prices while all others are going up has caused distortions which were expensive and in some cases even disastrous. But in these instances, of course, it is more legitimate to speak of the *resistance* to inflation being the source of real problems, rather than the inflation itself.

This is also substantially true of the idea that 'inflation creates unemployment', repeated endlessly like a mantra by governments and central banks desperate to legitimise their recession-creating policies. There *are* some senses in which inflation may be said to create unemployment, but they were hardly uppermost in the minds of monetarist politicians during the early 1980s. The main cause of increased unemployment at this time was precisely the attempt to *reduce* inflation.

For all that, inflation is far from irrelevant. The degree of harm it does largely depends on how well the system is adapted to it. The insouciance of the 'inflation is irrelevant' school is based on the premise that inflation is fully expected by everyone in the system *and that everyone is able to embody their expectations in all prices*. Once this stage has been reached, the losses from yet faster inflation may well be minimal.

In countries with endemically high inflation this may be a reasonable picture of reality, for then no pretence is made about the integrity of money values. Important agreements or long-term arrangements whose values could be devastated by inflation, if they are not indexed in local currency, are made in a foreign currency (usually dollars) in whose real value the transactors can have faith.

For systems with moderate inflation, however, of the sort that most of the industrial west has experienced for 50 years, getting *everything* adjusted to inflation is difficult. It involves abandoning the assumption that money values have meaning, and that abandonment has costs. It might be worth it for individual businesses to incur these costs at high rates of inflation, but not at moderate rates. So the system operates with some costs and prices adjusted to inflation and others not.

The Great Deceiver

Quite apart from whether the system is free to adapt to inflation, there is also the matter of whether individuals understand the inflationary process enough to want to make adjustments to money values when they are free to do so. There is plenty of evidence that they do not properly understand it. Inflation is the Great Deceiver. It confuses people about relative prices at any point in time, and about real values over periods of time. If we believe in individuals' ability to make decisions for themselves, then to the extent that they are deceived by inflation they must make inferior decisions.

One part of the economy which *does* fully adjust for inflation, and arguably overadjusts for it, is the financial system. Governments have tended to use high short-term interest rates, which are under their control, to contain inflation. As a result, in the 1980s they raised rates by even more than the level of inflation justified, that is to say, the level of *real* interest rates was increased. Meanwhile, investors in bond markets were so paranoid about inflation that they pushed up the yields on government bonds, the key determinant of interest rates and asset values throughout the whole economic system, far more than was justified by current inflation.

This puts paid to one of the arguments that inflation has been beneficial. Once the financial system has incorporated the fear of future inflation, far from benefiting debtors and hurting creditors, it does the reverse. And the result of higher real interest rates, both short and long, is to discourage real investment in such assets as plant and machinery and thereby to restrict economic growth.

Let alone high real rates of interest, high *nominal* rates can have a devastating effect on cash flow. This is serious for small businesses but it also plays havoc with personal finances. With high interest rates, homebuyers are heavily burdened in the early years of a mortgage and then are let off lightly at the end. Pensioners enjoy a decent income when they retire only to find it is squeezed as they grow older. Deposit holders think they have a good income from their capital, only to find later that it buys less and less as time goes on, and that the real value of the capital has been eroded.

Perhaps these effects are less serious for the *macroeconomy* (that is to say, the economy in total) than the inhibiting effects on investment, but it is difficult to regard them as self-cancelling for the individuals concerned. Even if they fully understand what is going on, it is impossible for them to make adjustments which leave their income and its distribution over their lives the same as it would have been without inflation.

In the business world, inflation creates distortions just as serious. These are exacerbated by the tax system which, in general, is not fully adjusted for inflation. Nor are company accounts, so that under persistent inflation these cease to give true readings of a company's profitability. In addition, as I argue in Part II, perpetual inflation has encouraged firms to operate with low volumes and high margins and has strengthened the tendency towards short-termism.

Moreover, the battle to reduce inflation has involved running the economy at lower levels of capacity utilisation, and higher levels of unemployment, than would otherwise be necessary. So once it is acknowledged that perpetual inflation is licked, then western economies can be run with lower levels of unemployment.

The Dangers of Disinflation

This discussion makes it sound as though the world economy is standing on the brink of a golden age. And indeed it could be. But life without perpetual inflation will not be all roses. For those companies and individuals who fail to perceive the change in the environment and who carry on as though nothing has happened, the end of inflation could be ruinous. The shift to the new environment has already brought a severe price adjustment in the property market which could be only a foretaste of what is to come when the general level of prices falls.

People are having to come to terms with a revolution in their personal finances which they do not understand, and often do not like, even if, in reality, they are no worse off. Money values which they were used to going up inexorably, often at double digit rates, now go up sedately if at all – not only prices in the shops, but also pay, houses and pensions. In laying bare the real facts, the end of inflation should bring the benefits of clarity. At the moment, though, it is bringing pain and confusion.

And precisely because so much of our economic and social system has become geared to inflation, whatever the benefits of zero inflation once the system has adjusted to it, if the process of *disinflation* is not properly managed by the authorities, it could bring about financial crises every bit as serious as those associated with the upsurge of inflation in the 1970s. In particular, as I discuss in Chapter 4, the financial markets present a serious problem. Having been so badly burned by the inflation of the 1970s they now insist on bond yields which are too high for a world without perpetual inflation. They refuse to accept the evidence that things have fundamentally changed. Theirs is the triumph of fear over experience.

If governments and central banks fail to perceive the dangers posed by the combination of high debt and high interest rates, the west could end up losing most of the gains promised by advancing technology and trade by erecting protectionist trade barriers and suffering large-scale unemployment. If the new state of affairs is managed badly, this could prompt a macroeconomic disaster. The result could be a depression just as serious as that in the 1930s. The stakes couldn't be higher.

Imagination and Experience

The key to avoiding financial disaster, gaining advantage from the end of inflation and deriving full benefit from the remarkable developments in technology and the economic advance of Asia, Latin America and eastern Europe, lies with governments focusing their policy on sharp reductions in public borrowing combined with a shift to sustainable, low interest rates. This will promote financial stability, make possible increased investment and underpin faster rates of economic growth.

But interest rates will have to fall to levels that have seemed fantastical during the last quarter of a century. Levels of rates which were regarded as the bottom of the interest rate cycle over this period – 4, 5 or 6% – must now be the peak, or even the crisis peak.

The first challenge to consumers, businesspeople, governments and economists is a mental one, requiring imagination, courage and insight. For both the opportunities and threats which now confront us amount to a complete reversal of the economic conditions of the last 25 years, and the overturning of the established wisdom which they spawned.

As I argue in Chapter 2, what is happening now is not only a dramatic increase in the world's productive potential, but also the emergence of a constantly shifting, dynamic process of concentrating production on the cheapest source, both within countries and between them. By undermining the confidence of both businesspeople and consumers, this is limiting their inclination to spend and borrow. But it is also destroying producer power and directly reducing the price level.

This change is on such a huge scale that it is likely to be the dominating theme which shapes our inflationary experience over the next few decades.

Blind Faith and Heresy

In arguing this way, I am turning the conventional wisdom of modern economic theory on its head. When thinking about inflation, most economists would completely disregard the various real, structural forces operating on the price level, on which I place so much emphasis in this book. They view such factors as price reductions brought about by eastern competition as completely irrelevant for inflation. These are, they would say, just changes in particular prices. Inflation, by contrast, refers to an increase in the *general* price level and that is determined by 'the money supply'.

In September 1995, a leader in *The Economist* pronounced:

The hard fact is that inflation is a function of the macroeconomic relationship between growth and the money supply, not of structural
changes in technology or competition. For this reason, the chief influence on inflation is still monetary policy.[19]

The Economist, and indeed many economists, may well regard my stress
on real, structural forces as anti-inflationary influences as tantamount
to professional heresy.

I doubt very much whether general readers will be greatly troubled
by this, but economists may well be. I must crave their indulgence in
postponing full consideration of such theoretical issues until Chapter 8.
But for their sake, I should at least briefly explain my theoretical
position now.

I do not seek to reject the idea that increases in the money supply
are the proximate cause of major inflations, or that they are at least
associated with even moderate inflation. In the light of the historical
evidence (which I discuss in Chapter 7) how could I? But I do reject the
rigid tenets of *monetarism*, including the notion that the eternal monetary verities explain all, and that no institutional changes or historical
forces matter for the analysis of inflation, save as a possible way of
explaining why monetary growth turned out the way it did.

The monetarist view of the world is attractive because it is full of easy
certainties. Yet for the open minded, both theory and experience undermine this faith. For something supposedly so concrete, 'the money supply' is remarkably mercurial. It is almost impossible to define satisfactorily and consequently there are several different measures of it, often
pointing in different directions. Although the amount of money people
need to conduct economic life is supposed, according to the theory, to
be stable and predictable, societies seem to be able to make do with
remarkably different amounts. And even where the links between the
quantity of money and the level of money income are very close, we do
not know whether it is the change in money supply that causes changes
in the level of prices and money incomes, or the other way round.

This point is extremely important. If it needs to, money can respond
to prices, as well as prices to money. This leaves the way open for real,
structural forces sometimes to affect the price level, with monetary
influences following in their wake. This is part of the theoretical

approach to inflation which I expound in Chapter 8.

It also holds the key to vital questions which must by now be nag-ging both general readers and economists alike. *Why* the period of about 60 years during which prices only ever went up? *Why* was this time, which for most of us contains all of our experience, so different from almost everything which went before? And *why* the inflationary explosion in the 1970s?

The answer given by conventional economists is refreshingly simple. The post-war inflation was due, they would say, to lax control of the money supply by governments and central banks in a misguided attempt to sustain unemployment at too low a level. When inflation took off in the 1970s, this was merely the delayed, but inevitable response to this erroneous policy.

This answer is also simplistic. As I describe in Chapter 7, issues of demand management and economic policy were indeed very important and the shift in the attitudes of policy-makers during the 1980s was profound. But this is not the end of the story.[20]

Not All Inflations Are the Same

History is littered with examples of inflations caused directly by exces-sive growth of the money supply. But the inflation experienced in most of the industrial world after the Second World War had distinctive characteristics. Although it was persistent, it was, on the whole, fairly moderate from year to year.

Furthermore, prices hardly ever fell *even* when demand conditions were slack. Indeed, slack demand did not produce much of a fall *in the rate of inflation*.[21]

If this experience were restricted to one or two industrial countries, we would have to seek an explanation in terms of the unique charac-teristics of those countries. But it was not. It was shared throughout the industrial world.

The Management of the Market

The explanation lies with the institutional structures of the economy which diminished price competition and inhibited the working of normal market mechanisms. In the 1930s, these structures reduced the extent to which pay and prices could fall to absorb the impact of depressed demand. As I discuss in Chapter 7, in the process they exacerbated the misery of mass unemployment. In the buoyant demand conditions of the post-war world, these same factors produced perpetual inflation. But what were they?

Beginning in the early twentieth century, but only reaching full expression in the years after the Second World War, the economy evolved from competitive capitalism into a new form – *managed capitalism*. Whereas nineteenth-century economic structures had been little more than conduits for the flows of supply and demand, the economic structures and institutions of the twentieth century were strong enough to resist, modify or even divert them. *Producer power* had arrived.

At the root of this change was technology – the economies of large-scale production and the discovery and exploitation of the mass market. This naturally led to monopoly and concentration in industry. In 1909 the largest 100 firms in US manufacturing accounted for 22% of total output. By the mid-1970s this figure had risen to 34%. In the UK, the rise was more spectacular – from 16% to more than 41%.[22]

Enterprises were now managed in accordance with strategic goals rather than the immediate pressures of a competitive market. In the new world of large corporations, prices were *decided*, not determined by the impersonal interplay of supply and demand. Indeed, the demand for the product was managed by the creation of an image, the use of branding and advertising. Price was only one element of the positioning of a product in the market.[23]

Meanwhile, all this management had to be conducted by someone – the managers. As companies expanded, vast bureaucratic structures grew up within them – strategic planners, market research and marketing departments, management development, building, catering, and even economics departments, personnel departments, liaison and co-ordination officers and, of course, managing all the managers, layers of still more senior managers.

What was such a company for? The answer was often *the managers and employees*. As a result, large businesses were not tough in resisting cost increases. In short, they blunted the competitive edge of markets.

One Strong Power Creates Another

But producer power was not confined to the sellers of goods and services. The same forces which produced the mass market also produced the mass workforce, and the power of large industrial corporations was mirrored by the power of organised labour.

The nature of the dominant technology placed labour in a strong position. For although the mass production techniques of the early twentieth century sharply increased productivity, they were still essentially *labour using*. Large numbers of unskilled people were required to pull levers, push buttons, stand by a production line and perform the same simple task, repetitively, all day long. Essentially, the machinery could be thought of as a sort of large and sophisticated tool, only with a mass workforce, rather than an individual, as the operator.

Throughout the industrial west, this power was harnessed and projected by trade unions which grew enormously in membership and power.[23] Their influence was supported by the growth of the welfare state, which sharply diminished both the fear of unemployment and the sense of uncertainty about the future, and in many countries by both a strong legal position and a widely acknowledged strong *moral* position after the hardship, economic mismanagement and class antagonism of the inter-war years. This helped unions' influence on pay levels to spread beyond the sectors where the workforce was unionised.[25]

Three's Company

The influence of big corporations and organised labour grew hand in hand with the emergence of a third repository of producer power – the state. In the US, although even the great utilities remained privately owned, the state's influence was felt through direct public employment in administration, education and public services, through the multifarious state agencies and regulators, and through the dominating role in the US economy of the military–industrial complex, closely tied in to state spending on defence and, later, on space exploration.

In most of Europe, the state's tentacles stretched deeper into the economy, with not only all the great utilities, education and healthcare publicly run, but also the shipbuilding and coalmining industries, and often even major car manufacturers and important banks, in public hands.

The goals of publicly owned entities were unclear, but the maximisation of profit was certainly not at the top of the list. Cost-plus culture reigned. Moreover, aggression over wages was often strongest in the state-owned sector, not least because the potential downside from industrial action, namely a reduction in the number of jobs and ultimately bankruptcy of the enterprise itself and the loss of all the jobs, simply did not arise. The assumption was that public ownership provided access to a bottomless purse – the endless supply of taxpayers' money or public borrowing.[26]

Equally, consumers had little or no ability to resist such price increases because of lack of alternative sources of supply. (In some cases alternative supply was even forbidden by law.) This contributed to the inflammation of inflationary expectations.

The Pay–Price Spiral

All these factors which inhibited, suppressed or modified pure market forces were features of an economy dominated by mass-market manufacturing. But this was itself characteristic of a particular period in history. Before the twentieth century, most economies were dominated by agriculture. In the middle of the nineteenth century, for instance, agricultural output accounted for almost half of French and German production.

This was important for the behaviour of the overall price level because, in contrast to the mass-manufactured products which proliferated during the twentieth century, the prices of agricultural products could fall as readily as they could rise. Indeed, this is still true even today. (In Europe, though, in a perverted throwback to the old days of controlled prices, the Common Agricultural Policy currently prevents market forces from having full sway over food prices.)

As the twentieth century wore on, however, the role of manufacturing was itself challenged in importance. Rather than the production of *things*, more and more of national output now took the form of *services* of one kind or another – transport, education, healthcare, catering, advisory services, cleaning, communications, the list goes on and on. But far from relieving the structural rigidities of the manufacturing sector, the tension between the manufacturing and service sectors became an important source of inflationary pressure. For the growth of productivity was generally faster in manufacturing. In many services, indeed, there was very limited scope for any increases in productivity at all. This meant that even very low increases in pay would automatically lead to increased prices.

If the overall price level were to remain constant, then the price of other parts of national output would have to *fall* to offset the increases in the price of services. There was scope for this to happen in large parts of manufacturing since rapid productivity growth there would allow employers to absorb the impact of reasonably modest pay rises.[27]

But in the years after 1945 everything in the system conspired against this happening. Managements sought to *raise* the prices of their products by successful marketing and advertising. The idea that their prices should fall year after year was alien to them. Meanwhile, workers in manufacturing enterprises agitated for pay rises which reflected the increases in 'their' productivity. And because of higher productivity, managements could often accede and still enjoy an increase in profits.

The problem was rather in the service sector. After all, the car worker did not 'deserve' higher increases than a nurse or teacher. The car worker's higher rate of productivity growth was not the strived-for outcome of harder work, but quite simply the automatic result of capital accumulation and advancing technology. So, seeing manufacturing earnings rise, service sector workers pressed for comparable increases. The result was that all pay went up by similar amounts. Inflation was the inevitable result since the pay rises in the service sector were not fully offset by productivity growth.[28] But the vital link in the pay–price spiral lay in the manufacturing sector, in the failure of its prices to *fall*.

The issue was how to distribute the benefits of productivity growth between competing groups. In a competitive free market this would not be a problem because without producer power no one would be able to arrogate the benefits to themselves. Where productivity growth was high, prices would fall. This is precisely what happened in the nineteenth century. But it is precisely what did *not* happen in the post-war period. The distribution of the benefits of increased productivity was left to a system of interlocking, self-interested, quasi-monopolistic producer groups. Scarce wonder that perpetual inflation was the result.

Sparks Galore to Set Inflation Ablaze

This inflationary structure gave birth to, and was then affected and eventually sustained by, an inflationary *culture*. The continual upward march of prices and pay became accepted as the norm, and once inflation was built into people's expectations, inflation itself became the source and cause of more inflation. In this new world of perpetual price rises, any new external shock could cause the price level to explode. All it needed was a spark.

In the event, there were several at once. The early 1970s saw an enormous rise in the price of raw materials, the breakdown of the international monetary system and a massive rise in the price of oil – turning the 1970s into the west's inflationary nightmare. The 1970s were to inflation what the 1930s had been to depression. And just as in the 1930s, the old economic orthodoxy was powerless to explain or prescribe, and governments and central banks seemed impotent. Hence the revolution in economic thinking and policy, relying on very high interest rates which, for most of the industrial west, resulted in unemployment reaching levels unimagined since the 1930s.

History Moves On

I have described the period of perpetually rising prices in the years after the Second World War as a historical aberration. What produced it was an intertwining of economic structure, institutions, ideas and historical circumstance. But as time moves on, so do they. By the early 1990s, just as the triumph of anti-inflationary monetary policy seemed complete, so the structural forces which had produced the tendency for continually rising prices were collapsing. The inflationary era was drawing to a close. The zero era was about to begin.

2

The Triumph of Competitive Markets

What man that sees the ever-whirling wheel
Of change, the which all mortal things doth sway,
But that thereby doth find, and plainly feel,
How mutability in them doth play
Her cruel sports, to many men's decay?

Edmund Spenser[1]

...forty-seven Vietnamese or forty-seven Filipinos can be employed for
the cost of one person in a developed country, such as France.

Sir James Goldsmith[2]

THE WORLD IS IN THE GRIP OF OVERWHELMING FORCES WHICH ARE transforming the economic and business landscape and the lives of ordinary people. The roots of the economic changes ripping through society are diverse – technological, organisational, ideological and psychological. But they have a common theme. They all contribute to the emerging dominance of competitive markets. And in the context of anti-inflationary macroeconomic policies, collectively they have a dramatic result – the end of perpetual inflation in the west.

Now that the philosophy of tight anti-inflationary control is accepted everywhere, so the inflationary forces which have blocked the normal operation of competitive markets, and which, in the process, have made inflation such a formidable opponent for so long, are retreating, to be replaced by powerful new *anti*-inflationary forces. Throughout the industrial west, the old cost-plus, bureaucratic system of interlocking quasi-monopolies is now collapsing.

Technology and the Demand for Labour

Over the last 15 years, a technological revolution has occurred in manufacturing industry and much of the service sector, based on the spread of automated processes, made possible by the computer, microelectronics, advanced communications and (to a lesser extent) the robot. This technological revolution is altogether different from the first industrial revolution which was still essentially *labour using*.

The new technological revolution which has swept over the world is predominantly *labour saving*, especially of unskilled labour. No longer are armies of unskilled or lightly skilled workers required to operate vast arrays of machinery. Throughout the industrial west, former bastions of working-class solidarity have crumbled – in the steel industry, in car manufacture, in the coalmines, in fact just about everywhere. Millions of workers have lost their jobs, to be replaced, if at all, by some sort of automated process.

But these changes do not stop with what had formerly been widely thought of as the massed armies of the industrial working class. After an initial hiatus, the introduction of the personal computer, together with modern communications technology, has cut a swathe through traditional middle-class areas of employment in the office.

And the structural changes stretch deep into the service sector. In transport, for instance, computerisation greatly reduces the number of people needed to run a railway system. The *potential* developments in service industries are huge. Education is one service industry where there is massive potential for the use of labour-saving technology, with electronic access to the best teachers or the replacement of teachers with electronic teaching systems.[3]

In the US, the power of the changes in labour demand is already apparent, but given American flexibility and the recently strong pace of demand growth it does not show itself in high levels of unemployment. Rather the effect is visible on rates of pay. As Figure 2.1 shows, even though the unemployment rate has fallen sharply in recent years, the rate of increase of hourly earnings has risen only marginally.

Moreover, the position is starker at the lower end of the income distribution. The Economic Policy Institute in Washington has calculated that the real hourly incomes of the bottom 80% of male employees and the bottom 70% of female employees in the US have been stagnant or declining over the period 1989–95. This is closely related to the increasing importance of education and skills. Fifteen years ago, a male college graduate earned 49% more than a man whose education ended with a high-school diploma, but by 1993 the difference was 83%.[4]

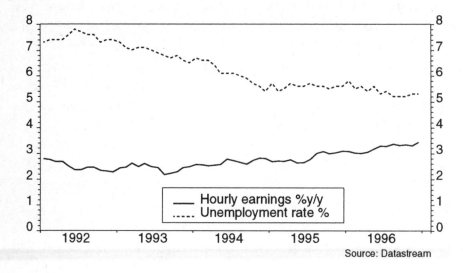

Source: Datastream

Figure 2.1   US earnings growth and unemployment, 1992–6

In most of the European Union, the effect on real income levels is not so clear cut, largely due to the overregulation and inflexibility of the labour market. But the same underlying force, namely weakness in the demand for labour, is nevertheless to be seen in the high rates of unemployment, particularly among unskilled males. In 1996, unemployment was over 10% of the workforce in Germany, over 12% in France, about 12% in Italy and nearly 23% in Spain.

In Britain, in the light of its more flexible labour markets, the same forces are more clearly seen in rates of pay, as in the US. One of the results has been to reduce the share of national income going to pay to its lowest level since records began 40 years ago. In the second quarter of 1995 the share of income from employment in GDP was down to 62%, compared to a peak of 72% in 1975.[5]

But this isn't just a story of technological change. The very nature of employment itself is changing. The old assumption of one full-time job, taking a person from their late teens or early 20s up a progressive career ladder finishing with retirement at 60 or 65, is fast becoming old hat. Increasingly, work is part time, temporary or contract based, and people are having to juggle several jobs at once or to string together a series of 'engagements', rather as actors have always done. The concept of 'portfolio people' has emerged. The proportion of workers in full-time tenured employment in the UK has dropped from almost 70% in 1975 to nearer 45% today, and looks to be on course to fall below 40% in the next few years.[6]

Furthermore, *new* employment opportunities are even less likely to have full-time, tenured status than are established positions. So for those in the market for new jobs, the opportunities are already predominantly of the insecure variety. And as new hirings more accurately reflect the new realities of the labour market, they are tending to be increasingly badly paid. Whereas the ratio of earnings of those entering work to those already in employment was 63.6% in 1976, in 1990 it was down to 53.4% and is now quite possibly below 50%.

The Changing Nature of Pay

These changes have gone hand in hand with dramatic changes in the structure of earnings, even for those in full-time employment. In the old days, pay was dominated by the 'rate for the job'. In factories, rates were often negotiated by unions for different types of work and applied nationally across umpteen different locations, whatever the circumstances.

In the offices of the large, bureaucratic companies, as well as in the public sector, salaries rose according to certain scales. If you were a 'Grade 8', that meant a particular level of income, benefits and, where applicable, even a certain type of company car, size of office and thickness of carpet. And Grade 7s and Grade 9s would know what the differences were, in minute detail.

This system of rigidly determined rates of pay is now breaking down. More and more employees are having to come to terms with both differences in their pay compared to others whom they may regard as comparable, and variations in their own pay as circumstances change. There is a move towards plant-level rather than national bargaining and towards pay packages where a significant proportion is not guaranteed but rather tied to profits, or performance. In 1995, the Chief Executive of Lloyds Bank, Sir Brian Pitman, proposed that the rates of pay for retail bank employees should vary depending on where they worked, rather than being set, as they traditionally have been, at the same rate across the whole of Britain, from Land's End to John O'Groats.

In short, the price of labour is now being treated by employers just like other market prices rather than as part of a hierarchical social structure. These changes to the pay culture help firms to contain costs and also themselves contribute to the reduction of labour power by fragmenting the workforce. They amount to a revolution in the *social technology* of business. The central concepts of job, career and salary were the social reflection of the hierarchical, protected, bureaucratic structures of the old order. Now they are crumbling. In the process, employers are transferring much of the natural uncertainty of economic life to those who used to be called employees.

The contrast with the 1970s could not be greater. In the US and Britain, many employers are running riot, *dictating* pay, hours of work, terms and conditions of employment – and with barely a murmur from their workforces. In much of continental Europe there is an attempt to cling on to old ways, but the pressures for change are mounting. In Germany, Gesamtmetall, the metal industry employers' federation, put forward proposals in early 1996 for labour market deregulation. They include calls for pay restraint, lower entry-level wages, more working time flexibility, and a greater regional devolution of the bargaining process.[7] Even in the powerhouse of Europe, competitive pressures are being keenly felt. The message for the future is clear: the period of labour power and labour militancy is over.

Trade Unions in Decline

The weakening of labour's bargaining position due to technological change has gone hand in hand with a weakening of labour unions. Where unions had previously presented a serious problem they are now largely emasculated. Britain is often thought of as the home of militant trade unionism. But membership of trade unions has declined from a peak of more than 52% in 1979 to 35% in 1993. This more than reversed the increase in unionisation which occurred in the late 1960s and 1970s. By the mid-1990s, the rate of unionisation was back to levels last seen in the 1940s.

In the US also, as Figure 2.2 shows, there has been a substantial decline, though from a lower level. The picture is even more striking if you exclude the public sector. In the US, only 11% of private sector employees now belong to a union.

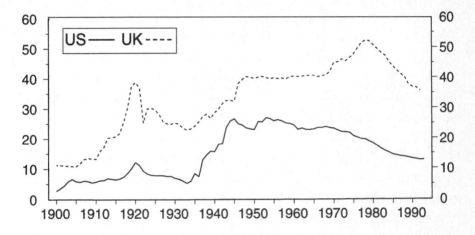

Source: *Historical Statistics of the United States*, US Bureau of the Census 1975, Bureau of Labor Statistics; for the UK, The Employment Department

Figure 2.2   US and UK union membership as % of workforce

In France, less than 10% of workers belong to a union, down from 22% in 1970, although the power of organised labour is far greater than this figure suggests, not least because more than 90% of the French workforce is covered by collective bargaining agreements. Indeed, the continuing power of organised labour was evidenced by the wave of public sector strikes in December 1995.

But the decline in the influence of unions is an international phenomenon. A recent OECD study compared the percentage of the workforce that was unionised in 21 member countries in 1970, 1980 and 1990. In the decade 1970–80, 12 of the 21 countries experienced increases in union membership. In the decade 1980–90, by contrast, only 2 of the countries saw increases – Finland and Sweden – and they have since suffered a collapse of centralised bargaining. Everywhere else, in countries as diverse as Ireland, Japan, Portugal, Austria and Italy, trade union membership was in decline.[8]

Centralised bargaining is still very much the norm in Germany, although even there things are changing. In March 1995, in a Munich hotel room, an agreement was sealed by two negotiators which would settle pay rates for 3 million workers in the German engineering industry, in precisely the way that has been normal in Germany throughout its economic miracle.

But this time there was a difference. Far from welcoming the deal, many employers vowed 'never again', and since then several companies have quit Gesamtmetall, the employers' federation. Indeed, union membership itself is on the decline as older members retire and young employees refuse to join. Having swelled to 3.7 million at the time of reunification, the membership of IG Metall, Germany's largest union, is down to 3 million.

Moreover, IG Metall now appears to have realised that current competitive pressures require changes in its behaviour. In November 1995 it said that when the existing wage deal expires in 1997, it is prepared to accept wage rises in line with inflation (i.e. no increase in real terms) if employers give certain guarantees on levels of employment.[9]

So what explains the ebbing power of unions across the industrial world? Partly it has been a response to much higher levels of unemployment, but structural factors have generally magnified the effect of this, including the decline of mass manufacturing as an employer. As traditional factory floor jobs have disappeared, employment has grown in the service sector, in areas where it is more difficult to organise and where unions have traditionally been weaker.

Moreover, the nature of employment itself has been changing. Union members typically used to be male, full-time, manual workers. Not only is manual work now less important but, as I discussed above, employment is more and more of the part-time, flexible or contract variety and the workforce, in most western countries, is increasingly female. In addition, companies' insistence on greater flexibility in the way labour is deployed, as well as corporate restructuring and decentralisation, have made it more difficult to organise collective action by union members.

Furthermore, whereas in the past it often suited managements to negotiate with strong unions, now that organisations employ a huge variety of people doing widely differing jobs, and modern conditions demand constant flexibility, this appeals much less. And the fact that in this era of dynamic change unions cannot protect jobs has made them less appealing to potential members.

Even the social mood has operated against unions. Workers, particularly young ones, have become more individualistic and less interested in solidarity with their fellows. The major changes in both the nature of employment and the wider variety of lifestyle defining consumer goods have helped this development.

These factors applied to most of the western industrial world, but in some countries they have been compounded by sharp attitudinal changes arising from particular events. In the US, the strike by air-traffic controllers in 1981 was a defining moment. Up to this point these workers seemed to be one of a select number of employee groups which potentially had a stranglehold over society. When they went on strike it seemed inevitable that they would win. But President Reagan used military air-traffic controllers as a temporary stand-in and set about training new civilian personnel to take their place in due course. The strikers lost their jobs. They were now helpless. If the air-traffic controllers were not indispensable, who was?

In Britain, the defeat of the miners' strike in 1984–5 was a similar turning point. After all, the miners had been the *bête noire* of British governments trying to control wages. Their challenge to Edward Heath's pay policy had ousted his Conservative government in 1974. As well as having considerable industrial muscle, miners were also the workers who excited the greatest degree of public sympathy. If the government was able to defeat this group after a bitter struggle lasting many months, leaving the miners with nothing to show for it, and indeed considerably the poorer, what hope was there for other groups of workers?

The result of the miners' strike, coupled with significant legal changes to the position of unions, has had a profound effect on the attitudes of workers towards industrial action. Indeed, the number of days lost through industrial disputes in Britain plunged to such low levels that in 1995, when the German electronics giant Siemens announced a plan to build a plant in Britain, it cited the country's trouble-free industrial relations as one of the attractions.

Because most of the forces acting against unions are strongest in private industry, the strongholds of the union movement are now mostly in the public sector. But something else has arisen to threaten even these redoubts.

Privatisation

The old, bloated public sector enterprises, so long a protected haven from competitive pressures, are now increasingly subject to the cold blast of competition as they have either been privatised, are being prepared for privatisation, or are left to live in fear of it.

Whenever countries wish to extricate themselves from structural economic weakness, raise revenue or increase efficiency, privatisation now figures high on the list of what needs to be done. Yet before the middle of the 1980s, it would scarcely have warranted mention as an idea, never mind a reality. But the international scale of privatisation activity is now breathtaking. From Finland to South Africa, Canada to Korea, in the old industrial world and the new, in thrusting dynamic countries and backward ones, governments are divesting themselves of the ownership of economic enterprises.

Even France and Germany, formerly staunch supporters of the state's role in industry, are seeking to privatise large parts of the state sector. In November 1996, 24% of Germany's biggest monopoly, Deutsche Telekom, was sold to the private sector, raising DM20 billion (about $12 billion). There will be more stock to come. And the *real* consequences of privatisation will be enormous. *Business Week* suggested that Deutsche Telekom may need to cut 60,000 jobs, a quarter of its workforce, as well as slashing its prices in half to meet competition.[10] Opposition from the workforce and political wobbles in Bonn can be taken for granted. But this privatisation is working with the train of events and with the grain of market forces.

Not only is privatisation a dominating refrain almost everywhere, but telecommunications are in the front line. For instance, Korea is planning to privatise the state-owned Korea Telecom, a long-distance operator and sole provider of local services, and to liberalise its telecommunications market. The reason appears to be fear that Korea might otherwise not be able to take full advantage of the explosion in computer and information technology on which so much of future economic growth will depend.[11]

Even in the less glamorous utilities, once the very embodiment of complacent, inefficient monopoly, it is a similar story. They too can be subject to global forces as former national monopolies start to vie with their competitors on the world scene. When British Gas was privatised it employed 90,000 people. In March 1994 this was down to 65,000, but British Gas stated that it intended to reduce its payroll by a further 25,000 in the next five years.[12] Moreover, it is now worried about its competitive position in the gas *market*. Only a few years ago, this would have been unthinkable. The utilities were lumbering megaliths in competition with no one.

This is not an isolated story. Wherever industries have been privatised, the results have been the same – a flood of job losses and a new focus on lower costs and responding to the market. As Robert Skinner of the Paris-based International Energy Agency (IEA) recently put it:

> The control of the power sector as an instrument of social policy is giving way to its decontrol in support of economic policy.[13]

Hence we see sweeping deregulation in the electricity industry in New Zealand, Chile and Argentina, takeover mania in Britain's privatised utilities, and the encouragement of private investment in the power sector in Eastern Europe.

The contribution of privatisation to the achievement and maintenance of low inflation is many faceted. The substantial reduction in the workforces of privatised industries can play a significant part in the softness of the labour market and in the transformation of workers' expectations. Moreover, the emergence of competition, albeit to a limited extent, and more importantly the threat of more to come, puts pressure on managements to keep costs down and improve efficiency, and contributes directly to lower prices.

Meanwhile, the removal of industries from public control denies them access to the public purse as an ultimate source of finance for pay increases, thereby helping to reduce the size of the public sector deficit and improving monetary control. This has been particularly important since, with ultimate access to public money and relatively secure employment, public sector workers have often been among the most militant, while their managers have had little incentive to be tough. Public sector settlements have often been among the pace setters for pay settlements in the private sector.

Large-scale privatisation can make a significant difference to the whole shape of the economy. For instance, in the UK in 1979, employees in public corporations accounted for 7¼% of the total workforce. By the second quarter of 1995, the equivalent figure was less than 1½%.[14]

The End of Cosiness

Yet the devastating changes in employment have gone beyond the mere replacement of labour with machinery, or the collapse of union power and the shift of industries from public to private ownership. The structures of business are being streamlined and the very focus of business organisations turned upside down. In the process, the dominant ethos in the world of work has changed. It is the *end of cosiness*.

There has grown up an intensely *competitive culture* in which every established practice now has to be justified, as if each institution and structure were starting again from scratch. Whole layers of middle management have been cut out and head office staffs slashed. Sometimes people are now even obliged to reapply for their own jobs. 'Downsizing' and 'delayering' are the buzzwords of the day.

Consider the big banks, now busily closing branches, sharply reducing the numbers of tellers and other junior bank staff while also cutting a swathe through the senior management cadres. Why? To reduce costs and increase profits, of course. But why now? Why did they not do something similar before? Many of the changes have been made possible by technological advances, but many banks have been overstaffed for years. Now they are under pressure to cut costs to the bone and deliver 'shareholder value'. Their managements are focusing on costs and profits as never before.

Or consider what has happened to head office staffs in the great industrial corporations in the west. Twenty or thirty years ago, these were typically vast, bureaucratic structures of people, mostly underemployed, but ensconced in a cosy world of middle-class security – well-paid jobs, perks, promotion, pensions.

Not any more. America set the pace with concentration on lean and mean organisations and focus on measuring results. In-house functions were contracted out and management staffs were severely trimmed. The upshot was burgeoning middle-class unemployment and insecurity – thousands upon thousands of forty-something executives in danger of never getting a job again.

Their main problem is that what they had acquired was company-specific knowledge. Their whole lives had been built around ascending the corporate ladder, doing things the corporation's way. They knew all about the corporate structure and its own institutions and practices, but not much about the world outside. They had value for these corporations, while things carried on in the same old way – but once outside the warm corporate embrace, they were dead. Now the corporation spewed them out in their thousands.

The Competitive Whirlwind

It is wrong, though, to think that these changes represent an accretion of further power to employers, because they are themselves caught up in the competitive whirlwind. In the corporate world, many old-established mega-corporations are floundering. They are being forced not only to shed labour, but to refocus and respond to the market.

General Motors, for instance, for so long a symbol of American corporate strength, made a loss in 1980 for the first time since 1921 – $763 million of it – and was reduced to fighting for corporate survival. Its reaction was an internal revolution and a purge of jobs. It was prepared to decimate employment in Flint, the town of its origins, by laying off 30,000 workers, even while it set up new plant in Mexico.[15]

For most of its life, IBM has been the ultimate symbol of the secure and paternalist employer and in 1989 it performed this role for no less than 400,000 employees. Renowned for its ethos of lifetime employment, the company and its employees were shocked when in 1992 it registered the largest loss of any company in history, and had to reduce staff through voluntary retirements.

But it isn't only companies in trouble which now make radical changes. The imperative of cost reductions and profit maximisation is affecting everybody. In August 1995 came news that Chemical Bank and Chase Manhattan, two big banks on their own, were set to merge. They planned to shed 12,000 of their combined 75,000 payroll.[16]

In Europe, with the exception of Britain where industry was devastated in the recession of the 1980s, managements have been, on the whole, slower to accept the need for change – but the pressure is now on with a vengeance. In 1995, Wolfsburg, Germany, was a city living on its nerves. It is a company town *par excellence*, utterly dependent on the car manufacturer Volkswagen. The company had always reciprocated with a sense of responsibility towards its people and the community. It helped to build swimming pools, theatres, kindergartens and flats.[17]

But in 1993, Volkswagen threatened to cut 30,000 jobs unless the workers accepted a four-day week. The workers reluctantly accepted but then the management demanded more changes, including the threat of work on Saturdays as normal, without the payment of over-time. The workers simply could not understand the need for more changes. Union posters carried the words 'Daddy belongs to us on Saturday'. But as far as modern managements across the western world are concerned, if Daddy has a job, he doesn't.

The Will to Survive

What explains this shift to a much more cut-throat and competitive climate? The organisational structures and methods which dominated in the 1950s and 1960s had grown up to suit the older technologies, and they had grown fat on it. Protected by their established positions in markets, mega-corporations acquiesced as their cost bases burgeoned. Labour power consolidated in both large privately owned companies and in the public sector.

In the more competitive US, sustained high rates of economic growth blunted any need to adapt and organisations became cosy and sleepy. Meanwhile in Europe, this atmosphere was strengthened by the prevailing acceptance throughout industry and business of the need to maintain a social consensus. Many large companies openly accepted obligations not only to their workforces but also to their local communities, especially where their history was closely bound up with a particular town or city, such as Volkswagen in Wolfsburg or Imperial Tobacco in Bristol. Anyway, business was good. Why rock the boat?

The sharp deterioration of the west's economic performance during the 1970s, followed by the deep recession of the beginning of the 1980s, forced a change. The need to survive bred a mood of intense competition. Yet this mood was intensifying even as the economy was recovering. Something else was afoot.

Financial Market Pressures

In the US and Britain, part of the answer lies with stock market influences. The accent on share price performance grew stronger, partly as a result of the rapid development of the fund management industry. And increasing financial sophistication and deregulation provided more opportunities for financially driven changes in corporate control and organisation. Even at the very top end, virtually no company was so large as to be immune from takeover. And everywhere, even at the very bottom end, sections of businesses could now be readily sold off to the managers, perhaps with a substantial shareholding for the workforce.

In the US, between 1987 and 1989, 2730 publicly quoted firms with an aggregate value of $860 billion were acquired by takeover. And there were some spectacular individual episodes. In 1985 the tobacco giant R.J. Reynolds took over Nabisco, the huge food company. A few years later, the chief executive, Ross Johnson, then famously tried to perform a leveraged buyout. The corporate raider T. Boone Pickens managed to bid (admittedly unsuccessfully) for none other than Phillips Oil and then Gulf Oil, while through the use of junk bonds Michael Milken made virtually any deal seem financeable.

In the UK, the examples were less spectacular but the trend was the same. Hanson bought EverReady, Imperial Tobacco and Consolidated GoldFields. The Hanson raid came to be deeply feared throughout industry. Everywhere the formula was the same – cut out head office costs, rationalise, sell off. At Imperial Tobacco, Hanson managed to cut the number of employees in half.[18]

The effects of these changes spread far beyond the list of companies which were threatened with bankruptcy or gobbled up by rivals. In short, the whole corporate culture changed. And some of the results were extraordinary.

Some mega-corporations even volunteered to be broken up – the very antithesis of the empire-building ethos of yesteryear. In the US in late 1995, AT&T was planning to split itself into three parts, and it is thought that 20,000 jobs will be cut from its payroll before the split is completed by the end of 1996. The break-up is being driven by awareness of the company's inefficiencies, and their reflection in a sluggish share price. 'The market value of AT&T was being buried,' said Mr Robert Allen, AT&T's chairman. 'Investors could not understand the strategy of the combined company... Investors will clearly understand the strategy now... I'm trying to shape the future rather than react to it.'[19]

In Britain, the textile firm Courtaulds split into two separate parts and the industrial giant ICI split itself into two independent businesses – ICI, concentrating on chemicals, and Zeneca, which develops and manufactures pharmaceuticals – something which would have been unthinkable only a few years ago, let alone to the founding fathers of the corporation. In a massive restructuring in 1990, the oil giant BP even abandoned its prestigious corporate headquarters which used to occupy all 32 floors of Britannic Tower in London. The headquarters staff numbers were reduced by two-thirds and the headquarters was moved to a much smaller building, with most of Britannic Tower left empty.

Barclays Bank, which a few years previously had apparently seen its main function in life as trying to be bigger than its rival NatWest, hired a dynamic, young chief executive, Martin Taylor, who not only set about sharply reducing costs but openly touted the merits of Barclays trying to be *smaller*. He floated the idea of Barclays buying back its own shares in order to improve returns to shareholders. This was nothing novel in the US, where many companies had been doing this for years, and there had even been some isolated examples in Britain, but for Barclays to do this? Unthinkable!

Stockmarket influences have traditionally been much less important in continental Europe but things are starting to change even there, partly due to the increasing internationalisation of both business and financial management. According to *Business Week*, 'of some $500 billion in stock issued by Europe's privatised companies, about 20% went to US institutions, which demand more transparency and better returns than most European companies have ever been subject to.'[20]

And there have been some high profile examples of investors flexing their muscles. In 1995, the Chairman of Suez, the giant French holding company, was forced out for failing to give shareholders an adequate return on their investment. This followed major institutional shareholders forcing out the management of Navigation Mixte, a large holding company with diverse interests, for lack of 'strategic vision'.[21]

Although such events are still small fry compared to what happens in the US, they illustrate the mounting financial pressures to produce decent returns for shareholders even in continental Europe.

The Information Revolution

But aside from financial pressures, at the root of corporate unease across the western world are the speed and nature of technological change. The emergence of new processes and new products means that there are few areas where businesses can feel comfortable with standing still. Even when you are making good profits you have to make sure that you are doing your utmost to keep costs under control and to reduce them through new technology and corporate restructuring, or you will find your market being cut from under you. In short, profit maximisation is back in fashion – for survival as much as for success.

The current wave of technological advance is so closely bound up with the explosion of communications and information technology and the associated cheapening in its cost that the term 'information revolution' is in vogue. The acquisition, interpretation and dispersal of information have become substantial economic outputs in their own right, as well as being vital inputs in virtually all production processes.

Yet this development, which has already brought enormous changes, is surely still in its early stages. It seems likely to be every bit as profound in its effects as the mass production revolution which overtook the world in the nineteenth and early twentieth centuries. But whereas that development was associated with factors which heightened the susceptibility to inflation – increased concentration, producer power, image branding and monopoly – the communications and information revolution brings several factors which help to suppress inflationary tendencies.

The availability of information is at the very root of the efficient functioning of markets – and the lack of it is at the root of the continued survival of many quasi-monopolies. Accordingly, the information and communications revolution is fundamental to the triumph of competitive markets. It is epitomised by the tremendous power now available to a single individual through the personal computer (PC), but 10 years ago the accent of computer development was on large mainframes which would enhance the power of large organisations over small. Whereas the old technology favoured large structures and producer control, the new technology favours small structures and producer responsiveness.

Over and above this, the information revolution has a direct impact on the effectiveness of competition because information about rival products and sources of supply is now readily transmissible. Just about the most readily transmissible piece of information is price. Shopping around for most goods and services has always been a physical activity requiring precious time (and, indirectly, costing money). The information revolution is already starting to change all this. With car insurance, for instance, independent brokers now input the customer's details into a computer and come up with the cheapest offer, more or less instantaneously. But as technological advance continues, this practice may come to be the norm rather than the exception, and soon without the intermediation of a broker.

You can clearly see the impact on the retail sector. In the US, about 11 million people have a modem attached to their personal computer which allows them access to electronic data networks. This has prompted a surge into electronic shopping by commercial networks such as Compuserve, America Online and Prodigy.[22]

Teleshopping is most advanced in the US but other countries are developing fast. In October 1995, Germany's first home-shopping TV channel went on air and is expected to launch a scramble by competitors to get into this potentially lucrative market.[23] In the UK, although teleshopping is undoubtedly still in its infancy, facilities are already available on satellite and cable TV.

In the future, it will be normal for purchasers to have screen-based access to information about the availability and prices of various goods from different suppliers. The consequent huge increase in information (acquired at virtually zero cost) will lay bare price differences and will greatly increase competition. The result is that the adverse volume response to a particular price rise will be greater and it will accordingly be more difficult for a particular producer or seller to raise prices.

Globalisation

The information revolution is a key component in another force which is intensifying competition – the globalisation of the marketplace. Whereas it had been possible in the past for all but the very largest companies to see themselves as operating in a national or even a regional market, responding only to local economic forces, now even many small companies can feel the beat of world economic forces at their door, while large companies are increasingly operating in a truly international environment.

The liberalisation of markets, the reduction of trade barriers, and the international mobility of capital and technology, combined with the modern communications revolution, have produced a large rise in international trade. But the change has gone beyond mere numbers to produce a different state of mind. Companies have begun to think internationally. National borders are now old technology.

If companies can manufacture just as effectively but much more cheaply in Mexico, then they move there. If they can restructure the production process so they can produce some parts locally and combine them with other parts imported from abroad, they do so. If they can have their administrative and clerical work done more cheaply in Bombay, why not?

What is happening is a global reallocation of production and a redirection of purchasing power towards the cheapest sources. This lowers costs and prices directly, but it also makes a large indirect contribution by the change it effects to the competitive culture. Scarcely any economic enterprise feels safe any more. Doing nothing is not an option.

The rise of the dynamic economies in East Asia and Latin America and the opening up of eastern Europe have massively extended the scope of this process of globalisation and given it added spice. Indeed, the forces arising from the incorporation of these fast-growing economies into the international trading network promises to transform the world economy. Its potential consequences are on such a scale that it can be regarded as the equivalent of the industrial revolution and the development of North America rolled into one.

It is not a single factor but rather a powerful combination which has unleashed these forces on the world – the employment in most of the dynamic economies of development-oriented policies, including a substantial advance in educational standards, the adoption of a market-friendly and outward-looking strategy, the collapse of communism, the operation of an open world trading system, the revolution in communications, the international mobility of capital and the transferability of technology. These factors have been interactive. Take one away and the effectiveness of the others would be much reduced.

Development on a Dazzling Scale

Of course, there is nothing new about rapid development in 'new countries', but the sheer size of the area currently enjoying rapid growth makes it different. It dwarfs the previous development zones. China's population, at some 1.2 billion, is roughly three times that of the EU.

China's progress so far has already been impressive, even though its rapid development began only very recently. After the implementation of Deng Xiaoping's economic reform plan in 1979, the growth rate quickly exceeded 10% and ran at double figures for most of the 1980s, until attempts to deal with inflation in 1988 and 1989 brought it down to 4%. It subsequently surged again.[24] Meanwhile, China's exports boomed from $15 billion in 1979 to $85 billion in 1992.

The frantic pace of development in many dynamic countries and its effect on international trade has already had a significant impact on the west. Whereas 'developing' countries accounted for 29% of US manufactured goods imported in 1978, by 1990 the figure was over 36%.[25] The bulk of this increase was accounted for by seven countries in East Asia (China, Hong Kong, Korea, Malaysia, Singapore, Taiwan and Thailand) together with Brazil and Mexico. These nine countries increased their share of total world trade from 7.4% in 1978 to 13.0% in 1990.

And the future prospects are staggering. According to two American economists, Professors Sachs and Shatz, US trade with China may grow by about 16% a year. Even so, China will remain a low wage economy for a considerable time. They say that whereas in 1990 Chinese average wages were 1.9% of US wages, after more than 10 years of rapid Chinese growth they will still be only 3.2% of the US level.

Although many of the most spectacular examples of rapid development come from the Far East, and particularly China, we must not forget the importance of the other areas of rapid development. Just as perhaps we can think of Japan as benefiting especially strongly from east Asia's development, so Latin America's development (and especially Mexico's) is of particular importance in exercising restraint on the US price level. Mexico registered a fall in GDP in 1995, as did Argentina, although Brazil managed to continue to grow by about 5% – but Mexican exports surged. Mexico continues to have excellent prospects as a manufacturing base.

Meanwhile, quite apart from the fact that *Europe* will also share in the benefits of Asia's and Latin America's development, it has a major development zone on its own doorstep, namely eastern Europe and the former Soviet Union. Although many of the countries in this zone are a long way back on the development road, there have recently been some impressive developments. The Czech Republic is growing again after sharp falls in GDP in 1991 and 1992, and it continues to act as a magnet for overseas investment. Although Hungary is finding the going tougher, by 1994 it too was expanding again.

Moreover, in both countries the high educational levels of the workforce combined with low levels of pay continue to give them a bright future as exporters – and not necessarily of low-tech goods. In 1995, average pay levels in Hungary were still about a seventh of those in western Europe, while for skilled engineers the fraction was a tenth. There are many individual examples of success which promise much for the future. The town of Székesfehérvár has attracted approximately $1 billion in direct investment from 14 countries, including money from Ford, Alcoa and Philips. From its Hungarian factory, Ford makes ignition coils and fuel pumps for use in plants throughout Europe.[26]

Meanwhile, Poland is booming. After sharp falls in GDP in 1990 and 1991, the economy grew strongly over the next four years and looks likely to continue doing so. In 1995, exports surged by 37% and there were thousands of companies exporting from Poland, compared, according to *Business Week*, to only 200 five years previously.

Moreover, a number of western, and even some eastern, companies have opened up production facilities in Poland, attracted by its low labour costs. Pepsi Co Inc, for example, is investing $500 million in the expansion of its operations in the country, while Daewoo, the Korean car manufacturer, has chosen Poland as a base for its production in Europe. By the year 2000 it plans for an annual output in Poland of 40,000 vans, half of them for export.[27]

The Effects on Costs and Prices

How does all this affect inflation in the west? It acts as a direct depressant on the price level. In many areas, eastern producers are able to supply goods (and sometimes services) into western markets at much lower cost, sometimes at a fraction of the western cost.[28]

And the result is to put massive competitive pressure on western producers and to undermine established oligopolies in the west. As they find they cannot compete on price, they either have to abandon whole areas of production, or source most of the product from the dynamic countries, or withdraw into higher value-added, niche areas, or make a determined effort to match the competition on price through substantial cost savings, including demanning and wage freezes and/or investment in cost-saving technology.

One response is for western companies to transfer production to the Far East, Latin America or eastern Europe in search of lower costs. This is the route recently taken by Morgan Crucible, one of the world's largest suppliers of industrial carbons and ceramics. In late 1995 it announced that it was going to move output from Belgium, the Netherlands and France to plants in Hungary, the Czech Republic, China and Vietnam. The managing director explained the decision by saying that labour costs in eastern Europe were $1.50 an hour compared to $26 in Germany. Meanwhile, at Morgan Crucible's new plant in Shanghai, workers are paid $1 an hour compared with $31 in Japan.[29]

This is far from being an isolated example. Many large companies, including Philips, the Dutch consumer electronics group, Carnaud Metal Box, the French packaging company, and BPI, Europe's largest polythene film producer, have recently shifted production to the east. Explaining the decision to move production from Britain to China, BPI's Chairman was explicit. He said: 'We had to go there or see our business disappear.'[30]

In September 1995, Helmut Werner, the chairman of Mercedes-Benz, said that the German car producer was planning to increase the proportion of its output abroad from 5% to 25% 'in the medium term'. At the same time the company aims to increase the proportion of components sourced from abroad from 20% to 30%. It is about to start production in India, has further ambitions for China and aims to set up new production capacity in Brazil. It also has projects on the go in South Korea, Thailand, Malaysia, Indonesia, the Philippines and Vietnam.[31]

Eastern competition is most commonly associated with manufactured goods, but it is also being brought to bear in a number of service sectors. India, for instance, has developed a burgeoning computer software business centred on the southern city of Bangalore – sometimes called India's Silicon Valley.[32]

This is an activity where some of the countries of the former eastern Europe could also do good business. As it is, they are starting to export a service to the west of rather older vintage – electric power. In October 1995 came news that the national electric power distribution systems of Hungary, Poland, Slovakia and the Czech Republic are plugging into western power grids. This could eventually lead to lower electricity rates in several west European countries.[33]

The influence of eastern competition on western behaviour is not restricted to the areas where the dynamic countries can currently compete. Even where the competition from them is not yet a factor, in many business areas it is seen as a threat on the horizon. The fact that eastern competition is not yet a problem does not necessarily mean that a particular industry has escaped the fate which has befallen so many other western industries. It simply means that industry has time – not time to do nothing but time to make adjustment.

Moreover, in a business world where the east will not only be an ever more important source of supply, but will also make up a larger and larger share of the world's *markets*, the increasing success of the dynamic countries in supplying their own markets poses a competitive threat to the west. The response of many western companies is to try to get in on the act. In India, many of the world's largest car-makers are either investing already, or are discussing investing in joint ventures in car manufacture for the Indian market. Honda has recently signed such an agreement, following in the steps of General Motors, Peugeot-Citroën, Fiat, Chrysler, Daimler-Benz and Daewoo.[34]

Peugeot-Citroën, the French car manufacturer, has recently signed an agreement with Proton, the Malaysian car manufacturer, to collaborate on a production venture in Malaysia. 'The most important thing for us is technology transfer,' said Dr Mahathir Mohamad, Malaysia's Prime Minister. 'The most important thing for us is to be in the Malaysian market,' said Claude Satinet, Peugeot-Citroën's Managing Director.[35]

The result of eastern competition and the globalisation of the marketplace is that the dominant business ethos throughout the western world consists of cost reduction and competitiveness to make sure of long-term *survival*, never mind success. The dominance of this ethos means that the effects on western business behaviour – including on rates of pay and price inflation – are greater than a mere measurement of the *existing* trade flows would suggest. The fact that BPI, and numerous other companies, have shifted production to China will not be lost on other groups of workers who fear that they may soon face a similar fate.

And there are plenty of examples of precisely this effect at work. For instance, when recently deciding where it should build a new line of compact cars, Germany's Daimler-Benz negotiated with officials in the Czech Republic, Britain and France. In the end it decided to build the cars in Germany – but only after workers there made concessions, including agreeing to wage increases below the level agreed nationally. Similarly, workers at the German company Robert Bosch agreed to more flexible hours after the company showed them plans for a factory in Scotland which would perform the same function.[36]

Getting Right to the Source of the Problem

Eastern competition hits particularly strongly at labour power because it is most powerful where it relies most heavily on low labour costs. So the western production which is displaced by eastern competition is heavily concentrated in labour-intensive areas such as textiles. And it is the unskilled or lightly skilled workers who are most at risk. The combination of this factor with the labour-saving nature of technological change, the collapse of union power and the changing patterns of work itself explains the restrained growth of pay in the west over recent years.

Competition, or the threat of competition, from cheaper labour in the dynamic countries has helped to ensure employees' passivity in the west, even in the face of dramatic increases in insecurity and poor pay rises. Workers in the west are caught in a pincer movement – labour-saving technology and organisational restructuring at home and cheap labour competition from abroad.

But the focus of eastern competition on manufacturing has also been particularly important. For this is precisely the area which was the locus of the west's persistent inflation problem, not because the prices of manufactured goods have typically gone up faster than others, but rather because they typically did not *fall* in the way that they had to if overall price stability was to be preserved. Labour and capital employed in these industries tried to bag the whole benefit of technological progress for themselves, setting off a struggle over relative incomes which expressed itself in inflation. The influence of this factor was set to peter out as the relative importance of manufacturing diminished and productivity growth picked up in many service industries. But eastern competition has given it a further kick.

Exposure to competition from the east has undermined the power of producer groups, both by replacing western domestic production with lower priced imports and by forcing surviving western domestic producers to pass on the full benefit of technological advances to the customer in the form of lower prices. This, combined with the phenomenon of falling production costs for high-tech goods, has produced a swathe of manufactured goods where prices have fallen – video-cassette recorders, compact disc players, mobile phones, computers and telecommunications equipment.

And the phenomenon of falling prices for some goods has also strengthened disinflationary forces through another channel – expectations. For several types of good, we now *expect* prices to fall.

These changes have been so powerful and interactive that the whole is now greater than the sum of the individual parts. A new competitive climate has been established in which people *expect* inflation to be low. This has started to transform business behaviour in ways which themselves help to suppress inflation.

Even that quintessential example of twentieth-century manufacturing, the car industry, has been engulfed. Formerly it was the home of large 'productivity' awards for workers and cost-plus pricing. Now western car producers are under enormous pressure from eastern competitors even in their home markets. The new threat comes not from the Japanese but from the Koreans. From a standing start, South Korean carmakers, led by Daewoo, had by 1995 captured 1.9% of the market in the European Union. And their market share looks set to expand rapidly.[37]

In October 1995 came news that Ford, the second largest vehicle company in the world, wants its suppliers to freeze their prices until the end of the century. With bought-in components now accounting for up to 70% of a vehicle's cost, this would be a key element in allowing Ford to meet Asian competition head on.

Ford wants suppliers to absorb all price increases on a component regardless of whether they are caused by improvements to the product or by general inflation. Technology holds the key. Ford's chairman, Alex Trotman, told *The Sunday Times*: 'By being ingenious, we simply will not accept cost increases.'[38] This represents a complete turnaround in the industry. It would have been unthinkable even a couple of years ago. 'In the old days, we would take a very relaxed attitude to engineering changes,' Mr Trotman said. 'We have to get off that mindset.'

This may herald the start of a trend towards falling prices for new cars. When this happens it will be clear that the benefits of technological progress in fast productivity growth industries can be passed to workers in other sectors without the need for inflationary pay rises elsewhere. The vital link in the post-war pay and prices spiral will have been broken.[39]

What Does the East Do With its Money?

Dramatic though these effects on the west are, they only look at one side of the coin. The east's success in selling goods to the west provides it with the opportunity to *buy* goods from the west, both to satisfy its own consumers and to help further the process of development.

But this does not mean that the disinflationary effects described above are negated. When two countries engage in international trade it makes both countries better off. Each imports the goods which are more expensive for it to produce and exports the goods which are cheaper for it to produce. This reduces the price level in both countries.

In practice, though, the reduction in the price level in the west may be greater than this discussion implies. For the evidence seems to suggest that for wide sections of economic activity, particularly in manufacturing, the costs of producing an extra unit may be broadly constant across a wide range of output, but average costs fall sharply with higher levels of output as substantial initial or fixed costs are spread over a larger number of units.[40]

Now if these conditions apply in the activities where the east wishes to buy goods from the west (and there is no reason to suppose that they do not), then the west's specialisation on the goods where it has a competitive advantage, such as in heavy machinery, aircraft and pharmaceuticals, would actually *reduce* the average cost of production in those industries. This in turn would aid dynamic development in the west because by making possible longer production runs it would enhance the prospective returns.

Setting in the West but Still Rising in the East

While the impact of dynamic growth in the east is to reduce western inflation, the same cannot be said of inflation in the east. Indeed, in many of the dynamic countries inflation is alive and kicking. Figure 2.3 shows how inflation in China over recent years has on the whole been of a completely different order from the older industrial countries (represented here by the US). Inflation in Hong Kong has been an intermediate case – decidedly higher than in the US, but never reaching the worst heights experienced by China.

In the cases of serious inflation such as China, or even more so in some former members of the Soviet Union, what is going on is classic monetary inflation of the sort referred to in Chapter 1 and discussed in detail in Chapters 7 and 8. Typically, governments run with levels of

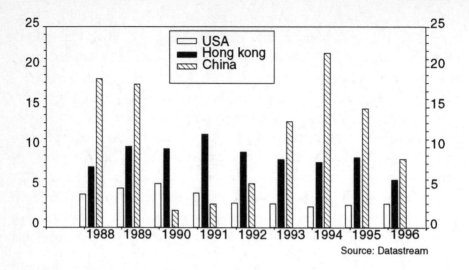

Figure 2.3   Inflation in the US, China and Hong Kong, % year on year, 1988–96

expenditure which they cannot or will not finance fully from taxation, leaving them with a large budget deficit.

This would be bad enough, but in many fast-developing countries the method of finance available in most western countries – namely sales of long-term government bonds – simply is not available on an adequate scale. The domestic capital market is not developed enough to be able to take up the volume of debt required to finance the deficit. So, the government resorts to printing money to cover the gap between government expenditure and government income. And the lack of an effective set of checks and balances within the political system allows them to get away with it. Russia, after the collapse of the Soviet Union, is a good example.[41]

In countries which have got the public finances under control, however, inflation tends to be moderate but persistent. This is inflation of a quite different type, more structural in origin. It derives from differential productivity growth, in a way similar to the tensions between manufacturing and services which plagued the west in the post-war years. It is the interaction with the more developed west which causes part of the problem. In the east, productivity growth in the sectors of the economy engaged in international trade is rapid compared to the domestic 'non-traded' sectors. But wage growth will be similar in the two sectors.

The only way for this to be compatible with a stable price level is for prices in the fast productivity growth sectors to fall, to offset price rises in the domestic sector. But in the international sectors, prices are effectively set on world markets. If the exchange rate is fixed, then traded goods prices cannot fall and the inevitable result must be that higher prices in the domestic sector then cause inflation of the overall price index.[42]

This is *development inflation*, a problem of economic success. It can be tolerated without necessarily leading to disaster. Even so, monetary authorities must prevent it from turning into a more virulent form which could be disastrous, without killing the goose which lays the golden egg. The key is to let the exchange rate rise against the main western currencies. This allows the dynamic countries to separate the trend of international prices from domestic prices.[43]

Why should the typical inflation experience of the dynamic countries of the east be so different from the current norm in the older industrial countries? Precisely because the two are at completely different stages of development. It is largely this difference which is driving the impact of the east on the cost and price level in the older industrial countries. And in the east it is also largely responsible for the inflationary pressures arising from the process of rapid growth and interaction with the west.

Equally, the frequent outbreaks of classic monetary indiscipline in the east are the result of ill-developed tax systems and capital markets and inadequate restraints on government, in what are usually politically immature societies.

So the east is still prone to suffer from both the classic monetary inflation which plagued the west periodically during its history, and the more moderate sort which arose from producer power and structural tensions in the post-war period. For some years to come, these two dishes could continue to appear as staples of the eastern diet, long after they have disappeared from the western menu.

Interestingly, though, there are now signs of much lower inflation even in the east. In 1995, inflation in the Czech Republic fell below 10%, having been over 20% two years earlier. And in booming Poland, although inflation was nearly 30%, it was on a downward track. In Brazil it was just over 20%, having been over 1000% in 1994, while in Argentina, a country with one of the worst inflation records in the world, it was down to 1½%. In much of dynamic east Asia, although inflation in 1995 was well above western levels, it was still below 10%. Singapore even managed to combine growth above 8% with inflation of only 2%. Under the twin forces of international financial market pressure on governments to operate disciplined monetary and budgetary policies, and more open trading policies, in years to come perhaps the contrast between inflation in east and west may not be so stark.

Consumer Wariness

If you draw together the themes of this chapter, they amount to the collapse of producer power in all its guises. On the face of it, this looks like extremely good news for consumers. Certainly, increased competition, the swelling tide of lower priced goods from the east and the ready availability of information all work in consumers' favour. This makes it sound as though people should be dancing in the streets – only the bosses should be downcast.

Yet this forgets that consumers are merely producers going shopping. The power people have gained as consumers corresponds to the power they have lost as producers. As consumers, people used to be taken for granted. Prices went up regardless; products and services were structured for a mass market; it was difficult to express or communicate individual preferences.

But in the world of work it was different. Here there was both security and power. In the big corporations, in the banks, the nationalised industries and government departments, for both ordinary office workers and executives, there was an implicit guarantee of jobs for life. On the factory floor, the unions stood as guardians and protectors of job security. Meanwhile, the general buoyancy of the labour market gave fallback security if things went wrong.

And in a wider context, there were fixed points by which to set your life. Not only did people have full-time jobs which lasted until they were 60 or 65, but earnings went up every year in both money and real terms. Workers in structured bureaucracies enjoyed their annual increments while manual workers benefited from the annual wage settlement, which was always in excess of prevailing inflation.

In the background there was another certainty – the housing market.

House prices constantly went up so that provided you owned your own home (and increasing numbers of people did) then you had God-given security, and tax-subsidised prospect for gain.

Now everything is turned inside out. Businesses everywhere are paying attention to what the customer wants and shaping products and services to individual preferences. And consumers wield power as they shop.

But so what? The consequences of the very power wielded by consumers are pushed down the production chain where consumers themselves feel them in their capacity as producers. There is no job security any more – virtually anywhere. Staying fully employed until you are 60 or 65 is turning into a minority occupation. Earnings can no longer be relied upon to go up relentlessly even in money terms, let alone over and above inflation. And more people's jobs are on a part-time or contract basis rather than regular employee status. What has happened is nothing less than a wholesale transfer of the natural insecurity of economic life from employer to employee.

Meanwhile, as I discuss in the next chapter, the property market is no longer the same. In many countries in the west, houses have fallen in value, and the prospects for the future look dicey. At the same time, the safety net extended by the state is being cut back and compromised. The new generation cannot rely on the state providing acceptable back-up support in sickness, old age or unemployment. In short, all the fixed points have been shot to pieces.

No wonder then, that the era of consumer power is also the age of uncertainty. Consumers may have power but they are anxious and wary, and reluctant to spend without good reason.[44]

Price Sensitivity

This has an important knock-on effect on the inflationary process. Consumers are now more concerned than ever with what they spend their money on. They have become discriminating and canny, price conscious and weary of gimmicks. Customer resistance is directly felt by anyone trying to pass on increased costs. People simply won't stand for it any more.

Much of the transformation in consumer attitudes is due to the real forces for change now ripping through the economy. These forces help to reduce inflation, but they do not in themselves derive from changes in the inflationary environment. But part of consumers' new canniness is directly related to low inflation itself and in turn it affects inflation.

Perpetual inflation stole power from consumers by confusing them. When prices are rising fast everywhere and people *expect* them to go up, if they observe a particular price going up, then without putting in an enormous effort to check out prices elsewhere they cannot tell whether the *relative price* of this product has risen or whether the rise in this particular price is merely part of the continuing inflationary process. And with the value of money itself changing the consumer cannot be sure whether the higher price for the premium provider of a good or service is justified by the higher quality, convenience or other non-price aspects.

This means that inflation makes consumers *less responsive to price increases*. In economic jargon, demand is less elastic. But in that case, it is in sellers' interests to raise prices more readily. In short, their degree of monopoly power is increased and they can increase their profits by exploiting it.

Equally, consumers' confusion about relative prices and comparative passivity over particular price rises leaves them with higher pay claims as the only means of defence against the threats to their standard of living. It is almost as though the cost-plus mentality which dominated price fixing in companies also affected consumers. As they became *less* sensitive to the micro changes to the price structure, so they became *more* sensitive to the macro changes to their incomes. Meanwhile, employers saw the onward and upward march of their labour costs as inevitable. Their only hope to maintain (or increase) profits was to operate an aggressive stance on pricing policy.

When inflation slows very considerably, as it has in most of the industrial countries over the last few years, these processes go into reverse. Firms find that customers are more price sensitive because greater price stability enables them to maintain their price markers more easily. When a particular price goes up they are more inclined to notice it, resent it, and be prepared to switch their custom elsewhere. (In the jargon, demand is now more elastic.)

The effects of changed perceptions of price sensitivity have been described above in terms of businesses contemplating their pricing strategy. But they may be equally relevant to the supply of labour.

Workers, both individually and through their unions, may be more inclined to 'supply' labour without pushing up its price when inflation is low than when it is high, because they perceive that their employers' demand for it is more price sensitive. This may go some way to explaining why in both the US and Britain the labour market has tightened, and in the US unemployment has even fallen sharply, without engendering any sort of pick-up in earnings growth.

Indeed, the fact that people are no longer confident they can drive up their pay to compensate for higher prices forces them to seek greater value when they spend their money. On the selling side, firms experiencing increased price sensitivity see two ways out: adopting a policy of lower unit margins but higher volumes, or tightly controlling costs.

High inflation breeds passivity in the face of price rises, but aggression in the pursuit of pay rises. Low inflation breeds sensitivity in the face of price rises and passivity in the face of 'low' pay rises. The result is that when inflation is established, diminished price sensitivity makes it easy for it to carry on. By contrast, the process is difficult to get going in the first place. Inflation will be more upwardly mobile when the rate is already high than when it starts off at zero, because resistances to it are that much weaker.

At the level of the macroeconomy, this means that once inflation has been subdued, it will be possible to operate at higher levels of output without igniting inflation than seemed possible when inflation was high.

Competitive Markets Rule, OK?

Consumer anxiety and price responsiveness complete the circle. Producer power is collapsing, but rather than thinking of power being transferred from producers to consumers, it is more useful to think of it dissipating altogether. It is *markets*, not consumers, that are in the ascendant. Managed capitalism has given way to competitive market capitalism – if you like, capitalism in the raw.

As I make clear in Chapters 7 and 8, it is still *possible* for governments to stoke up inflation by excessively expansionary budgetary and monetary policies, although, in the words of the distinguished commentator Peter Jay, in most of the industrial west this is currently 'about as likely as a plague of frogs'.[45]

It is widely believed that this stems from influences quite separate from the real forces which attack the world of business, and that it represents a temporary phase of uncharacteristic self-denial which could easily and rapidly change, giving way to a burst of irresponsible inflationary policy.

I think this view is quite mistaken. As I argue in Part III, the intellectual change behind the shift in macroeconomic policy has been profound and will not easily be shaken.

But more importantly, far from being above the competitive forces which buffet businesses and individuals, governments and central banks are now right in the thick of them. Because of the information and communications revolution, as well as the effects of deregulation, governments (and central banks) can control much less than they used to be able to. All the while, their financial and economic stewardship, particularly with regard to debt and currency values, is closely scrutinised by well-informed, sophisticated, global financial markets, able to give an adverse verdict at the drop of a hat. As a result, however immune they may be to competition within their own countries, governments are now seen by the markets to be in competition with each other. The result is that they can get away with very little. The costs of an inflationary strategy are quickly apparent and, for any rational, responsible government, this serves to deter the attempt. Thus the ultimate repository of producer power – the state provider of money itself and of economic management – is being tamed by globalisation.

Meanwhile, the competitive forces now dominating the world of business and work, which I have described in this chapter, are transforming the behaviour of prices and the way they respond to policy. They are serving to eradicate wage-push; they are transforming the climate of inflationary expectations, making inflation easier to suppress and to contain; they are helping economies to absorb adverse shocks to the price level from a devaluation or a sharp rise in commodity prices; and they are providing a continuous flow of favourable price shocks.

Perhaps most importantly, now that the inflation of the 1970s has been wrung out of the system, in response to adverse shocks, the institutional structure of the economy will now allow prices to fall – for the first time since the 1930s. This opens up the vistas, unseen for two generations, which I described in Chapter 1, vistas of both great promise and great peril.

Part II

Surviving and Thriving in the Zero Era

3

The Return of Ever Rising
House Prices?

Saving is a very fine thing. Especially when your parents have done it for you.

Sir Winston Churchill[1]

Among the things that money can't buy is what it used to.

Max Kauffman[2]

DURING THE INFLATIONARY ERA, PEOPLE IN THE US, CANADA, Australia, most of Europe and Japan had a love affair with property. They saw house prices escalate out of all proportion to initial purchase values, and they loved it. Or at least they loved it while it lasted, and they loved it if they owned enough property. For the inflation of property values was a powerful machine for redistributing wealth within society. Those who did not own property, or who did not own their share of it, lost out to those who did. They paid the higher prices for goods and services in the shops like everyone else, but they did not enjoy tax-free capital gains to compensate for it.

It is no exaggeration to say that over the last two or three decades, home ownership and home finance have dominated personal finances and, as a result, the consumer side of the macroeconomy. The economic imperatives of the average middle-class couple have revolved around housing – buying early, borrowing as much as possible, moving to larger and larger properties, extending or developing properties, putting up with umpteen inconveniences in order to maximise the 'exposure to housing' and, most of all, being prepared to forego ordinary pleasures and scrimp and save in order to devote the lion's share of the family income to feeding the mortgage monster.

Housing has had a symbiotic relationship with inflation. High and persistent general inflation has fostered high house price inflation and thereby promoted the idea of ownership of property as a speculative investment. Meanwhile, high house price inflation may have helped to stimulate general inflation, both by boosting wealth levels and hence encouraging consumer demand, and prompting higher rates of pay inflation to match the rising cost of housing.

In the zero era all this is changing, and it is leaving people bewildered. Property prices have fallen in most countries of the west and, even though in some countries there is now a real recovery under way (for instance, in the UK), in others it looks as though the market could continue in the doldrums. How will the property market behave in the new world without inflation? Will house prices now go up and up, as before? Could they fall back again? What would the consequences be of the end of perpetually rising house prices?

The Housing Money Machine

The numbers tell the property market story. In every one of the world's leading industrial countries (the Group of Seven or G7), house prices rose remorselessly during the heyday of inflation. Between 1970 and 1992, the *average* annual rate of increase of house prices in Britain was 12½%. Italy registered the same average rate in the period 1970 to 1989. Even in low inflation Germany, the average annual rate of house price inflation was 5½%. The US fell between these two extremes at 7¾%.[3]

Substantial rates of price increase of this order produce massive cumulative price rises. In Britain in 1992, house prices stood at more than 13 times the level at which they had stood in 1970. For the other countries, the equivalent figures are much lower but still pretty impressive – 6 times for Canada, 5 for the US and Japan. In the 12 years from 1980 to 1992 house prices in France more than doubled. Even in anti-inflationary Germany, house prices in 1992 stood at roughly 3 times their level in 1971.

The overwhelming bulk of these rises represented house prices keeping pace with the increase in general prices, so most of the capital gains were illusory. But in every single country in the group, there was something left over after inflation, that is to say, *real* house prices rose. In Britain and Japan, real house prices rose, on average, by 2½% a year, in Canada by 2%, by 1½% in Germany and the US, by 1% in France, but by only ¼% in Italy.

These real growth rates sound meagre compared to the growth experienced in money terms, but they have still produced heavy increases when cumulated over the period as a whole. In the UK, the cumulative rise in house prices in real terms was about 75%, and it was over 40% even in Germany.

But of course, these averages disguise huge variations over time and most of these countries have on occasions experienced booms in house prices, during which the rate of increase in prices was well above these averages. It was probably the ferocity of these booms combined with, until recently, the power of inflation to create illusions about real values which established and sustained the mystique of housing as an unbeatable investment.

Between 1985 and 1990, for example, real house prices in Japan increased by 12% a year, on average. In case you think that this is another example of outlandish Japanese numbers, it should be noted that the UK was not far behind at just over 9%. In Canada, the real capital gains were also substantial, at more than 7% a year, though the US registered only 1½%.

So what is going to happen to the housing market in the zero era? This is a question of keen interest in most countries of the west. But for the sake of comparability, in what follows most of my examples are drawn from the UK.

House Prices Without Inflation

Perhaps the most important question is what the end of inflation will imply for the demand for houses and hence for their *real* price. I'll come to that in a moment. But the place to start is what happens to the money price of houses, assuming that there is no impact on the demand for houses from the end of inflation. You might think that is another example of the 'neutrality' of inflation – take inflation away and you simply get changed money values with no real consequence. But in fact it is quite the opposite. Even if a regime of zero inflation would have no systematic implications for the real price of houses, the process of dis-inflation would have enormous implications.

After all, people take out mortgages which are fixed in nominal terms. That was the source of their gains from housing during the infla-tionary era. The value of their housing assets rose while the value of their mortgage liabilities remained constant. And what happens to the nominal price of houses is vital to the plight of the people caught with 'negative equity', where the value of their house has fallen below the value of the mortgage.

In 1995 in Britain more than a million households were in this predicament and probably another million had equity so small as to be insufficient to cover the incidental expenses of moving and a deposit on another property. They were effectively trapped in their current proper-ties, regardless of the suitability of these to their jobs or personal lives. These were some of the people left high and dry by the collapse of infla-tion. They were victims of the transition to the zero era.

In a sense there is a sort of symmetry about this, for it was those who borrowed heavily to 'invest' in housing who were the biggest gainers from inflation. But this does nothing to relieve the pain of those caught with negative equity and it cannot even be called rough justice, because those people who have lost out through inflation's demise are, in general, quite different individuals from those who gained from it in the first place.

Pursuing the marine analogy, if inflation can be thought of as a stead-ily rising water level, even the most stranded hulks will be floated off in time. And, of course, the faster the water level rises, the sooner each will find itself afloat. This was precisely one of the most appealing charac-teristics of inflation for property investment. You might buy at the wrong point of the cycle; you might buy the wrong sort of property, in not quite the right location; you might pay rather more than you should. But in the end inflation would lift you off. It was only a matter of time.

However, if house prices do not rise, the mistakes live on to haunt those who made them. There is no easy or guaranteed way out simply by waiting. Those submerged by negative equity will not be bailed out. And that is one of the painful consequences of the end of inflation – no relief for those unfortunate to be caught at the moment the music stopped.

Swings and Roundabouts

In fact things are not quite as simple as this, because property prices are inherently volatile, moving up and down in cyclical movements. That is not how people have typically seen them – they have seen houses as assets which only ever go up in price; which, until recently, was broadly true *in money terms*. Figure 3.1 shows the annual rate of price inflation against the annual percentage change in house prices (the Nationwide Index). It brings out both the sharp swings in house price inflation, and the general tendency for house price rises to outstrip general inflation.

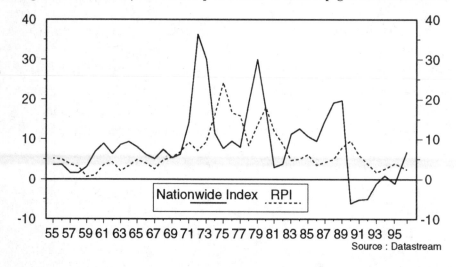

Source : Datastream

Figure 3.1   House and retail price inflation, % year on year, 1955–96

But this has not been true in every year. Indeed, if you subtract general inflation from the rate of house price increases to get a measure of what has happened in real terms, then you can see that real house prices have fluctuated a lot. Even in post-war Britain, the home of rampant house price inflation, the rate of general inflation has exceeded the rate of house price inflation (i.e. the real price of houses has fallen) on a number of occasions – in the early 1950s, after the boom of the early 1970s, again slightly at the beginning of the 1980s, and more familiarly in the early 1990s.

The reason the early 1990s experience made such an impact is clear from Figure 3.1. Because there was so little general inflation, the fall in real house prices had to take the form of a fall in nominal prices, for the first time in recent memory. By contrast, the sharp fall in real house prices in the mid-1970s caused less of a stir because it was achieved while house prices continued to rise in money terms. Rampant general inflation made all the difference.

The early 1990s experience, which seemed so extraordinary at the time, is the shape of things to come. In the zero era the level of real house prices will undergo cycles, just as it always has, but without perpetual inflation this will mean that house prices will rise in the boom years but fall in slack years, *even in money terms*.

If, as I argued in Chapter 1, the world of zero inflation overall is one in which the price level, far from being static, fluctuates up and down, then house price swings will be wider. For the cycles in general inflation will probably be closely linked with the cycles in real house prices. Accordingly, the fluctuations in *nominal* house prices will be more extreme than the fluctuations in real house prices. In that case, people will then have to get used to significant movements in house prices, up and down.

And therein lies an acute danger. It may be all too easy for people to be sucked into the housing market on the current upswing, just as they were before, believing that this heralds the return of the 'good old days', the never-ending property price spiral. If they *are* sucked in, then they could be hit hard by another bout of negative equity as house prices fall again from their peaks. Everyone who wants to avoid this trap should remember that, although in many countries the market is currently enjoying a recovery, this does not mean that house prices are now set to move up relentlessly. In the new world, the bursts of excessive optimism in the market will be followed, not by a pause, but by a reversal.

The Real Reasons for Rising House Prices

Was the fact that house prices not only kept pace with inflation but exceeded it causally connected with inflation itself? That is to say, was it inflation which made houses such a good investment? If so, then zero inflation *could* imply not only an initial fall in real house prices, but also no continued rise in the real price of houses thereafter. This would spell the end of housing as a speculative investment.

This conclusion is resisted by most economists and housing market professionals. They argue that general inflation should be reflected in the money price of houses, but that changes in the real price of houses will be caused by real factors. In most western countries, they say, there have been powerful real factors at work tending to raise the real price of residential property, including increasing population and rising levels of real incomes and wealth. These would have been operative without inflation. All that inflation did was to alter the money values. Accordingly, the end of inflation will make no difference to the real price of housing. The real factors which caused real house prices to rise in the first place may continue to operate, in which case real house prices will continue to rise; or they may not continue to operate, in which case real house prices will not continue to rise. But that is that.

I think that this is much too simplistic a view. There *are* significant real factors at work and indeed the balance of them in most countries probably continues to favour rising real property values over the long term. The most important factors are the pressure of rising populations on a limited supply of properties, with additions ultimately limited by the supply of suitable building land, and the tendency of people to want to spend more money on property as they become richer.

Equally, housing is still well treated from a tax point of view. Throughout the western world, the norm is for some part of mortgage interest to be tax deductible (although the extent of this advantage has recently been substantially reduced in the UK), for the imputed rent from owner occupation (that is to say, the benefit of living in the property) to be untaxed, and for capital profits on the property when it is sold to be free of both income and capital gains tax.[4] The glaring exception is Germany where there is only limited deduction of interest. Interestingly, Germany also has an unusually low level of owner occupation – about 40%, still higher than Switzerland, which comes in at 30%, but much lower than the UK at 67%, the US at 65%, France at 54%, Japan at 61%, and Italy at 70%.[5]

Moreover, housing has particularly attractive qualities as an investment, partly because of its attractions to lenders as a form of security. For most individuals there is no other way that offers them the opportunity to borrow large sums to finance an asset, thereby standing to make a profit on somebody else's money. The ordinary person would not be able to go to a bank and ask to borrow a sum for investment in the stockmarket, putting up as little as 10% of the money themselves (let alone nothing), and hope to receive a polite reply. And that is assuming that he or she would want to.

Inflation and the Real Price of Houses

Nevertheless, there are several good reasons for believing that persistent inflation has assisted the growth in real house prices and correspondingly that, other things being equal, the absence of inflation will see real house prices lower. This may imply that there is nothing necessarily aberrant about the recent fall in house prices in a number of western countries, and indeed that they may have further to fall, until the various real forces mentioned above underpin a slow, unspectacular increase.

For a start, there is the fact that as a real asset houses are some sort of inflation hedge, and for most western countries over the post-war period there have been few other attractive inflation hedges available. If inflation is a problem, then the quality of inflation protection is worth paying for. If it is not a problem, it is not worth paying for.

Tax Relief Eases the Pain of High Interest Rates

Moreover, persistently low inflation will reduce the tax advantages of housing as an investment. Favourable tax treatment is bound to have increased real house prices relative to what they would otherwise have been. This is widely acknowledged. But what is less obvious is that the extent of the attractions of housing originating from this source are greater at higher rates of inflation.

With tax deductibility of interest, the higher the rate of inflation and nominal interest rates, the lower is the *real after-tax* cost of borrowing. Indeed, at only modest levels of inflation and nominal rates, the real after-tax rate of interest will be significantly negative.

Suppose that inflation is 2% and the rate of mortgage interest is 6%, giving a real rate of interest before tax of 4%. But now assume that mortgage interest is tax deductible at 40%. In that case the after-tax nominal interest rate is 3.6%, giving a real after-tax rate of 1.6%.

Now suppose that inflation is 8% and borrowing rates are 12%. Again, the real rate is 4%. The after-tax nominal interest rate is now 7.2% (i.e. 60% of 12%), against inflation of 8%. So the real after-tax interest rate is negative.

And the same point affects the comparison with other investments. Interest on bank deposits or bonds is normally subject to income tax in the usual way, with no allowance for inflation. Suppose that inflation is 8%, interest rates are 10%, and tax rates are 40%. Depositors will then receive 6% after tax. But this means that they have been paid *minus* 2% in real terms. In effect, they have paid the bank for the privilege of depositing money with it. Moreover, if the pre-tax level of real interest rates remains constant, then the higher the rate of inflation and the level of nominal interest rates, the more negative will a depositor's real return become.

Accordingly, when someone compares a return like this with the tax-free return on housing, housing clearly wins. If you add in the tax deductibility of interest on money borrowed for housing purposes, then it becomes what the Americans call a 'no-brainer'.

In some countries the relative tax advantages with high inflation extend even more widely because while capital gains on owner-occupied housing are tax exempt, there is no indexation relief for purely inflation-related gains on other assets, such as equities. Where this applies, then again housing is relatively more attractive as an investment with higher rates of inflation.

Inflation as a Lubricant

All this created an attractive environment for house purchasers, but it also created an environment which mortgage *lenders* found attractive. For under conditions of high inflation, mortgage loans which initially represented a high proportion of the property's value quickly turned into low percentage loans as house prices rose, but the amount of the loan outstanding either stayed the same (with an endowment mortgage) or even fell (with a repayment mortgage). Similarly, as incomes rose under the impact of inflation, mortgage loans which initially represented a high multiple of the borrower's income quickly changed into low multiple loans. This substantially reduced the risks facing lenders. It might seem risky to lend up to 100% of the value of an asset, or up to five times a person's annual income, but time was on the lender's side, quickly reducing the risk.

Now you might think that this favourable influence on lenders would be offset by exactly the opposite consideration for borrowers. After all, the high nominal interest rates which accompany high inflation oblige borrowers to make very high repayments throughout the life of a loan. In the early stages, before inflation has boosted the borrower's salary, these represent an enormous proportion of his or her income. As time goes on and income rises with inflation, the proportion of income represented by interest payments falls. These high interest payments are a reflection of the falling value of money. They compensate the lender for the fall in the *real* value of the capital, which is tumbling throughout the currency of the loan, thanks to inflation. Effectively, the combination of high inflation and high interest rates forces borrowers to repay the real value of the capital earlier than they would under a system of low inflation and low interest rates.

You might think that this would deter borrowers and thereby offset the favourable influence of inflation on the position of lenders. But in fact it may easily work the other way. Borrowers may also like the idea that the burden of the debt will fall sharply over time, while the value of the house will quickly dwarf the outstanding value of the mortgage. In short, this regime which effectively imposes a high burden on them in the early years may make borrowers feel safer.

Competitive pressures among mortgage lenders may cause lenders to resist this conclusion, but the logic of this analysis is that without inflation, lenders should want to lend lower percentages of property values (and multiples of salary) and borrowers should similarly like to borrow smaller percentages (and multiples of salary). This factor should tend to put downward pressure on real property prices until the adjustment is complete.

Moreover, house price inflation provided a *lubricant* for the housing market. In the old inflationary days, after a few years' residence in a house its price would have risen sufficiently to show a comfortable 'profit'. This would then be used to cover the transaction costs of moving house and provide a deposit for a more expensive purchase. Without the 'profits' provided by inflation, householders will have to draw on their savings to cover transaction costs and any increase in the required level of deposit compared to their old property.

Now in equivalent conditions but without inflation, you could argue, householders' savings would be higher because mortgage interest payments would be correspondingly lower. They could readily find an increased deposit and fund the transaction costs of moving to a more expensive property out of these savings.

But there are two problems with this. First, there is what economists call *money illusion*, that is to say, the acceptance of prices or amounts of money at face value, and the failure to see how their real value has been changed by inflation. Even if a house has only gone up in line with retail prices so that in real terms there has been no gain, householders are unlikely to see it that way. They are more likely to regard the increase in the house's value as 'profit' and to consider it perfectly natural to play up their profit by borrowing more to buy a larger property.

By contrast, in the world of no inflation and low nominal interest rates, householders first have to decide to save rather than spend the amount they have avoided paying in higher nominal interest rates, and then they have to be prepared to sink the hard-earned savings into bricks and mortar and/or to finance transaction costs when this very asset, residential property, has yielded no 'profit' (or at least not much of a nominal profit) without inflation.

Secondly, the tax treatment of interest comes into play here too. In the case where you have high inflation and apparently high nominal interest rates, the interest which mortgage holders pay is (at least partially) tax relieved while the increase in the capital value of the property is tax free. In the case where all real variables are the same but there is no inflation, the interest which householders earn on the money they save to provide a deposit and/or finance transaction costs is fully taxed.

The result of all these factors is that inflation has caused house prices to rise in real terms, at precisely the time that in some countries (especially Britain) other real factors, including the interaction of demographic factors with a shortage of building land, was itself putting upward pressure on prices. The result was the generation of high real returns to investment in housing, and the creation of a speculative culture in the housing market which then stimulated yet more demand.

Ladders – and Snakes

The effect of this extra demand was both to persuade people to pay more for a given property and to encourage them to hold more property than they ordinarily would have done. If you like, added to the normal consumption demand for houses, there was now a speculative demand.

Young people felt compelled to enter the market earlier than they would otherwise like to. This had important real consequences for the market as a demand emerged for very small 'starter' properties, for example the one-bedroom flat, which often had to be carved out of larger properties to meet the demand for young people to get an early 'foot on the housing ladder', no matter how small or how basic.

Others further up the housing ladder may have been encouraged to anticipate future housing needs by buying bigger than they initially needed because they worried about the price slipping beyond their reach if they held off. In other words, these people were driven by fear and insecurity to hold more property than they otherwise would have done.

But there were also people driven by the hope of gain. These included not only those who actively traded properties, but also people towards the end of their life hanging on to large properties built as family homes, even though only one or two adults were now living there, because 'it's a good investment'. Still others left second homes empty for much of the year 'because once you take account of the capital appreciation it doesn't cost us anything'. The result of this is that at any given time, part of the demand for housing was speculative demand. In effect, housing has been hoarded.

What will be the consequences of zero inflation for the housing market? All of the above factors raised the level of real house prices. With the death of inflation these factors will drop away and some will even go into reverse. The market will go through a one-off adjustment process which, nevertheless, may drag on for several years. As real prices stagnate or fall, the speculative culture will be wrung out of the housing market. This, in turn, will cause excess property holdings to be released onto the market, thus depressing prices further.

Despite this, at some point the market will reach a new equilibrium. Thereafter, what happens to house prices will depend upon all the usual real factors such as the income sensitivity of the demand for housing, the degree of land shortage, demographic factors, etc. In many countries, including Britain, these should mean that housing at least keeps pace with inflation and perhaps continues to outpace it slightly (that is, real prices rise), reflecting the rise in real incomes. But without general inflation, we are talking very small numbers compared to the large increases which most people are used to. In Britain, a trend rise of something like 1–3% might be sustainable, not taking account of costs of repair, maintenance and all the other incidental expenses of owning property.

A Housing Disaster?

So far the picture I have painted doesn't sound too bad – house prices fluctuating in both nominal and real terms, a good chance that house prices will be lower because of the demise of inflation and may not increase much afterwards, but no collapse of prices. Every reader, however, should be aware of the possibility of something much more dramatic. The zero era *could* see a housing market disaster.

In 1995, Professor Douglas Wood of Manchester Business School forecast falls in British house prices of up to 30% in real terms over the next 20 years. As a central view of the future this strikes me as much too gloomy, but there is no denying continued downside risks. After all, there are instances of large house price falls in the past. In Britain, house prices fell persistently during the 1930s and they even edged lower in the early 1950s. The cumulative fall in the early 1990s recession so far is 12%. The Bank for International Settlements has recently studied house prices across 15 countries. Over the period between 1970 and 1992, all of the countries had experienced at least one bout of house prices falling by 7% or more; in seven cases, including the UK, countries had experienced a fall of 10% or more; and Finland and the Netherlands had experienced a fall of more than 30%.

If house prices could fall this much against the background of a continual upward movement of the general price level, what would it be like if the general level of prices fell, and fell persistently? The danger would come from mortgage indebtedness. As house prices plummeted, the value of mortgage debt would remain unchanged. True, interest rates would presumably be much lower, even close to zero, but, as I explained in Chapter 1, they could not be negative. So the financial position of borrowers would deteriorate. They would surely panic, cutting back on their spending and hence worsening recessionary tendencies and putting further downward pressure on the general price level.

Now *someone* in the system would have to gain from the borrowers' loss. It would be the holders of financial assets such as bonds and bank deposits. In many cases, of course, these would be owned by the same people who had mortgage liabilities. But there would be a substantial mismatch. And even individuals who held an equal quantity of mortgage liabilities and fixed money assets, so that inflation was neutral on their overall balance sheet position, would be unlikely to *feel* unaffected. Much of their monetary assets would be held in pension funds and life insurance companies locked away for long periods. They might not even realise that the real value of these assets was rising. By contrast, the falling value of their house would be evident, as would the rising real value of the regular mortgage payments.

In practice, this could not produce a real disaster without falls in pay levels. For if prices were falling and pay was constant (the contrast being made possible by rising levels of productivity), then real incomes would be rising. People would be anxious about the falling real value of their houses but at least they could easily meet their mortgage obligations. And provided that pay levels were constant, thus sustaining cost levels and limiting the ability of companies to compete by slashing prices, price deflation could not proceed at a very rapid rate – 3 or 4% perhaps (influenced primarily by the rate of growth of productivity).

Things are altogether different, however, if pay levels can fall. Then there is, in principle, no limit to the rate at which the prices of goods and services can fall, and no protection for individuals against the rising real value of mortgage payments. This mortgage nightmare would be quite different from anything in the 1930s, because then levels of home ownership and personal indebtedness were much lower. Then the dangers of downward price spirals lay largely in the financial and corporate sectors. And the onset of depression psychology which made it so difficult to restore normal levels of output and employment and which so troubled Keynes was again a problem of the financial markets and industrialists. Consumers were largely immune. They were thought to respond more or less automatically to whatever economic impulses were generated in the corporate and financial worlds.

But not now. If we were ever again trapped in a downward spiral of pay and prices, then the large level of mortgage debt would ensure that consumers were engulfed and that they would succumb to depression psychology. Indeed, they would probably be at the very centre of the problem. Let us hope that the mortgage nightmare can remain locked in the realm of all our worst dreams.

Consequences of the Transformation of the Housing Market

Even without a housing disaster, and even after the acute pain caused by the sharp adjustment of house prices has passed, the new environ-ment will be such a sharp contrast with what has gone before that there will be major structural changes in the practices and institutions of the housing market.

There will probably be a major change in the structure of mortgage lending. Without persistent inflation, mortgage lenders may become more cautious. At the very least, in a world of zero inflation they must dramatically scale down the amount they are prepared to lend, both as a percentage of a property's current market value and as a multiple of borrowers' incomes.

For without inflation, the real value of their exposure on the loan will be higher for longer. Or, putting the matter another way, it will take much longer for their security for the loan, the value of the property, to reach any given margin of safety over the value of the loan. In the light of this, it would be rational for lenders to charge higher rates for loans which represented a higher proportion of the value of a house.

Without inflation, prospective purchasers will be under less pressure to buy or move up market. Accordingly, the average age at which peo-ple first take out a mortgage may rise. Indeed, it will be normal for young people to save in order to accumulate enough for a deposit, in contrast to the culture of the 90% or even 100% mortgage prevalent over recent years in some countries.

As I argue in the next chapter, in a regime fully adjusted to zero inflation, long-term interest rates would be much lower than they are today. As a result, long-term fixed-rate mortgages might become much more common. One result of this would be to make the economy less sensitive to changes in short-term interest rates as householders would be immune to movements in short rates. If householders typically had a lower proportion of debt and more equity, the effect would be the same, although if the debt were floating rate there would still be some sensitivity to short rates.

With house prices rising much more slowly than in the past and mortgage debt rising more slowly, the business of mortgage lending institutions will also grow more slowly. This is bound to put strong competitive pressure on these institutions, probably leading to smaller margins, but also to rationalisation and mergers among lenders.

The new environment of zero inflation is likely to reduce the level of housing turnover. The absence (or reduction) of speculative opportunities will remove the compulsion to move frequently to keep 'full exposure' to the market. Moreover, the much attenuated automatic generation of 'profits' by property ownership may, by removing the ready source of equity to support increased borrowing and finance transaction costs, also deter frequent moving.

After the collapse of the property market in Britain in 1990, turnover did fall and in 1995 it was languishing at levels which housing market professionals regarded as unusually low. They still clung on to the idea that things would at some point 'return to normal'. The penny had not dropped that what they regarded as normal was in fact abnormal, in the sense that it was the result of the distortions created by the growth of the speculative culture in housing.

Because of the reduction in housing turnover, all the activities which depend upon the market will be affected – solicitors, removal firms, mortgage lenders and arrangers, decorators and the like. The home improvements industry, however, is subject to a two-way pull. One of the motives for extensions and developments to homes is surely financial – the view that the money will be well spent as it will serve to enhance the value of the property when it comes to be sold. Without house price inflation, this activity will surely suffer a serious blow.

But on the other hand, one of the effects of house price inflation is to disguise the deterioration in properties which occurs without repair and maintenance, from such things as rotten window frames, leaking roofs and ruptured damp courses. Without such expenditure, the value of residential property may fall by perhaps 1 or 2% per annum. Without inflation house-holders will have a clearer incentive to undertake this expenditure and mortgage lenders will have a greater incentive to ensure that it is done.

The housebuilding industry will be adversely affected by the lower real price of houses as this will imply, other things being equal, a lower real price for new homes also, but at least some of this effect will be absorbed by a reduction in the prices paid for building land. Moreover, the changed structure of the market could have profound implications for the sort of new homes which people want to buy, perhaps fewer starter homes, more family homes to live in for some time, and smaller properties to trade down to at the end.

A Subdued Housing Market Equals a Weak Economy?

To many observers and commentators, (not least those directly con-nected with the market), the weakness of the housing market is an eco-nomic disaster. They point out how much economic activity is bound up with housing in some way or other, and stress the effects of the weak market in depressing consumer confidence and therefore consumer spending. We won't get a real economic recovery, they say, without a recovery in the housing market.

As a statement of how important the market has been to the economy in the past, they are right. And in the transition phase to the new regime, the 'abnormal' behaviour of the housing market is playing a major role. But the fact that a high proportion of economic activity has in the past been connected with the housing market does not make it either good (i.e. efficient or growth promoting for the economy) or inevitable.

Nor does it mean that once the transition has been made there will be a permanent hole in the economy where the housing market used to be. Indeed, quite the opposite. Despite its past dependence on the housing market, and with the market now in desperate straits, after 1992 Britain managed a very decent recovery, led mainly by net exports. Moreover, the pace and type of the British recovery were directly related to the depression in the housing market. For it allowed the authorities to set interest rates sufficiently low to maintain a competitive pound and help business, without setting off the usual housing boom and surge in consumption. Far from being a disaster, in terms of macroeconomic policy, the state of the housing market was a boon.

Furthermore, there are deeper and more long-lasting benefits from removing the artificial stimulus to the housing market which inflation provided. Britain is the quintessential example of a society obsessed with housing values, but the lessons from the British case apply much more widely. The obsession with housing has diverted resources away from more productive activities. It is sometimes alleged, for instance, that Britain has invested too much in bricks and mortar. Clearly, though, to have any economic significance, this needs to be true of the amount of resources spent on new housebuilding, and not just the amount of *money* spent on recycling secondhand houses. In fact, new housebuilding activity in Britain has been low by international standards.

But the recycling of the housing stock has itself had a substantial cost – the real cost of churning the property portfolio. Walk along any high street in south-east England and you could be forgiven for thinking that the leading economic activity in the country was buying and selling each other's houses – mortgage providers, mortgage brokers, estate agents, removal firms, surveyors, solicitors, decorators and kitters out, and little else.

Even so, this has probably not been the most important sort of distortion – that prize goes to the effect on people's attitudes. For throughout the long period of persistent house price inflation, buying property was commonly viewed as a way, if not *the* way, of getting rich. Indeed, for many ordinary people it was for a long time just about the only way of ever amassing a substantial capital asset. People saw others borrowing a lot, moving house often, and progressing up the wealth ladder. They drew the conclusion that this is where wealth came from – created out of thin air in the housing market.

A court case which produced its verdict in September 1995 provides food for thought. According to the report of the case in *The Times*,[6] in

1988 Julia Verity, 55, a teacher, and Richard Spindler, 36, an acupuncturist, had borrowed £150,000 from Lloyds Bank. They bought a terraced home in Henley for £126,500 and spent £25,000 on renovations, expecting to sell the house for £160,000 within a year. For security, they gave the bank not only this property but also two other mortgaged properties, one of which was the family home. In the event, the property market collapsed and it took them two years to sell the house; even then they only raised £135,000 from it and had to sell one of their other properties, still leaving them substantially out of pocket.

The couple brought an action against Lloyds Bank for negligent business advice which they claimed ruined their lives. The essence of their case was that they had read Lloyds Bank's pamphlet *Starting Your Own Business*, which stated: 'Your bank manager will help you to decide how much you can afford to invest.' They won their case and were awarded £77,500. But Lloyds filed a counter-claim for money owed on four other loans and in January 1996 a High Court judge ruled in the bank's favour, awarding it £104,000.[7]

It is not for me to comment on the legal rights and wrongs of this particular case. But gross misperceptions of the housing market were common at this time. It is startling that ordinary people could borrow large sums for property speculation, sometimes owning a clutch of mortgaged properties. It is perhaps more startling that they could regard property speculation as *investment* and even see the organisation of the activity as a business. Napoleon is supposed to have called England 'a nation of shopkeepers'. At this point in the late 1980s, it would more aptly have been described as a nation of property speculators.

Yet how can a *society* be enriched by the fact that its housing stock trades at higher and higher values? Many individuals *did* feel better off as a result of house price inflation, but they failed to take full account of the fact that they needed to live somewhere, and the prices of all the other places they might live were also rising. For many, there was a gain over and above this, because they traded houses for a profit or because they planned to 'move down' at some later stage. But it was offset by the *loss* endured by other people on the other end of the transaction.

So the wealth 'created' in the housing market was part illusion and part transfer from other people. For the individual, any return accruing from this process was rather like the profit from taking part in a chain letter. Or, to change the metaphor, it was like a society trying to get rich by everyone agreeing to take in each other's washing.

Most accounts of the surges in the housing market speak of them being driven by *greed* as people dived into the market in search of quick profits. Undoubtedly, this was one aspect. But at least as important, in my view, was another powerful emotion – *fear*. As house prices rose, people feared being left behind. If they did not yet own property, it was fear of never being able to afford to do so. If they did own a small or starter property, it was fear of never being able to own the family house they would need when the children arrived.

Many people were indeed shut out from property ownership altogether by the rapid rise in prices. Still others found themselves rushed into buying more property, and buying it earlier, than they needed – in order to be able to 'secure their place' before someone else did. Yet when the professionals talk about the housing market they seem to forget about *these* people and their emotions. You would think that rising house prices equalled joy for everyone and falling house prices equalled pain for everyone. But rampant house price inflation was not all about profits and confidence, even for those in the market. It also bred fear and insecurity and in the process wasted resources.

There will still be rises and falls in house prices even if the general price level turns out to be completely stable. But once the truth has sunk in, the death of perpetual inflation will put a stop to this frantic merry-go-round which spun off such powerful and destructive emotions.

Viewing Property as Somewhere to Live

What is the right attitude for people to take towards the ownership of residential property in this new world? It should be viewed solely on its merits as a provider of housing services, not as a source of profit. True, once the adjustment to zero inflation is complete, house prices may well continue to creep up, and property still has advantages as an asset, including tax privileges. But there are also expenses. These may have seemed insubstantial in the days of rampant house price inflation, but they will not now. The conclusion is that, in general, housing is still likely to be a reasonably good store of value, but will be far from the money-spinner of yesteryear.

This means that people should aim to buy property when it makes sense in relation to the rest of their life, and buy the right sort of property in the right place. In short, it means treating property just like any other major consumer purchase, differentiated by the long life of the asset, but not as a counter in a complex speculative game. It is a measure of how much our values have been distorted by inflation that this principle seems bizarre, if not naive.

Because property prices will go up and down and, in general, pay will rise only slowly, it also means that people need to adopt a cautious and conservative attitude towards borrowing money for house purchase. The 80, 90 or even 100% mortgages which were prevalent in the heyday of the housing market at the end of the 1980s could now be downright dangerous.

And remember the risk of falling prices and even falling pay. Just about every inflation rate could go negative – house prices, general prices and pay. But *not* mortgage rates. The mortgage nightmare which I described earlier should scare borrowers into keeping their borrowing levels low so that they can survive a spell of outright deflation.

A New Form of Mortgage Misery

The mortgage nightmare could arrive sooner and be all the more serious for borrowers who take out *fixed-rate* mortgages. Of course, there are times when these are a good idea. Indeed, sometimes the terms offered by lenders are all but irresistible. In some countries, there are fixed-rate mortgages which allow you to repay early *without penalty*. These are potentially a very good deal because they effectively amount to a one-way option. If interest rates rise you are sitting pretty with your fixed-rate mortgage, but if rates fall you can terminate the fixed-rate agreement and refinance with a cheaper variable-rate mortgage.

But these are exceptions. Where a one-way option does not exist and the interest rate is genuinely fixed, unless it is deliberately fixed by the lender at a low level as a marketing ploy to entice new borrowers, then the very quality which makes fixed-rate mortgages attractive when interest rates go up can make them dangerous when interest rates fall. If you borrow on fixed rate and then the economy enters a down-swing, the monetary authorities are likely to react to this by dropping interest rates to very low levels, just as the Japanese authorities did in 1995. But if you have opted for a fixed-rate mortgage you will be committed to continuing to pay the same interest rate until the expiry of the agreement, even though the general level of interest rates is very low and the value of the house is falling, and even if the general price level is falling and perhaps your income level is falling as well.

The fact that mortgage borrowers are naturally inclined to see fixed-rate offers as a bargain, as long as the rates are equal to or only slightly above variable rates, is a reaction to the history of the last 25 years. Borrowers are caught in a time warp. They still fear the times of double-digit interest rates which devastated their finances only a few years previously. Few have yet even imagined a world where most prices are falling and interest rates are at minimal levels yet they are stuck paying 7 or 8%. But this, rather than mortgage rates of 14 or 15%, represents the more likely threat of mortgage misery in the future.

4

The Financial Markets:
Our Future in Their Hands

A bird's eye view of the history of interest rates will unsettle most pre-
conceived ideas of what is a high rate or a low rate or an average rate.
Each generation tends to consider normal the range of interest rates with
which it grew up; rates much higher suggest a crisis or seem extortionate,
while rates much lower seem artificial or inadequate. Almost every generation is eventually shocked by the behaviour of interest rates because,
in fact, market rates of interest in modern times have rarely been stable
for long. Usually they are rising or falling to unexpected extremes.

Sidney Homer, 1977[1]

THE FINANCIAL MARKETS ARE THE CENTRAL FOCUS FOR THE FORCES
which will determine the fate of the western economies in the
zero era. The key questions concern interest rates. How low
will they go? Will the markets allow them to fall low enough to stave
off depression and outright deflation? But also, how will markets be
affected by the onset of falling prices?

The answers to these questions will have implications for all the
subjects examined in other chapters – property, pensions, cash management, personal finances, business investment and company
finances. They also have implications for the world of stocks and
shares, commercial property and real assets, which I discuss here.

How Low Can Interest Rates Fall?

Lower interest rates are one of the main benefits to be had from the end
of inflation. At the very least, rates should fall in line with inflation and

that should bring cash flow advantages to borrowers, as I argue in other chapters. But they should fall even further than this. As I explain in Chapter 7, in reaction to the inflation of the 1970s, long-term real interest rates rose as investors demanded compensation for the risk of inflation in the future. Meanwhile, governments used high real short-term interest rates as a way of reducing inflation.

So, if it becomes generally acknowledged that inflation is permanently subdued, then not only should nominal interest rates fall, but real interest rates, both short and long, should also be lower. How low might interest rates go? The evidence, both past and present, suggests *very* low.

In several countries, including Canada, Australia, Denmark, Israel and the UK, there are now indexed bonds in existence which allow us to have a clearer idea of the *real* returns currently demanded by the market, that is to say, the ordinary rate of interest which would be demanded by the market if it were confident that there would be no changes in the value of money.[2] The market for indexed bonds is most highly developed in the UK. The real interest rate on these British indexed bonds has mostly fluctuated between 3 and 4%, in other words, not a million miles away from the return on bonds in the nineteenth century which I discuss in Chapter 7. As Figure 4.1 shows, it is also the yield level which Japanese bonds reached in 1994–5, when current inflation was just about zero (although they have since fallen even further).

Short-term interest rates, though, could reasonably be expected to be lower than this in normal conditions, as they were for most of history. The US Federal Reserve recently operated a policy of setting short-term real interest rates at roughly zero. In the conditions of the time, with inflation at about 3%, this implied short-term rates of 3%. But if inflation had been zero, it would have implied rates as close to zero as possible. And in Japan, as Figure 4.2 shows, at the end of 1996, with official interest rates at ½%, short-term interest rates (represented here by the three-month rate) were only just above zero.

It needs to be emphasised, however, that despite the force of the above arguments, inflation and its implications are only one influence on the level of long interest rates. Other factors could compound or offset their influence. The prime candidate for the role of offsetting influence is the effect of rapid economic growth in the dynamic countries, which I discussed in Chapter 2.

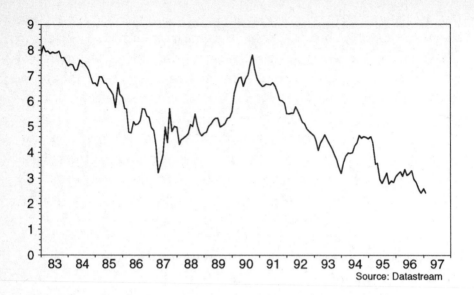

Figure 4.1   Japanese 10-year bond yields, %, 1983–96

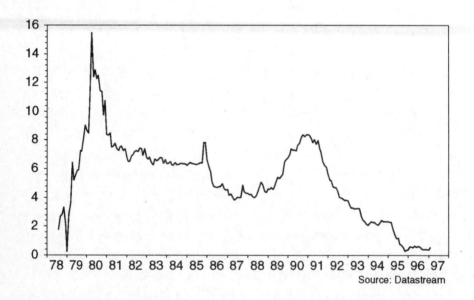

Figure 4.2   Japanese 3-month interest rates, %, 1978–96

The result could be a period of very high real returns on investment in these countries, which could spill over into higher required returns on all investment instruments around the globe. Equity funds would be drawn towards these higher yielding markets, raising required equity yields in the older, established markets. Higher equity returns would drag up required returns on bonds. Indeed, there are some suggestions that this has already been happening.

So what happens to real interest rates could be the result of a tug of war between high (but risky) real returns in the emerging markets and the influence of low inflation and low short rates in the west. The outcome is far from certain. Perhaps the result will be divergent for different instruments – bond yields being dragged down by low short rates and low inflation, but equity yields dragged up by higher prospective returns in the emerging markets.

The Importance of Expectations

The effects of low inflation on the world of investment can already be glimpsed from recent experience. For as inflation has been trending down in the western world over the last 15 years, so has the level of interest rates and bond yields.

Even if inflation falls no further in the west but simply remains continually at current low levels, there will still be major changes in interest rates and investment relationships. The financial world has not yet adjusted to the current reality of low inflation, let alone to the possibility of falling prices, to which I shall turn in a moment.

This is because it does not expect the currently low rates of inflation to continue. Rather, it expects inflation to pick up, admittedly not to the levels that it reached in the 1970s but, depending on the country, to somewhere in the 3–6% range. Indeed, more or less throughout the disinflationary trend of the 1980s, the financial markets' expectations of the future seemed to be along these lines – not as much inflation as before, but more than currently. As inflation trended down, so that financial markets tended to be proved wrong, they nevertheless stuck to this same view. This is still largely true today. At the beginning of 1996 a large number of investors in the US bond market were starting

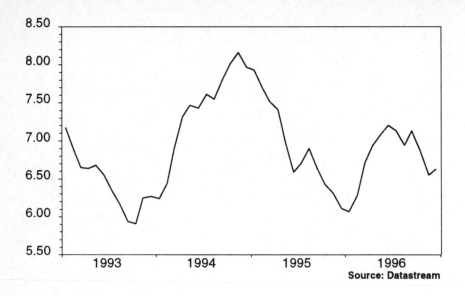

Figure 4.3   US long bond yield, %, 1993–96

to believe that inflation would not return to higher levels, and the rate
of interest on long bonds fell to just over 6%, but as Figure 4.3 shows,
later in the year their pessimism returned.

Indeed, use of the very word 'expectation', which is so common in
markets as well as in academic and policy circles, fails to capture the state
of mind of investors. They do not really 'expect' anything. Rather, they
operate with a normal *presumption* and then add something for protection
against an outbreak from normality. But such is the state of mind of
investment markets today that, as far as inflation is concerned, just about
the only conceivable breakout from the normal presumption is upwards.

This state of mind not only has important consequences for financial markets but it also presents a serious danger for the economy. If
inflation disappears but the markets do not believe it, then we will be
stuck with interest rates which are *higher* in real terms than they were
before. This not only offsets any benefits from the death of inflation but
threatens economic disaster.

Beliefs, Conventions and Shocks

Why are financial markets proving so slow to recognise the collapse of inflation which is now so evident to many businesspeople and consumers? The short answer is because in trying to look forwards, they always start by looking back. And, of course, the history of the last 30 years is of high and unstable inflation. But the problem created by this is more systematic. After 15 years working in the financial markets, I have come to believe that there is something strange about the way financial markets form their expectations.

Market practitioners are trapped by the impossibility of knowing the future. Financial institutions frequently invest in financial instruments with a life of 20 or 30 years. Yet how can anyone begin to know what the world will be like in 20 years' time, let alone how a particular company or government bond market will fare?

Market practitioners deal with this problem in two related ways. First, they assume that although the instrument itself is long lived, they can dispose of it when they wish by selling it to someone else.

Secondly, they try to assess the future by looking at the past. What the market appears to do is to go back perhaps 15–25 years, to form a basic assumption about the norm, and then modify it by giving special weight to very recent experience and current trends. Why 15–25 years? There is no logical reason, but the explanation may be because this corresponds to the working lives of the senior people and the living memory of just about everyone in the markets. This history forms the markets' expectational hinterland.

When you put these two methods of dealing with uncertainty together, they begin to make more sense. If the owner of an asset expects to sell it at some point in the immediate future, it is not of key relevance how the market will perform over 20 years. What he or she needs is some assurance that it will trade well in the immediate future, in relation to what was paid for it, even though at that point in the immediate future, the far future which is relevant to the asset over the whole of its life will be just as uncertain as it is now.

Each investor can do this by adopting *conventional assumptions* about valuation. If the market as a whole tends to assume that inflation over the next 20 years is going to be the average of the last 20 years and you are buying an instrument which you might well want to sell in the immediate future, then it makes sense for you to judge it as an investment against that conventional starting point. This is essentially the view propounded by the great economist John Maynard Keynes in the far from inflationary 1930s. But this view of market behaviour has the same penetrating relevance today as it did then.[3]

'Expectations' which are formed in this way *may* be believed, but they do not have to be. They are used in the formation of market prices because they are useful. What makes them useful is that others use them. They can be thought of, if you like, rather as a form of currency. Dollar bills or pound notes are accepted as payment not because they are intrinsically valuable but because others will accept them.

How do such conventional expectations become established? The answer lies in the realms of group psychology. Market participants search for a set of financial expectations which others will adopt when each is simultaneously searching for the expectations which everyone else will adopt.

It sounds impossible that markets could reach a set of mutually accepted assumptions in this way, but in fact individuals and societies are remarkably good at finding solutions to such problems. Suppose that you have to meet somebody in Paris on a certain day. Neither you nor the other person is told the time or the place and no communication is possible. Each is to guess where the other will choose to meet, knowing that the other person is confronted with the same problem. You would think that the chances of meeting your partner are vanishingly small, and that both of you will be left milling about all over Paris for the whole day. Yet it is surprising how often pairs of people who are posed questions of this sort manage to find a solution which works.

What they do is to search for a convention which they believe is familiar to the other person and which, they think, the other person will believe is familiar to them. In the example I have given, the effective 'conventional' answer is 12 noon at the foot of the Eiffel Tower.

For markets, the far future is the equivalent of a whole day's milling about in a capital city in search of your other half. Markets deal with this problem by adopting conventional assumptions. But when expectations are formed in this 'conventional' way, they are difficult to dislodge. The mere passage of time may eat away at them as the convention comes to seem more and more incongruous when set against current reality. But this can be a very long process. It may take a sudden jolt to dislodge them, a defining event which shakes the imagination into life.

The markets' expectations of inflation are currently in the process of being whittled down, bit by bit, as the high inflation of the 1970s gradually fades out of their conventional memory and is replaced by recent years of much lower inflation. But on this basis it could take ages to grind inflationary expectations out of the financial system, with the result that, in relation to current inflation, interest rates and yields are set too high. This in turn will tend to depress demand, thereby making inflation lower and, indeed, risking a descent into serious recession and a period of falling prices.

It isn't only the markets which are affected by conventional expectations. The monetary authorities are also drawn in, for they set interest rates at levels which seem appropriate given the level of inflation expectations in the market. This means that even if the future corresponds to the very low continuous inflation vision they hope for (and perhaps now expect), it may be many years before short rates are low enough in relation to the new low inflationary world. The authorities too need a jolt.

The adjustment to low inflation would be quicker (and perhaps less costly) if some way could be found of shaking the conventional expectation of inflation. I believe that the most likely candidate for this role is a period of falling prices in the west. Recent Japanese experience already partly qualifies for this role, but it has not had much impact on market psyche outside Japan because it can so easily be dismissed as peculiarly Japanese. If the US were to experience falling prices, however, then that *would* shake market psychology. That would, in my judgement, be a defining event, creating a step shift in the expectational climate, the abandonment of the previous conventional expectation and the search for a new one.

The Dangers and Pitfalls of Transition

The adjustment of expectations is one of the problems thrown up by the process of transition from a world dominated by inflation to one without it. As well as the macroeconomic problems to which I have just referred, the transition can bring serious *financial* problems. For much of the financial structure is based on the same conventional expectation which rules the minds of investors. In particular, borrowers who have paid 8, 10, 12% or more for fixed-interest money for periods which may be as long as 30 years have only done so in the belief that inflation would continue at reasonably high rates. If it does *not* continue, then these high nominal interest rates translate into high real rates – rates of 8, 10, 12% or more. Interest rates such as these could be crippling.

The problem is most serious for the public sector. Forget the emerging markets; the developed world has several countries with enormous public debts, whose financing difficulties are already serious but whose position would become much more serious without inflation. In 1996, Italy's ratio of outstanding public debt to national income, or Gross Domestic Product (GDP), was more than 120%. In Belgium, the rate was even higher. Sweden's rate was 80% and Canada's was running at nearly 100%. In recent years, these countries have all borrowed at high interest rates, in Italy's case at rates well in excess of 10%.

The Italian predicament looks particularly serious. The annual budget deficit, which was recently 10% of GDP (as was Sweden's) was reduced in 1996 to 7%, but this is comprised wholly of interest payments. Italian hopes for achieving sustainable public finances rest on its becoming a founder member of the European single currency, the Euro. (See the discussion of EMU in Chapter 9.)

The danger that all these countries face is of an explosion of the national debt. Raising taxes or cutting government expenditure in order to pay interest is unattractive. So instead they borrow to pay interest, but this borrowing increases the total debt and thereby increases the level of interest payments in the next year, when the same issue confronts them, only now in more virulent form. If the national income is growing fast, the problem may be contained as the tax base normally grows roughly in line with national income.

It has traditionally been believed that inflation offers a way out for heavily indebted countries, by devaluing the debt. All nominal values go up in line with goods prices, including the nominal value of tax receipts, but *not* the nominal value of fixed-interest debt.

However, this is only true if the markets do not react to the inflation. For once markets get a whiff of inflation, they will only lend in that currency at higher interest rates, thereby increasing the government's need for funds to cover interest payments. It is clear that this is the predominant reality today. Inflation does not fool the bondholders any more.

Of course, such growth of public debt is unsustainable in the long run. But this is precisely what the debt crisis is all about. While debt levels are low, even unsustainable growth of debt interest is tolerable for a while. Everyone will tend to assume that something will come along to stop the unsustainable growth in the end. But at high levels of debt, this ceases to apply and a new factor begins to appear – fear on the part of investors that they may not get their money back. This risk justifies still higher interest rates which in turn make the debt service problem still worse. Not for nothing is this syndrome known as the debt trap.

There is no doubt that a slide into high inflation is a real possibility for some of the heavily indebted countries. But even if it were to happen in one or more debt-burdened countries, it would not carry the rest of the developed world along on an inflationary tide. After all, when various countries in Latin America have had their periodic bouts of very high inflation, this has not infected other countries because the inflating country's currency has depreciated so as to adjust for high inflation.

In fact, the effect on other countries might be strongly anti-inflationary because the financial markets would fear the loss of assets held in the fast-inflating country and, having seen the mess that countries can get into fiscally, they might drive bond yields higher in any but the most prudently managed economies. This, in turn, would put pressure on governments to cut spending and/or raise taxes in order to reduce their borrowing.

But it is by no means inevitable that any of the heavily indebted countries will suffer very high inflation. Even for those most perilously placed, there are ways out. Given that debt interest is at the heart of the problem, a fall in world interest rates and bond yields would reduce debt service costs even in the heavily indebted countries. Provided this benefit were used to reduce public borrowing and not squandered on increased government expenditure or lower taxes, it could then serve to bolster confidence in these markets and hence reduce the costs of funding still further.

The issue of index-linked securities and short- rather than long-term debt would also reduce the costs of financing a heavily indebted government if inflation turned out to be low, and hence bolster market confidence that such governments would choose to resist rather than give in to inflation. Most importantly, the countries at risk still have time to make a major effort to reduce their budget deficits.

Worries for Investors

The worsening financial position of government borrowers is, of course, matched by an improving position for those who lend to the government, namely the bondholders. But even for them, the process of disinflation is not an unmixed blessing. For they now have to worry about whether they will get their money back, or at least get it back in quite the form they expected.

Similar arguments apply to company borrowing, although the scale of the debt problem is much smaller. The income stream from which the borrower intends to meet the fixed-interest payments and eventual repayment of capital is now not the tax base but the company's profits. Without inflation, this stream will grow more slowly in nominal terms. For a company with low levels of fixed-interest borrowing this need not create a serious problem, even though it will definitely inflict a real loss, which will be reflected in the price of the company's shares. But for heavy fixed-interest borrowers, the effect could be devastating. Accordingly, the emergence of a prevailing assumption in the market of no inflation would lead to a rerating of company debt and equity on the basis of relative levels of fixed-interest borrowing.

Companies with high levels of variable-rate borrowing (e.g. overdrafts) should not be adversely affected, provided interest rates fall to reflect lower inflation. Nevertheless, in the transition phase, as I argued above, interest rates might not fully adjust so there would be some increased cost even to companies with only variable-rate debt. Accordingly, on this basis, the companies with the highest levels of borrowing would do worse than others and the values of their shares should reflect this.

Falling Prices

All the above factors would operate on a heightened scale if and when the general price level starts to *fall*. Theoreticians may be tempted to see the change from prices rising to prices falling as a mere quantitative phenomenon. The change from, say, 7% inflation to 2% inflation, you could argue, is just the same as the change from 2% to -3%; both simply involve a decline in inflation of 5%. The fact that in the second case inflation turns negative is not significant.

But it is a *qualitative* change. It is bad enough for investors to see that the institution, be it government or private company, which pays the interest on their bonds is going to find it much more difficult than it originally thought to pay interest and repay principal, because its revenue stream is no longer rising much without inflation.

However, think of the position if the revenue stream is actually *falling*. The general level of prices is falling with the result, let's say, that both government tax receipts and company profits are falling in nominal terms. Yet still the fixed-interest investors are entitled to the same interest payments, and repayment of principal, in nominal terms, so the financial difficulties of individual companies and governments rise constantly, year after year after year. Given that no one in those institutions will know how long and at what future rate this position will continue, the effect would be to engender raw fear on the part of *both* borrowers and lenders.

Moreover, it is now right to speak of *all* borrowers and lenders being affected because, since interest rates cannot go negative, when prices fall even variable-rate borrowers are caught in this particular trap.

Partly because of the fear of the unknown and the uncertainty about how far and how fast prices might fall, and partly because of the sense of things developing beyond anyone's control, the onset of falling prices could bring panic and disarray to investment markets.

Investment in the Zero Era

How can investors expect bonds, shares and commercial property to perform in the new world of zero inflation? And what about investments in real assets such as gold, or art and antiques which were so fashionable until very recently?

The fall of interest rates (short and long) from levels appropriate to continued high inflation confers capital gains on holders of long-term bonds. This last happened on a significant scale in 1993 when bonds surged as short-term interest rates fell. In the US, at the peak of the market, the rates on long-term bonds dipped as low as 5.7%. This is, of course, exactly the reverse of the process which occurred in the late 1960s and for most of the 1970s, when higher inflation and higher short-term interest rates caused bond values to plummet, in the process decimating the real value of many a person's savings.

If, by contrast, you hold savings in short-term or variable-rate instruments such as ordinary deposits with banks or building societies, then the interest rate received will fall with the process of disinflation, as has tended to happen over the last 15 years. You will not lose money, but neither will you profit. There will be no capital gain comparable to the gains enjoyed on long-term fixed-interest bonds. When prices *fall*, however, you will gain since interest rates will not go negative.

But earlier I highlighted an important caveat for the bond investor. The investor's capital gain on the bond is the borrower's capital loss. You have to be sure that the borrower is strong enough to withstand this loss, and to repay the original capital amount as well as continuing to meet the interest payments during the life of the bond. This puts a premium on high quality bonds. Locking in a high fixed rate of interest to be paid by a borrower who is about to go bust is not a good idea.

When the adjustment process is complete and we have entered a period of zero inflation, the opportunity to profit from holdings of long-term fixed-interest bonds will have passed. The market values of the bond will have adjusted so as to give a rate of return to its holders congruent with the new regime and the new lower level of short-term interest rates. Nevertheless, bonds will still deserve a place in personal portfolios as a protection and ballast in times when the general level of prices falls, along with the value of most equities (shares) and most dividend payments.

But the hope for decent long-term returns will still rest with equities. Even though, in contrast to the recent past, they will not rise much in nominal terms over long periods, and even though they may sometimes fall quite sharply, they are the instrument from which the investor can hope to gain a share of the real improvements which the technological and organisational revolution can bring, as well as the economic gains from the end of inflation itself.

This may seem paradoxical. After all, by and large, the cult of the equity has coincided with the inflationary era. Correspondingly, it may be thought that its end may sharply detract from the attractions of equities. In fact, this is probably grossly overdone. After all, at the simplest level, if we think of pricing and all other corporate decisions in real terms, the rate of inflation should make no difference to the real level of profits. Accordingly, you might think that the real price of equities should remain the same. Of course, without inflation, the nominal price of equities would rise more slowly than it would under inflation, but that has no *real* significance in itself.

Matters are not quite as simple as this, because the death of inflation will have real consequences. If the change from high inflation is 'a good thing', then it should have beneficial real consequences. I argue in succeeding chapters that there are several potentially large benefits from low inflation – improved allocation of resources and improved decision taking without the distortions and illusions created by inflation; a higher rate of investment, prompted by lower interest rates; the possible adoption of a more expansionary policy by governments. These effects should help to make possible a faster rate of economic growth for a sustained period.

This would imply a higher level of real equity prices at each stage even if the level of real bond yields and the rating of equity risk were the same. In fact, as I argued above, real interest rates are likely to be lower. Taken on its own, this argues for higher real equity prices.

As to risk ratings, it is often argued that a world without inflation and with accompanying low interest rates would be so much more stable than its inflationary predecessor that the risks attaching to equities would be seen to be lower. Again, this argues for higher real equity prices and a higher price/earnings (P/E) ratio (that is, the ratio of the share price to the company's earnings, either in the current year or estimated for the year ahead).

But this is not the whole story. Without the fear of persistent inflation, investors would not be willing to pay for inflation protection. And they have traditionally regarded equities as an inflation hedge. This argues for lower real equity prices and a lower P/E ratio.

Moreover, what about the risks associated with *deflation?* All the nightmare aspects discussed above would haunt equity investors – falling product prices, the rising real value of company debts, the financial predicament of heavily indebted governments, the higher and perhaps rising level of real interest rates and the danger of financial collapse. These argue for investors to view equities more cautiously.

I think the upshot is that, except at times when the market actively fears deflation, the advent of zero inflation is likely to result in higher real equity prices. But when it does actively fear deflation, it is a different story altogether. Moreover, in the new world where deflation is a continuing real threat on the horizon, the dangers of a serious collapse of equity prices appear to be much greater. Perhaps the awareness of this danger will restrain their performance even when deflation is not an immediate prospect.

Wide Disparities in Equity Performance

Another caveat is in order regarding equity investment. Some of the forces driving inflation lower, I have argued, are real – technological and organisational change and intensified competition. These forces themselves, quite apart from their anti-inflationary consequences, will have momentous distributional effects even within the corporate world. They present a twin challenge and opportunity – the chance to develop new products or exploit new markets on the one hand, and the chance to restructure the production process and redirect the sources of supply on the other. Some industries and sectors are almost bound to do badly out of these changes, just as some are bound to do well. But within different sectors, both the winners and the losers, some companies will adapt well and others will adapt badly.

Moreover, in Chapter 6 I stress that the change from high to low inflation will imply the need for sharp changes in business behaviour with regard to pricing strategy, the rate of discount used in assessing investment projects,and the structure of company finances. Well-managed companies which understand the extent of the changes implicit in a world of low inflation and are flexible enough to adapt to them need not be inconvenienced and can even profit from the changes.

Companies that do not understand the changes or are too rigid to adapt to them will pay a severe penalty. So will the people who invest in them.

Equities Versus Bonds

In the 1950s, it was normal to speak of the yield gap – measuring the excess of the dividend yield on an equity over the yield on (long-term government) bonds. Such an excess was supposedly required in order to compensate investors for the greater risks of holding equities rather than bonds.

All that changed with the recognition of persistent inflation. It became customary, instead, to speak of the *reverse* yield gap, that is to say, the extra return on bonds over equities, required to compensate bond investors for the prospect of inflation, which would erode the real value of their investment. More recently still, the yield *ratio*, that is to say, the ratio of gilt yields to equity yields, has been in vogue. Sometimes calculations use the *dividend* yield on equities, to give the dividend yield ratio, and sometimes total company *earnings*, to give the earnings yield ratio. Over the five years 1991–5, the dividend yield ratio averaged just under 2½ in France, Germany and the US but stood at just under 2 in the UK, and over 5 in Japan. The earnings ratio averaged about 1½ in France, the UK and the US, but 2 in Germany and 2¾ in Japan.

These ratios are often used to judge whether equities are cheap or dear against bonds. For instance, in the UK between 1970 and 1995, aside from a few brief periods, the dividend yield ratio fluctuated in the range 2–2½, giving support to the widely held view that equities are cheap when the ratio is 2 and expensive when it is 2½. On this basis, at the end of 1995 British equities were cheap, as the ratio dipped below 2.

In fact this is a potentially dangerous rule of thumb. For a start, the dividend yield ratio will be strongly influenced by company policies with regard to what proportion of their earnings they pay out as dividends (the 'payout ratio') and this both changes over time and differs substantially between countries. International comparisons are also sullied by differences in tax treatment, earnings reporting conventions and the prospective growth of earnings (which is linked to the rate of economic growth).

But this rule of thumb has a more serious drawback which is directly related to inflation. Bond and equity yields only have a meaningful relationship given some assumption about inflation. If the inflation rate were to fall to zero and to be widely expected to stay there, then a yield ratio of 2 would, in ordinary circumstances, make British equities *extremely expensive* against bonds. Zero inflation will force the investment community to rethink radically its investment yardsticks, just as the belated recognition of inflation in the 1960s overturned the old investment nostrums.

There are three general forces which impinge on the relationship between bond and equity yields – the prospects for inflation, the prospects for real dividend growth and capital gains, and the inherent riskiness of equities compared to bonds. If the market came to believe in zero inflation, and if there were no prospect of any real growth in dividends and capital values, then equities would have to stand on a higher yield than bonds in order to compensate for their riskiness – in other words, both the earnings and dividend yield ratios would have to be below 1, meaning, in the older terminology, a return to the positive yield gap. In fact, once you take account of the prospect of real growth in dividends and capital values, this result is considerably modified and, in my view, the end of inflation is unlikely in normal circumstances to see a return to the old yield gap. This could easily happen, though, in times of deflation. But even without the threat of deflation, as financial markets come to believe in zero inflation, there is scope for yield ratios to shrink substantially from the levels recently regarded as normal.

Bank Deposits and Indexed Bonds

Cash and deposits would still have some investment role in a world of zero inflation and very low interest rates, particularly for defensive purposes during phases of price deflation. However, given that without the need to offset inflation the monetary authorities would be likely to set nominal interest rates at very low levels, the real returns on bank deposits would normally be very low, in marked contrast to the 1980s when deposits performed very well as an investment.

One asset which investors might be tempted to discard altogether would be index-linked bonds. After all, these are usually thought of as a hedge against inflation and when the general level of prices falls, their dividend payments and final redemption value fall in tandem. So holding index-linked bonds when you know the price level is going to fall means holding an asset whose value you know is also going to fall. It doesn't sound very attractive.

In fact, it is not quite as bad as it sounds. For a start, investors will not *know* that prices are going to fall over the year ahead and even if they feel pretty sure, they will not know by how much. The valuation of other investment assets, such as fixed-interest bonds, will reflect the prevailing expectation.

Moreover, although the value of dividend payments, and perhaps also the market value of index-linked debt, would fall in times of falling general prices, they would not fall in real terms. Unlike equities, they would not carry the risk of a sharp drop in real dividend payments or real capital values, or the danger of insolvency.

Once investors see themselves facing a future in which prices may rise or fall, index-linked bonds take on an added attraction – they give security of real value of both income and capital. Holders will know that in phases of rising prices they will be protected. Meanwhile, in times of falling prices their income and capital will only fall in line with this general deflation, thereby leaving the real value intact. (For investors such as pension funds with liabilities fixed in nominal terms, however, index-linked bonds would be positively dangerous in times of falling prices.) And, of course, index-linked bonds will still offer protection against the sudden burst of high inflation which could appear out of the blue as a result of a war or natural disaster. So, far from being an asset which investors should discard, they will have decided merits in a world where there is uncertainty about movements in the price level.

Commercial Property

In a world of zero inflation, should we expect commercial property prices still to rise or would they, in general, remain flat? Is there in prospect a sharp downward adjustment of commercial property values to mirror what has happened with residential property?

At the outset, a distinction needs to be drawn between land and buildings. Land has value because of the activities which can take place on it. Except for agricultural purposes, it does not decay, require maintenance or become obsolescent.

Moreover, as a non-reproducible scarce resource, as income and production levels increase (reflecting both per capita rises and an increase in the number of people), then non-agricultural land prices should rise, even without general inflation. (As I pointed out in Chapter 2, this factor is particularly strong in many of the dynamic countries in Asia and is a major source of continuing inflation there.)

This is not true of buildings which, rather like capital equipment, should depreciate in real value as use, the passage of time and changing needs and technologies reduce their operative worth. (Of course, when property is purchased, whether it is for residential or commercial purposes, we usually buy the land and buildings as one so it is difficult to unbundle the two parts, although in principle their prices may behave quite differently.)

Although the world of commercial property has been racked by speculative ramps and subsequent collapses, rather like the market for residential property, two factors have kept it from the wilder speculative shores. First, investment in commercial property for professional investors has not been subject to the same tax incentives as investment in residential property has for owner-occupiers. Secondly, the fact that commercial property investment produces a definite and measurable income means that it is typically valued against bonds and this provides an inbuilt restraining mechanism. If inflation takes off and bond yields rise commensurately, then there is no reason for the value of commercial property investments to rise, as high prospective rental payments are offset by higher rates of discount (derived from bonds).

Indeed, because of this, commercial property investments do *not* seem to have been a very good hedge against inflation: sometimes the reverse. For an upsurge of inflation can only be reflected in rental payments once rents come up for review. So the result is that in the period before all rents are adjusted to the rate of inflation, the real value of rents falls. Moreover, since inflation has recently been associated with higher real rates of interest, both short and long, a lower real value of rental payments must now be discounted at a higher real rate of discount. Scarce wonder, then, that property investment may not perform well as an inflation hedge.

Property seems to have been a better inflation hedge in the US than in the UK, although still not a good one. The difference is probably due to the differences in lease terms. In the US commercial leases are typically 5 to 10 years, whereas in the UK they are typically 25 years. Although UK leases are usually reviewed every five years, there is no systematic indexation of rents to the general price level. In the US, by contrast, clauses which automatically link rents with the Consumer Price Index are not uncommon.

You would expect the end of persistent inflation to change some of the UK's peculiar practices in the property market, such as upward-only rent reviews, and indeed this has started to happen. There has also been a move towards leases with shorter break clauses. These trends are set to continue.

The idea that commercial property is not a good inflation hedge may sound puzzling, since it is often viewed as a real asset with equity characteristics. But it is in fact a hybrid financial asset with both debt-like and equity-like components. Fixed-value, defined-term leases are effectively fixed-interest investments; the entitlement to undefined income beyond the expiry of the current lease constitutes the equity component.

In the long run, though, it is true that property values are related to the general price level. Interest rates will not go on rising. They may go up to reflect a higher rate of inflation, but once inflation has risen and the adjustment in interest rates has been made, that is that. Thereafter, prices will still go on rising at the higher rate of inflation but interest rates will not. At this point, property prices will rise with the general level of prices. The result is that property offers reasonable protection against anticipated inflation (that is to say, inflation which is already reflected in the level of long-term interest rates), but is not a good hedge against unanticipated inflation.[4]

Bearing this in mind, how will commercial property behave in the zero era? To the extent that investors, including the financial institutions, have regarded property investment as an inflation hedge, then it should fall in real value. But the facts of recent property performance argue the other way. Rental values which have been fixed for some years in advance, reflecting the expectation of general inflation on the part of both lessors and lessees, will now be worth more than anticipated in real terms as the general rate of inflation turns out to be lower than anticipated. This will produce higher property values. Moreover, as real interest rates fall this will also support higher property values.

So, paradoxically, the end of inflation may at first see an upward movement in commercial property prices. This is certainly what happened in the UK after 1992 when, although inflation turned out to be unexpectedly low, long-term interest rates fell substantially.

Agricultural Land

The value of agricultural land reflects the profitability of agricultural production. This is broadly and loosely related to movements in the general price level but with substantial variations, reflecting changes in the relative price of agricultural products and changes in levels of efficiency in agriculture.

This is the pattern shown by the price of agricultural land in Britain. In terms of 1990 prices, between 1785 and 1995 agricultural land in Britain has fluctuated between a low of about £500 an acre and a high of about £4000 an acre.[5] But there have been some sharp differences of trend within the period. During the first 80 years of the nineteenth century real land prices were rising, presumably reflecting the pressure of increased population on the demand for food, but after 1880 they plummeted, stabilising at a low level between the two world wars. This sharp fall reflected at first the enormous increase in imports, particularly from North America, and then later the slower growth of population.

But from the early 1950s onwards the real price of agricultural land has been on an upward trend, reflecting the policy of protecting and encouraging agriculture and improving productivity. Indeed, since 1970, the link between the value of farm land and the value of wheat produced from the land has been very close, thereby reflecting not only the nominal (and real) prices of wheat, but also the yield of the land in terms of wheat produced.

Just as in the case of commercial property, the value of agricultural land will benefit from a shift to lower real interest rates, but it will also be heavily influenced by changes in the price of agricultural produce and agricultural productivity. There is a good chance that eventual reform of the EU Common Agricultural Policy could reduce agricultural prices and this, despite the trend towards enhanced productivity and the helpful effects of lower interest rates, may depress agricultural land prices throughout western Europe.

Gold and Real Assets

Real assets are held partly for *defensive* reasons, that is to say, in order to avoid the risks which, over and above inflation, bedevil financial assets – the risk that a financial claim will not be honoured; the risk that a sharp political change, perhaps a war or revolution or currency change, will render previous financial instruments invalid and reduce their value; the risk that wealth tied up in a financial asset will not be transferable internationally. Moreover, ownership of many real assets is much more difficult for the authorities to track, monitor and tax, and accordingly they have a special attraction for those living on the fringes of legality, or beyond.

But in contrast to land and property (which produce rent), non-income-producing real assets can only *make money* for their holders if their price goes up. Without general inflation, can these assets still offer the prospect of a return?

The answer is that it all depends. For some assets which are scarce and non-reproducible, and for which people will be prepared to pay more as they get richer, the answer is yes. Gold is the classic non-income-producing real asset, but it does not meet the strict test because it is possible to expand the supply of it. Indeed, this is happening all the time. However, gold does offer, *par excellence*, the defensive qualities referred to above.

On the face of it, gold has been a good investment during the inflationary era. At the beginning of 1968, it stood at just over $35 an ounce. In October 1995 its price was just over $380 an ounce, giving a compound return over the period of some 9% per annum. If you adjust the $ price for US inflation, however, the return falls to about 3¼% real.

But this came after a period in which the gold price was artificially held down, and it disguises enormous variations within the period. As Figure 4.4 shows, gold's heyday was the 1970s and its price reached a peak in dollar terms in 1980, at not far short of $700 an ounce, thereby giving those who had bought at any stage in the previous 10 years a spectacular return – provided they sold in 1980. For thereafter the price slipped, and it has oscillated around the $400 mark for the last several years. This means that even someone who bought in 1985, after the big fall in the price was over, would have lost some 15% in real terms. More recently, the price has fallen even further, making the returns still worse.

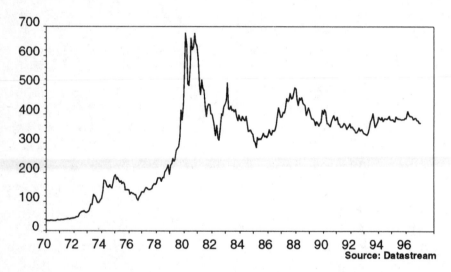

Figure 4.4   The price of gold, US$ per ounce, 1970–96

What happens to the gold price in a world of zero inflation will depend on what happens to the real cost of producing gold, and on how both the commercial and industrial demand for gold and the asset demand based on security respond to increasing levels of income and wealth. Without general inflation, there is no reason to suppose that the gold price would necessarily trend up over time. Indeed, if investors came to believe in zero inflation, then because this would rob gold of one of its investment attractions, namely protection of real value against the ravages of inflation, the gold price might fall somewhat and then hold its lower level. This probably goes some way to explaining its poor performance over recent years.

On the other hand, if the level of real interest rates falls as a result of lower inflation, as I argue here, then the income foregone by holding gold will fall, and this could give a boost to the gold price. Even so, once the adjustment has taken place you are back to the same point – zero inflation would probably mean something like a static gold price over long periods, but with fluctuations.

A period of *falling* prices might be expected to see the gold price falling *pari passu*, but in fact it could hold up rather well. For gold would not be subject to the worries about financial soundness which would afflict all financial assets, and as the general level of prices fell, at an unchanged price in money terms, its *real* value would rise.

Antiques, Works of Art and Collectable Assets

The ownership of real assets is the traditional way for people to protect themselves against the ravages of inflation and, taking the process a stage further, the fleet-footed try to use inflation to make positive gains by taking large positions in the assets which will benefit most from inflation. As we have seen, gold is the classic non-income-producing real asset and can be subject to wild speculative swings. But perpetual inflation caused an investment and speculative culture to grow up around assets which we normally associate with simple enjoyment.

It is easy to see why an investment culture grew up around works of art and antiques. For a start, they tend to hold their real value over the long term so that, at the very least, they give protection against inflation. Over and above this, some tend to rise in line with incomes and wealth (or even faster) rather than with prices. In this case, they generate a real return, similar in principle to the return on a conventional financial investment. And the way in which the return arises, solely through a higher price, may have attractions from a tax standpoint.

But in the surge in asset prices produced by inflation, the combined power of money illusion, self-fulfilling speculation and greed took over. Now almost any real asset was a candidate for investment status simply by virtue of the fact that it was a physical thing rather than a mere piece of paper. The definition of works of art was broadened and loosened; all sorts of old bric-à-brac were now wheeled out as 'antique'.

Moreover, classic cars, postage stamps, coins and fine wines were all drawn into the investment net and traded at ever more fancy prices, not principally for the pleasure of ownership or use, but in the prospect of being able to sell on later at a still more inflated price. And for a long time, just like housing, it all seemed inevitable. All you had to do was buy and hold. Nothing could be simpler. Then the music stopped.

In 1995, average sale prices at Christie's auctions in the US and UK were less than half their 1990 level. And in some of the more esoteric markets like classic cars, the carnage was greater. Some speculators were wiped out by the plunge in the market.

The history of the prices paid for works of art at public auction is fascinating. *The Daily Telegraph* Art 100 Index, which I show here in Figure 4.5 in terms of US$, measures the prices paid for the works of 100 leading artists. The index starts at a value of 1000 in 1975 so I have compared it with the level of consumer prices (the CPI) in the US, by rebasing this to 1000 in 1975. (Although this comparison with US consumer prices is only directly relevant to someone judging their investments by reference to the US dollar, or someone who lives in the US, comparisons in other currencies reveal a broadly similar pattern. For changes in exchange rates broadly correspond to the differences in inflation performance between countries.) So whenever the art price index (the solid line) is above the dotted line, then art prices have beaten inflation in the period since 1975.

The figure shows that art prices had a bumpy ride in the mid-1970s. (Indeed, the art index fell by 25% in 1976.) It was not until 1979 that prices regained the 1975 level. In fact, by the end of 1979, they were showing an increase over the 1975 level of 14% which, although not good, at least does not seem that bad. The trouble is that, by that stage, US consumer prices had risen by 38%. So in real terms, art investors were still well down.

Although they must have been cheered by the continued increases in prices in the early 1980s, in fact it was not until 1986 that the art index overtook the index of consumer prices to give a gain in real terms from the starting date in 1975.

The next few years were boomtime, and people who bought art in the mid-1980s, *and* sold at the top in 1990, enjoyed enormous profits.

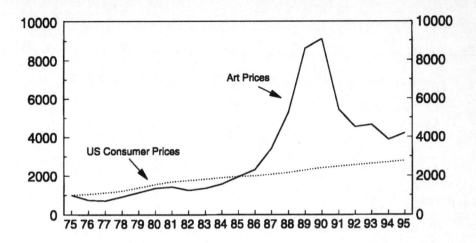

Source: Data on *Daily Telegraph* Art Index supplied by Robin Duthy, Art Market Research; US CPI data taken from Datastream

Figure 4.5   Art prices – The Daily Telegraph Art 100 Index, US$, 1975–95 (1975=1000)

From the end of 1985 to the end of 1990, *The Daily Telegraph* Art Index increased by more than 350%, while consumer prices increased by a mere 22%.

Doubtless it was this phenomenal performance which gave rise to the idea that, just like housing, 'you cannot lose money in art'. But the period after 1990 is a different story; in the early 1990s, prices plunged. Nevertheless, according to the index, if you had bought art in 1975 and held on to it through thick and thin then, even after the sharp falls of the early 1990s, you would still be showing ahead in 1995 and managing to beat inflation as well. In fact, this would not have been a lot to write home about, because the cumulative increase in art prices since 1975 amounts to an average annual increase of some 7½%. The equivalent figure for consumer prices is some 5¼%. So the average annual real return to holding art over the period was about 2¼%.

Moreover, if you bought art at the top of the market in 1990 you underwent a disaster. Figure 4.6 brings it out more clearly by showing art prices and consumer prices compared against a base of 1000 in 1990. Art market professionals may make much of the recovery in art prices in 1995 – up, according to the index, by about 8½%. But this did not

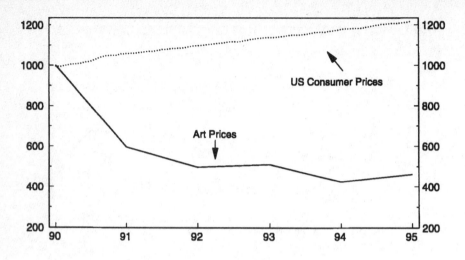

Source: Data on *Daily Telegraph* Art Index supplied by Robin Duthy, Art Market Research; US CPI data taken from Datastream

Figure 4.6   Art prices – The Daily Telegraph Art 100 Index, US$, 1990–95 (1990=1000)

even recover the ground lost in 1994, never mind the early 1990s. Meanwhile, consumer prices continued to rise.

In fact, if the art price index rose at 10% a year from now, it would take more than eight years to reach its 1990 level. If it grew by 5% a year, then it would take 16 years. If art prices increased from now at 5% a year and consumer prices stood still, then it would take 20 years for those people who bought art in 1990 to be back to where they started in real terms. Evidently, art is not such a straightforward investment after all.

Aunt Mabel and Picasso

In the speculative boom of the late 1980s, people had lost sight of a fundamental truth about investment in non-income-producing real assets. They can only produce a sustainable 'return' if society values them more in real terms in the future than it does at present. For some unique, non-reproducible assets, such as the truly great works of art, something like this appears to be true. As society gets richer, the values it places on Van Goghs, Picassos or Turners increases, not in line with general prices, but rather in line with income and wealth, or even faster.

But the idea that this can apply to all works of art, let alone all real assets, including Aunt Mabel's ormolu clock, is based on a fundamental misconception. It presupposes that the process of continued enrichment created by economic growth, although it produces more money, produces nothing of lasting value for people to collect and treasure. It is a process of continually increasing demand meeting completely fixed supply. The assumption seems to be that all the real assets people might want to hold were produced in the past – Chippendale chairs, Picassos, Ming vases, etc.

Yet this cannot make sense. After all, the self-same argument could have been advanced before the birth of Messrs Chippendale and Picasso and even, for that matter, before the Ming dynasty. The truth of the matter is that as societies get richer, they not only have more money to 'spend' on the unique or non-reproducible real assets left over from the past, but they also create new unique or non-reproducible real assets for people to hold in the future.

These new real assets can take strange, unimagined forms. In this century, for instance, vintage cars have become a collector's item and, for some, an investment asset. Even children's toy cars (Dinky toys) and old newspapers have become prized as collectors' items. Yet these items would have been unimaginable in the nineteenth century as stores of value, let alone attractive assets for investment. Who knows what real assets, including works of modern art, which are being produced now will become the valuable assets of the future?

Correspondingly, some works of art are prized when the artist is alive or only recently dead but become less highly rated as time goes on. Apparently, this fate has already befallen the works of Andy Warhol.

It is only when a society advances dramatically in wealth but without producing a comparable supply of new 'collectable' real assets, including, in particular, works of art, that it will be right to assume 'ever-increasing' real values for collectable real assets. Could modern industrial societies exactly fit this description? It is too early to tell.

Prices and Values

The upshot of all this is clear. It will always be possible to make money in antiques, or art or vintage cars or fine wines, by skilfully or luckily selecting an as yet underappreciated specimen and waiting until its qualities are widely accepted and fully embodied in the market price. Equally, there will always be price fluctuations in the markets so that it will even be possible to make money by trading in a general asset class – provided that you correctly judge the ups and downs of the cycle. (Of course, it is not possible for *everyone* to do this.)

Moreover, there will probably be particular items in any asset class which are so special (e.g. Van Gogh's *Irises*) that perhaps their value to collectors can increase at a rate equal to or even faster than the rate of return available in financial markets, and accordingly that they can offer decent investment returns, although prospective investors have to be careful about how much of this prospect is already embodied in the current price.

But for ordinary, run-of-the-mill real assets this cannot be generally true. After the current phase of downward adjustment is over, for some the market price may rise more than the general price level so that they produce a real return, but they are unlikely to produce a return equal to the return available on orthodox investments. Moreover, more probably they will simply hold their price alongside the general price level, thereby acting as a reasonable store of value, but not as a good return-producing investment. And if they are bought too expensively, they will produce a very poor return indeed. It is just like residential property; without the perpetual upward movement created by inflation it really does matter to the ultimate outcome *which* specimen you buy and *when*.

Shorn of the value conferred by the protection they offer against inflation, and viewed in the cold light of day without the illusions created by inflation, many real assets will simply fall out of investment consideration altogether, and will be returned to their original status as things to be valued and treasured for what they are. Or not. And quite right too.

5

Personal Finances in the Zero Era

Never mind the inflation, Mr Bootle. It's the price rises they ought to stop.

Cleaner to an impecunious student, 1973

THE DEATH OF INFLATION IS ALREADY WREAKING HAVOC WITH people's lives, just as the emergence of inflation did after the war. It is redistributing income to and from the personal sector as a whole and within it, between winners and losers from the disinflation process. It is leaving people baffled and bewildered as the illusions created by inflation are stripped away. And it is making them fearful of the future as the old financial certainties crumble.

Alice in Wonderland

One of the consequences of inflation, alluded to in Chapter 2 and fully developed in Chapter 8, is that it confuses people about relative prices. But the confusion it creates about prices in the here and now is nothing compared to the confusion it creates about prices over time.

Future money values are in a sort of never-never land. Even so, it is one that we have to visit whenever we consider taking out a long-term financial contract, such as a pension, life insurance or savings scheme. We are often invited to imagine investment returns rolling up at 10 or even 20% per annum so that, at maturity or at retirement, a person's savings are worth so many million dollars, French francs, pounds – it might as well be so many billions for all it means to most potential beneficiaries. They understand what so many dollars or French francs mean today, but how are they to relate that to the apparently fabulous sums they will receive later?

You can adjust every price by the movement in the general price level to bring it into real terms. It is rather like converting sums of money expressed in different currencies into a single common currency. And just about everything can be reassessed in this way – the level of real returns, the real interest rate, real wages, the real exchange rate, real share prices, and so on and so forth.

But people do not find it normal or easy to treat a dollar in one period as different from a dollar in another, treating it, indeed, as though it were a dollar in one period and a French franc in another. They find it most difficult when they are called upon to make long-term financial decisions or assessments of money amounts in 20 or 30 years' time, or to make adjustments between income and capital to compensate for inflation. In these cases, they end up confused. In particular, they suffer from what economists call 'money illusion', that is, the failure to see through the money amounts to the underlying real values.

As I show below, the contrast between real and money values, and the difficulty which people regularly experience in distinguishing between them, bedevils all the major financial aspects of their lives – the growth of incomes, the behaviour of property values and mortgage payments, pensions and money saved in the bank.

The Power of Compound Interest

Money illusion is devastating when applied to long-term financial arrangements, because even small differences in annual growth rates can make huge differences to capital amounts or income flows when the growth rates are sustained over many years.

If incomes rise at 2% per annum, then after 20 years they will be nearly 50% higher. Similarly, of course, a house which appreciates in value at this rate will be worth 50% more, and a pension fund which grows at this rate will be worth 50% more. After 30 years, the sum in question will have grown by about 80%. It takes 35 years to double in value. (Remember, this is the rate at which real wages might reasonably grow and, indeed, the rate at which nominal wages might grow in a world without inflation.)

Raise the growth rate only slightly to 3% and the figures become 80% after 20 years, and about 140% after 30 years. The sum now doubles in less than 24 years. Go up another gear to 4% and the figures are now 120% after 20 years and more than 220% after 30 years. The sum doubles in less than 18 years. The power of compound interest truly amazes for higher growth rates. At 8% the growth after 30 years is more than 900%. The sum doubles in 9 years. At 10%, the growth after 30 years is more than 1600%. The sum doubles in just over 7 years.

The higher rates of growth may seem fanciful, but they are not. These are precisely the sorts of growth rate to which all money values were subjected in the era of inflation – wages, house prices, goods prices, pension values. And, of course, they were completely meaningless.

Most countries in the west have undergone inflation rates in excess of 10% and some have undergone rates in excess of 20%, while the real growth rate has been 2% or less. It has been this apparently meagre real growth rate which has ultimately governed both the real growth of wages and investment returns, thereby affecting pensions. Consider the numbers: 2% growth over 30 years gives an 80% increase in the value of a capital sum; 10% growth over 30 years gives a 1645% increase. We are talking about differences of 20 times. It is scarce wonder that people might have been confused about real values during the inflationary process.

Getting Used to Pay not Rising Much

Many people regard inflation as something which affects only prices. Pay rises are something quite different. They reflect the fruits of one's labour. Accordingly, if only inflation (meaning price rises) could be stopped, we would all be better off!

Clearly, this is nonsense. Rates of pay are simply another price – the price of labour – which is affected by inflation. As inflation proceeds, all prices – goods prices, asset prices and pay rates – are driven up, but quite possibly at different times and speeds. And of course, intertwined with the pure inflationary effect on pay, there are the real influences which will be there whatever happens to inflation – the effect of *real* productivity growth on the real incomes earned by labour, and the effects of changing supply and demand on the incomes derived from different types of labour. Inflation confuses people about these two influences – general inflation on the one hand and *real* influences on the other. Even in the world of zero inflation, these real influences would still have their effect.

So suppose we are living in a world of zero inflation. By how much could the average employee expect his or her pay to increase? The answer will have profound implications for financial planning and particularly for the ability to pay interest and repay debt.

The average level of pay is determined by the overall level of output (or income) and the share of that output which accrues to labour. That is a tautology, of course. It is useful, nevertheless, because it decomposes the question of the growth rate of pay into two tractable components – the share of labour and the overall rate of economic growth. If the share of labour were to remain constant, then the rate of growth of labour's real income would be given by the rate of growth of real output.

But why should labour's share of real income remain constant? There is no reason why it should, although it can only change by comparatively small amounts in a year, and there are limits, in both directions, to how far it can go. It could be argued, though, that the two major economic forces of the rapid progress of technology and competition from the dynamic countries could work to reduce the share of labour in national income, and indeed there are clear signs that this has already been happening.

So suppose the share of labour holds its own. What could we expect to happen to pay in a world without inflation? It would depend upon the rate of economic growth. In a world of zero inflation, if economic growth were 2%, then pay on average would grow by 2%. If 3%, then by 3%. If 8%, then by 8%. (Individuals might do better than this average rate over time by acquiring valuable skills or experience, or gaining promotion. But in today's environment these opportunities are restricted, and in any case, in general, they will not be large enough to offset the effects of the death of inflation on the growth of nominal incomes.)

In most western economies, the sustainable rate of growth is thought to be in the range of 2–3%, having been lower than that in the 1970s. Now whether this sort of rate is indeed achieved in the future will depend largely on the effect of the real forces alluded to repeatedly in this book – the effects of rapid technological advance, organisational change and the development of the dynamic countries, as well as the direct effects on economic growth of low interest rates, and the improved allocation of resources stemming from the death of inflation.

Pessimists will see these factors as having no effect on growth potential, or perhaps even a negative effect. The early 1990s have seen pessimism in the ascendant. Yet to me this view seems scarcely credible. Once the western world and its policy-makers have adjusted to the new opportunities, then the sustainable real growth rate should be higher than before. Accordingly, the sustainable rate of growth of real incomes may be higher than 2–3%.

Even so, it surely will not come anywhere near the rate of growth of pay in the dynamic countries in the Far East and elsewhere. With economic growth rates, in some cases, of 8 or even 10%, these countries will be able to sustain increases in pay levels at this rate *even in real terms.* Accordingly, if they still have continuous inflation (even as the west has none) then the increase in their money incomes would be above this rate, even well into double figures, apparently mimicking recent behaviour in the west when double-digit pay rises were the norm. But, of course, the two experiences would be quite different.

For when workers in the west used to receive double-digit wage rises every year then hardly any of this represented a real increase in their incomes and living standards. Most of it represented inflation. By contrast, the prospect for many fast developing countries is that *real* incomes might rise as fast as 8 or even 10% per annum.

And whereas in the western economies real incomes (including the level of real pay and real dividends) will double every 35 years if they grow at 2%, in the dynamic economies they would double every 9 years, if they grow at 8%, and in just over 7 years, if they grow at 10%.

Mortgages and Disposable Incomes Over a Lifetime

What people earn is one thing, but in many western societies the scope they have for discretionary spending is heavily influenced by their mortgage payments. The way inflation has affected these payments has had a huge effect on the distribution of disposable income across an individual's lifetime, squeezing it at the beginning and boosting it at the end. Its demise will have a similarly large effect in the other direction – provided interest rates adjust.

Consider this simple example. Inflation is 10% and our imaginary mortgage borrower is buying a house for $200,000, all of which she is borrowing, on an interest-only mortgage, when all the capital is paid off at the end (known in Britain as an endowment mortgage), at an interest rate of 14%. Suppose her salary is $60,000 and, to make things simple, let us assume that this too is set to rise at a rate of 10% per annum, which is also the rate of house price inflation. In the first year, the borrower has to pay $28,000 to service the mortgage out of a salary of $60,000, before tax and other deductions. That is some chunk of disposable income pre-assigned. Indeed, after tax deductions, and perhaps pension contributions and life insurance payments, as well as the ordinary expenses of living, there will be next to nothing left.

But look what inflation does to this picture. After 10 years, she still has to pay $28,000 a year but her salary is now $156,000. The mortgage payments are now a still significant, but not troublesome expense. After 25 years, when the mortgage payments would still be $28,000 per annum, her salary would be some $650,000. At this point, the mortgage payments have become insignificant. By the way, just to complete the picture, by this stage the house for which she paid $200,000 is now worth more than $2 million!

In this example, the constancy of the mortgage payments over time gives a totally misleading impression of stability. In fact, there is a powerful process going on which is redistributing disposable income across the mortgage holder's life – squeezing it at the beginning and boosting it at the end. This effect is due to the interaction of inflation with normal mortgage structures.

To see the difference *without* inflation, let us go back to the previous example. There is no inflation at all and the borrower can borrow at a rate of 4% but, to make life simple, without general inflation, neither the level of house prices nor the level of salaries rises at all. To service the mortgage, she now has to pay only $8000 per annum ($200,000 at 4%), and she goes on paying that amount every year until the end of the mortgage, just as before. But now her salary remains the same year after year. So as she gets older there is no increase in the amount she has left over after paying the mortgage.

Incidentally, the value of her house is also unchanged from when she bought it – it is still worth $200,000. Even so, she is no worse off in real terms compared to the previous example when inflation of general prices, salaries and house prices was 10%. The real value of the house has remained constant, just as in the previous example.

But the difference is in the distribution of disposable income across her lifetime. There is no squeeze early on and no corresponding let-off later in life.

There is a way, of sorts, for the borrower to even out the level of disposable income across her lifetime when inflation does apply, if that is what she would wish, by borrowing money to add to her disposable income in the early years, paying the debts off later when inflation has done its work on the level of her salary. Something like this does take place, on a limited and *ad hoc* basis, but few people can begin to do it systematically.

For a start, how many homebuyers understand this process and its implications for their real standard of living? It may be particularly difficult for them to conceive of borrowing *even more* money for consumption purposes at just the time they have entered into the biggest financial transaction of their lives. And that is assuming that they would be able to secure a loan for these purposes at that stage. The usual lending agencies would be liable to consider them to be fully 'loaned up'.

Moreover, they would have to pay interest to borrow money in this way so that they could not, in fact, achieve the same standard of living overall by borrowing in order to sustain consumption in the early years in the world of inflation as would happen automatically in the world without inflation.

It is possible for borrowers to use a 'low start' mortgage where, even on the assumption of unchanged interest rates, the monthly mortgage payments rise over time, hopefully in line with the borrowers' earnings. But this type of mortgage is not particularly common and it was even less common in the days when inflation and interest rates were much higher.

The upshot is that the death of inflation will bring a sharp change in the distribution of income across lifetimes. This has the potential to bring with it a radical shift in lifestyles and spending patterns. Young couples, normally strapped for cash, unable to afford to go to 'smart' restaurants or on 'smart' holidays or to wear 'smart' clothes, could be thinner on the ground. Meanwhile, we might not see so much of their counterparts in later life – the people who have next to no mortgage obligations and, now that the children have left home, have oodles of money to spend, often when they do not know what to do with it. The result could be a marked shift in consumption patterns which retailers and providers of consumer services would do well to anticipate.

The result could be to bring Anglo-Saxon lifestyles closer to their continental European counterparts. In many of these countries – Germany, Switzerland, Austria, Benelux – fairly low inflation and interest rates have been the norm for some time. Accordingly, when people bought property they were much closer to the zero inflation world described above than were people in the mainly more inflationary Anglo-Saxon world of the US, UK, Canada and Australia. (Until recently, France and Italy were high inflation countries and Italy still is relative to other countries, although not by comparison with its own past.)

Moreover, in some of these countries, and particularly in Germany, it has been more common for people to rent their homes than has been the case in the Anglo-Saxon countries. This has been significant because when people rent, it gives the same sort of income distribution over time as a system based on ownership and mortgage borrowing with zero inflation.

The Impact on Savings Behaviour

There is, however, a major qualification to this picture of changed consumption patterns. Part of the effect of the reduced percentage of incomes taken by mortgage payments in the early years may fall, not on consumption, but rather on savings. Perhaps people will want to provide for a higher standard of living later on. Perhaps the conventional mortgage systems with high nominal interest rates, far from squeezing people's finances in the early years *against their will*, inadvertently catered for a latent desire for long-term saving.

For when someone buys a home they not only settle their accommodation, but they also enter into a lifetime savings plan as well. This is, after all, primarily what distinguishes owner-occupation from renting – the gradual accumulation of a stake in the property. But during the inflationary era this aspect took on added importance. People made substantial financial sacrifices during the early part of their lives in order to service the mortgage, but at the end of their lives, perhaps having moved several times and increased the size of their mortgage several times, they would have complete ownership of a real asset, their house, now worth considerably more than they paid for it.

In the simple story I told above of a balanced 10% inflation, in money terms, the value of the house had gone through the roof. In fact, in real terms, the house had merely retained its value. In practice, as I pointed out in Chapter 3, houses did much more than retain their real value – they increased in value substantially. So owning property was not only a way of protecting wealth, but also a way of accumulating it. Indeed, for many people, their home was far and away their largest asset. It formed a central part of their strategy for old age. The aim was eventually to sell up and move to somewhere smaller and cheaper and use the funds released in this way to provide income. If you like, their house was a central part of their pension plan. Moreover, it was the bulk of what they hoped to pass on to their children.

Now suppose that, due to lower inflation and various other factors, house prices will no longer rise and investing in housing will no longer provide a way of accumulating wealth. How will people adjust?

At one extreme is the story I told above. Homebuyers will simply spend the money which they used to find themselves paying over to service the mortgage in the early stage of their lives. That might credibly be the result to the extent that people did not previously count on the appreciation of housing values as part of their life's financial plan.

At the other extreme, they will seek out some alternative form of long-term savings in order to replace their houses as a form of asset accumulation. This might plausibly be their reaction to the extent that during the inflationary era people consciously viewed their homes as appreciating assets as part of their wealth portfolio. In this case, the effect of low inflation would be to persuade people to save more. This will present a new challenge and opportunity to financial institutions to put together suitable savings instruments for people to hold – not only the established products such as life insurance and pension schemes, but new ones to cater for the desire for long-term savings with limited access which could serve simultaneously as a fund against a rainy day or as a possible pension fund.

I suspect that because of the atmosphere of general uncertainty and depression that is accompanying the death of inflation, and because of the lingering fear of a return to high rates of interest, in many countries the predominant reaction may at first be more towards the savings extreme. But in sunnier times, once the adjustment to the end of infla-tion is complete, the reaction may veer more towards the opposite extreme and freer-spending young people, no longer overburdened by mortgages, may emerge in greater numbers.

Life Insurance

Life insurance is an area where long-term savings and mortgages often interact. The typical life insurance policy (or life *assurance* as it should more properly be known) combines insurance against death with long-term savings.

When a person takes out a life assurance policy they commit them-selves to paying a fixed monthly premium to the insurance company until the maturity of the policy at some specified date in the future. If the person should die before the maturity date then a specified capital sum (the death benefit) is paid to the deceased's estate.

If the policy holder survives to the maturity date, the policy also guar-antees to pay out a certain sum at maturity (usually known as the basic sum assured). Typically, this sum is increased each year by 'bonuses' which reflect the investment return on the sums paid to the insurance company. And at the end of the policy's life, again assuming that the *policy holder* is still alive, then a *terminal bonus* is added to the sums accu-mulated to make a grand capital payment. (In the circumstances, the use of the word *terminal* to describe the bonus can be judged a little unfortunate, but that is the term that companies employ.) After the maturity date, no further payments pass in either direction, and there is no further insurance against death.

But what links the monthly payments to the sums paid out at maturity are the investment returns earned by the insurance company, and these returns will be strongly influenced by the rate of inflation. Indeed, in practice they have been dominated by it. In January 1996, Norwich Union, one of Britain's leading life insurers, said that its 25-year endowment policies (more on these below) with premiums of £50 a month maturing in 1996 would pay out £92,535. According to the group finance director, Richard Harvey, this would give an average annual return of 12½% over 25 years, compared with the average rate of inflation of 7½%.[1]

These figures would indeed represent a very sound result – a return of 5% in real terms. But what would the nominal rate of return have been if inflation had been zero? This is a more complicated question than it looks because it depends on the mix of investments between bonds and shares and how these different investments respond to the transition to zero inflation. Once the financial markets have adjusted to zero inflation, assuming that zero inflation itself does not affect real returns, then the return on such life insurance policies in the future will be much lower than 12½%. In fact, under the same conditions which produced the 12½% quoted above, the return would be 5%.

We are still a long way from returns as low as this, but the size of bonuses paid on policies, and the overall rates of return, have been falling since the late 1980s, reflecting lower investment returns achieved in the context of lower inflation.

These lower returns have left many policy holders feeling aggrieved, but have they really lost out? Does it matter if bonus rates fall? The answer, I'm afraid, is that it all depends. And what it depends on is our old friend, the distinction between nominal and real returns.

If the real returns which insurance companies earn are the same without inflation as they are with inflation, then the amounts paid out to policy holders should also be the same in real terms and they should feel no worse off. That most people do not see things in quite this way is further tribute to the power of money illusion. People got used to seeing the value of their policies rising at a rapid rate and to the idea that at maturity they would be worth so many hundred thousand dollars, pounds or whatever. By and large, they did not convert these sums into real terms and judge subsequent 'bonus' announcements or maturity amounts by this standard. As a result, anything less than the nominal sums they had been expecting comes as a disappointment.

This disappointment has a more concrete foundation when the life insurance policy has been taken out with the explicit objective of producing a certain sum of money at a particular time. This is precisely what happens with *endowment mortgages*. In this case, in contrast to a repayment mortgage, where a borrower repays both interest and capital during the life of the housing loan, the borrower simply pays interest on the loan but takes out a life assurance policy on which he or she pays regular monthly premiums. The idea is that at the maturity of this policy, the capital sum accumulated is enough to pay off the loan and (under most policies) with something left over for the policy holder to keep.

What links the regular monthly payments with the capital sum at maturity is, of course, the rate of return. A lower rate of return means a lower capital sum at maturity. But no such adjustment is made to the mortgage amount outstanding. So if the assumptions about rates of return made when the policy was taken out prove too optimistic, then the capital sum at maturity will be smaller than expected and it may even prove to be too small to repay the mortgage. In this case, the householder may be left in the unfortunate position of being required by the mortgage lender to increase premium payments, to ensure an adequate capital sum, or may simply be required to find the difference out of his or her own pocket at maturity.

This is precisely the prospect which confronted many British people in the mid-1990s. They had taken out endowment mortgages in the 1980s when investment returns were high. In reaction to the collapse of inflation, and hence investment returns, in the mid-1990s, many of them discovered that their policies might not be sufficient to pay off their mortgages when they matured.

Pensions

Pension provision is the area where individuals perhaps come closest to the severe problems of analysis and interpretation presented by the distortion of money values by inflation. Whether we are referring to a self-administered or a managed pension fund or an American Individual

Retirement Account (IRA), or indeed any capital sum or investment contract which, although not called a pension, is intended by the beneficiary to provide income in retirement, the problem is the same – how to connect money values now with money values in the future.

In a world of inflation, left to their own devices, there may be a systematic tendency for individuals to underprovide for their retirement because they are taken in by the high nominal rates of return which bear little relation to reality. For instance, when life insurance companies and pension funds tout for business in the UK, they are obliged by law to quote returns on their policies assuming annual rates of return of 6 and 12%, recently reduced from 8½ and 13%. The result is that even comparatively modest sums can accumulate to apparently fabulous amounts after 20 or 30 years. But what do such amounts mean?

They are literally meaningless. It is like telling someone that if they pay in so many French francs every month then at the end of 20 or 30 years they will receive so many Japanese yen in return, but without saying anything about the exchange rate between francs and yen. The result is probably, in most cases, to persuade people that they will be better off than they in fact will be, and hence to leave them underprovided for the future.

When considering long-term investment returns, it is best to be cautious and conservative. What is a reasonable rate of return to assume on investment? It may be possible for those who invest your pension money to achieve real returns of 8 or 10% per annum, but it would be unwise to rely on this. If you invested in riskless, index-inked government securities in the few countries where they are available – Britain, Canada, Australia and Denmark, and a few other countries – you will receive between 3 and 5% real, and that would have seemed a remarkably generous rate 15 or 20 years ago. Admittedly, you should be able to do better than this by investing in a diversified portfolio of equities, and the good fund managers regularly do. But 8 or 10% *real*, year after year, is asking a lot.

Suppose your money earned 3% real which, after all, would have seemed a reasonable rate of return on savings for much of the nineteenth century. After 20 years, the initial capital sum would be worth 80% more. Now let us assume that when the capital sum matures, the rate which can similarly be earned on it is again 3%. Then every $1000 saved now will produce a permanent, continuing annual income of only $54 ($1000 × 1.8 × 0.03). You have to agree, this is not a lot.

Admittedly, you can edge this sum up by being a mite more generous on the assumptions. Increase the investment period to 30 years and, without changing the rate of return, the amount of income becomes $72. Raise the rate of return to 4% and it becomes nearly $130.

This is the sum which would be available to be spent annually, in perpetuity, while leaving the capital intact. Now, of course, many pensioners would not want to leave the capital intact. Indeed, in a specially designated pension arrangement, on retirement they would normally buy an annuity which would be predicated on the assumption that on death the payments ceased. Buying such an annuity, therefore, explicitly consumes the capital as well as the income. For this reason, annuity rates are higher than straightforward interest rates. (There is more on this below.) With a nominal rate of interest of 4%, the annuity rate for a male aged 60 would be 7¾%. This would then give an annual income in the case discussed above of $140.

Admittedly this is a fair bit higher than $54, but it is a long way short of the income which someone might think they were going to receive if their pension contributions were assumed to earn 10%. Just think of it – 20 years compounding at 10% and then the investment assumed to yield 10% at the end would given an annual income from the original $1000 of $672. And if the sum were allowed to compound for 30 years instead of 20 then the annual income, *without consuming any capital*, would be $1745 – every year, in perpetuity.

Now there's a deal to make your mouth water. Save any given sum now and after 30 years receive 1¾ times that sum every single year for eternity *and* still have the capital sum, now worth more than 17 times the original amount. What a deal! There is only one problem – as far as the opportunities available to most people are concerned, it's a lie.

Final Salary Pension Schemes

For many people, of course, pension income is not directly tied to the investment returns on capital sums invested during their working lives either by themselves or by their employers. Instead, their pensions are tied by a formula to their salary when they retire. For anyone some way distant from retirement, this still leaves the amount they will receive in retirement uncertain, in both nominal and real terms.

But they do have some sort of yardstick in real terms because they can compare themselves with other people in their organisations who are themselves approaching retirement. They can say: 'Suppose I make it to Smith's level by the time I retire. Smith is on X,000 a year. I would be entitled to $\frac{40}{60}$ (or whatever the formula is) of final salary, so I would be entitled to $\frac{40}{60}$ths of X.'

Now, of course, they cannot know what X will be in terms of money. But they don't need to. In fact they know something more valuable – they know how much Smith earns, and how much pension he will earn, in terms of *today's* money. They can reasonably expect to receive the same in real terms, provided they attain Smith's rank, and provided the system remains the same. Indeed, given the reasonable assumption that real incomes will trend upwards, including the incomes for Smith's successors, they can assume that on their retirement they would receive more in real terms than Smith currently does.

Provided they approach things in this way and do not mentally inflate Smith's salary at a compound rate of growth 8 or 10% over the next 20 or 30 years to reach a meaningless annual salary for people in Smith's job, they are spared the worst illusions about pension provision. In a sense, the system provides a built-in way of thinking in terms of real values.

Nevertheless, they do have two serious problems about the value of their future pension. First, will it continue to be possible to provide Smith's successors with the equivalent of $\frac{40}{60}$ths of Smith's leaving salary? The answer to this question depends not on matters to do with inflation, but rather to do with the cost of pension provision and the preparedness, in unfunded schemes, of the younger generation to go on paying for the pensions of the retired.

Pensions in Retirement

But the second problem is more explicitly tied to inflation. Moreover, it applies more generally to all pensions in payment, whatever the original source of their funding. It is all very well knowing the real value of Smith's pension when he first retires, but what will it be worth after 20 years of retirement? A pension fixed in money terms could start off seeming extra-generous at the point of retirement, but turn out to be almost worthless after 10 or 15 years. So Smith could end up on the breadline if he lives a long time.

Of course, many company pension schemes do upgrade pensions over time, but very few guarantee to match inflation fully. Indeed, this is widely regarded as 'too expensive'.

To anyone accustomed to thinking in real terms, the idea of it being expensive, let alone *too* expensive, to keep money incomes rising in line with prices is a curious one. Yet when the UK government reformed the law governing deferred pensions for so called early leavers, it decreed that deferred pensions should be increased by 5% or the inflation rate, *whichever was the lower*. Similarly, many pension schemes adopt something similar to this approach for the uprating of pensions in payment. This leaves pensioners with maintenance of pension values in real terms as their best hope. If inflation exceeds 5% then their pensions will fall in real terms. And yet many companies think they are being generous when they set up such arrangements!

What has happened with regard to pensions to deliver this result is rather interesting. It is another instance of the distortions created by inflation, a further example of the systematic confusion between real and money values. Most pension schemes have been explicitly constructed in such a way that *the pensioner is bound to suffer a reduction in real income from inflation*.

This problem is not created by inflation as such, nor would it be solved by the absence of inflation. For without inflation, nominal investment returns would not be as high. Accordingly, if in a world of zero inflation pensions in payment were held constant, then the cost of providing these pensions would be higher. *The problem is that the initial level of pension is too high to be sustainable in real terms throughout the whole period of retirement.* There is nothing magical about providing pensions which are structured to maintain their real value throughout retirement. This simply requires the initial pension to be set at a level which, on all the usual actuarial assumptions, can be maintained in real terms throughout the pensioner's life.

How Much Income Will an Annuity Provide?

This is precisely analogous to the problem that occurs when someone takes out an annuity on retirement. Let us say that the annuity rate is 14% and that the capital is $300,000. This gives an annual income of $42,000, which the pensioner will naturally think is there to be spent. But, of course, the income will carry on being $42,000 whatever happens to price inflation. In a world of persistent inflation, the pensioner's real income will decline, therefore, year after year. But this decline is not an accident. It is systematic. It is built into the very structure of the arrangement.

After all, why is the annuity rate 14%? As well as depending on actuarial calculations of life expectancy, it will be related to the rate available on government securities and that rate will be whatever it is *explicitly* to compensate investors for the prospect of inflation over the years ahead. The *real* annuity rate could not possibly be 14%.

In order to equalise their real income over their retirement, retired people should only consume that part of their annual income which represents a real annuity, and save the rest in order to be able to consume it later. But, of course, this is hopelessly complicated. Many people may try to do something like it in a simple way, but to do it properly is way beyond them. Even if they understand the concept of real annuities they will not know what the real annuity rate actually is in their case. Nor will they know how long they are going to live, so they will not know over how long a period they should seek to maintain their real annuity income constant.

The appropriate way to cope with this difficulty is surely to buy a *real* annuity from an insurance company. But when presented with this opportunity few people find it attractive, because they do not like the low initial level for their pension which seems so much less 'generous' than an ordinary annuity.

Will the death of inflation bring these problems to an end? The answer is yes, but not necessarily in a way which people will find immediately appealing. Their first reaction might be: 'Wonderful, 14% rates with no inflation.' But, of course, without inflation, annuity rates would not be 14%! The annuity might plausibly turn out to be 10%, or even 6%. At these rates, our pensioner with an initial capital of $300,000 is going to receive $30,000 or only $18,000 per annum.

The fall in annuity rates consequent upon falling rates of interest on government bonds has different consequences for pensioners, depending on whether or not the lower bond rates simply reflect a correct anticipation of the inflation outlook. If they do not, that is to say, if the *real* rates on government bonds fall, then the *real* terms on which prospective pensioners can use their capital to buy an annuity have deteriorated, and they will undoubtedly be worse off, in real terms, than if annuity rates had remained the same.

But if lower annuity rates simply (but correctly) reflect the prospect of lower inflation, then in real terms pensioners will not be worse off. Even so, they would be worse off initially, as the money value of the annuity will start off lower than it would have been if government bond rates had maintained their higher level. But without inflation, their annuity would go on being worth the same year after year. In later years, therefore, they would be better than they would have been with higher bond rates (and higher inflation). So the change in inflation, bond rates and levels of annuity income redistributes real income across the pensioner's period of retirement. This has the downside that things are not so rosy early on, but it does have the advantage of preventing the gradual slide into penury which has afflicted many pensioners over the last 30 years.

These issues are already posing serious questions for people who are soon to retire, as they witness annuity rates plunging. But these questions could become even more acute as and when the bond markets come to believe in zero inflation. When government bond yields are 8%, a male aged 65 can expect an annual income on an annuity of about 12% of the capital. A female aged 65 could expect about 10½%. (This is not another example of discrimination against women but simply reflects women's greater life expectancy.)

If interest rates on bonds were zero, so that the source of all of the annuity income derived from the gradual consumption of the capital over the pensioner's remaining life, then the respective rates would be 6¼% and 5%. That represents the rock bottom of annuity rates.

A more plausible assumption of 4% interest rates on government bonds would give figures of 9% for a male and 7½% for a female, aged 65. That is a fair bit better, but it is a long way from the high hopes, and illusions, still entertained by many people as they edge their way anxiously towards retirement.

Pensions Under Deflation

What about pensions when prices start to fall? Then all the old rules which applied in the inflationary era will go into reverse. A pension fixed in money terms without any alteration clauses becomes a boon, for its real value will increase as prices fall. Pension schemes which allow for a fixed uprating of 3% a year, or uprating by 5% or inflation, *whichever is the lower*, were framed in blissful ignorance of the idea that inflation might turn out to be negative. And in the UK, the 1995 Pensions Act included the stipulation that pensions in respect of past service may not be cut.

In countries where the legal position is unclear, there might be some interesting disputes about what should happen to pensions in times of falling prices. But even if the rule is applied to reduce pensions, the most by which they could be reduced would presumably be the rate of deflation, so presumably the worst that could happen would be pensions falling in nominal terms but remaining constant in real terms. As I pointed out above, this maintenance of real value is equivalent to the *best* which most pensioners can hope for under current arrangements if inflation continues.

But this analysis of pensions under deflation applies to the comfortable, steady, unthreatening sort of fall in prices which mirrors the low, steady inflation of the first 20 years after the war. In practice, the shift to a deflationary world, and the possibility of a more virulent deflation, raises the spectre of *unpaid* pensions, because the financial institution expected to pay the pension will have gone under, or because a supposedly fully funded pension scheme will have become underfunded, or because the promises to pay sums fixed in money terms will not all be able to be met when the value of money is itself rising.

This is a modern financial nightmare. There have been two fixed points in the post-war world of personal finances. The first is the sacred law of residential property: 'Thou shalt never lose money in houses.' The second is the sacred status of pensions. Both of these assumptions have been violated, the first by the widespread experience of falling house prices, the second by the dreadful plight of the Maxwell pensioners. In this case, of course, the cause of their plight has been a very particular phenomenon. But it has served to make people uneasy about one of the few things left about which they still felt safe – their pension. And under the general force of price deflation, this fear would become widespread.

Deposit Income

Many people, especially pensioners, supplement their income with the interest from short-term money deposits, in banks, savings and loans or money market funds (in the US) or building societies (in the UK). The income from these deposits has been grossly distorted by inflation. The end of inflation is already bringing a major adjustment, and a widespread sense of unease and even injustice.

When inflation is high, interest rates are high. The level of income on deposits is apparently high, higher than it is when inflation is lower and interest rates are also set at an appropriately low level. Accordingly, deposit owners are apt to think that they are worse off with low inflation and interest rates than they were with high inflation and high interest rates and that they therefore cannot afford to spend as much.

Yet if the level of *real* interest rates is the same in both cases, surely this cannot be. If interest rates are only lower to the extent that inflation is lower then their position must be exactly the same, and their ability to consume must be the same.

That people usually do not *see* things in this way is a result of inflation interacting with their misperception of what constitutes income. It is tempting for investors to think that their income in a given period consists of the amount they receive in interest or dividends during that period. In some cases this may be a reasonable approximation to the truth, but in many cases it will be grossly misleading.

The economist's definition of income is the amount someone can consume in a period while leaving their wealth intact. In the case of depositors being paid, say, 12% interest but experiencing 10% inflation, they cannot consume 12% while leaving their wealth intact. For the real value of their capital is being eroded by inflation. To maintain their level of wealth constant they must leave the bulk of their interest earnings in the bank to add to their capital. Only the small amount that remains is truly income to be consumed without reducing their wealth.

If they instead consume all of their interest earnings, they are in fact consuming capital, although they may not see it that way because they receive the interest as though it were income and do not need to reduce the nominal amount of capital. They could, of course, achieve exactly the same result in a world of low inflation and low nominal but equivalent real interest rates by supplementing their 'low' interest income by drawing on capital. However, so often you hear people in this position say, 'Oh, I couldn't possibly do that. I do not believe in consuming capital.' Yet this only amounts to doing explicitly what they would readily do implicitly, if only inflation and nominal interest rates were higher.

In fact, the interaction of inflation with the tax system strengthens the contrast between appearance and reality. For in most countries, interest income is taxable whether it represents real income or merely compensation for the erosion of capital value by inflation. This is as true for bonds as it is for deposit income. The result is that at high rates of inflation and nominal interest rates the real after-tax rate of interest can easily be negative.

Consider the case where deposit holders are receiving 10% interest in a world of 8% inflation and 40% tax. Pre-tax they are receiving 2% real. But of the 10% interest they have to pay 4% to the tax authorities, leaving them with only 6%, against 8% inflation. So in this case, their after-tax real return is *minus* 2%.

Now suppose that inflation fell to zero and interest rates to 2%. In pre-tax real terms things are the same, although many deposit holders might complain about receiving 'only' 2%. In fact, for taxpayers the position is now much better because the tax bill is only 0.8%, leaving a positive real return of just over 1% compared to minus 2% before.

So deposit holders are actually better off and are able to support more consumption than before. But scarcely one depositor in a hundred will see things that way. Instead, they are likely to see themselves as victims of the unjustly low interest rates.

After Britain withdrew from the ERM in 1992 and interest rates fell to levels which were very low compared to the rates which had ruled in recent years, MPs' and ministers' postbags were crammed with letters from people complaining vociferously about the low interest rates. And the British government had thought that lowering interest rates would be popular!

Confusion About the Past

Uncertainty about how to regard income on deposits is another example of the widespread confusion about the link between present and future money values which pervades the issues of mortgages and pensions, discussed above. In the case of deposit income, people do not appreciate that they are being paid compensation *now* for tomorrow's fall in the real value of their savings. But they are subject to a similar confusion about *past* money values. Indeed, persistent inflation isolates a society in the present, cut off from both past and future money values.

Past values cease to have a bearing on the present because they are in 'old money'. Comparing the current price for something with its equivalent five years ago, let alone fifty, is like comparing the price for something in Italian lire with its price in Swiss francs. When inflation develops into hyperinflation then the same point applies to comparisons between prices today and prices yesterday, and in really extreme forms, between prices now and prices an hour ago.

People are aware of this problem and they constantly try to make mental adjustments for it which then become habits of mind. But these adjustments are necessarily crude. 'I paid $20,000 for that car,' they say. 'And that was *then*.' Or, 'I earned $20,000 on that job. That was serious money *then*.' They are aware that $20,000 is not worth as much as it was *then*, but they have very little idea of precisely how much less it is worth now.

One consequence is that people are particularly bad, even after the event, at assessing the wisdom of even the simplest of transactions, like buying or selling a secondhand car. A frequent refrain runs as follows: 'You know, I owned that car for five years and I sold it for $2,000 more than I paid for it. So I actually made a profit out of owning and running it!'

Of course, you can hit lucky with a low purchase price or, at the top end of the market, choose a model which appreciates because it becomes a collector's piece. But the idea that by consuming the services of an ordinary wasting asset you can actually make a profit should strike you as pretty odd. And, as a rule, you cannot make a profit this way. This is another trick played by inflation. Because the value of money is falling, it is possible for the real value of the car to fall and yet for the *money* value to increase, thereby providing the happy owner with a 'profit'.

The separation of present from past values which inflation engenders can leave public attitudes hopelessly confused. In 1824, a British magazine called the *Economist and General Advisor*, whose principal journalist was one William Cobbett, opined on how to manage on a limited budget. A family of four, it aimed to show, could live on an income of one guinea (£1.05) a week.[2] Today that would just about buy a cup of coffee, but this gives no indication of how well or badly people could manage in 1824.

Interestingly, in 1914, before the First World War took off, the weekly earnings of a worker in the engineering sector, at 22s 10d (£1.14), were not much above the basic level which 90 years earlier the *Economist and General Advisor* had said was just sufficient. Another 80 years on, it seems the engineering worker is now incomparably better off with £276 per week. But a loaf of bread and a pint of milk now cost about 20 times as much, while a pint of beer costs 140 times as much. (In 1914 a pint of beer cost 2½ old pennies, or 1p in today's money.)[3]

You frequently hear people complain about how expensive things are now, not only basic goods but also luxuries and entertainment. By contrast, in the 'good old days', supposedly it was possible for two people to go out and have a wonderful time and still have change from £5. In 1914, for instance, you could buy a front stalls seat at the Royal Opera House for £1 1s (that is, £1.05), and have dinner at the Savoy for 7s 6d (or 37½p). You could even stay in a double room at the Savoy for £1 5s (£1.25). And the whole lot, for two, would have cost just over £4. It sounds wonderful – until you realise that, cheap though it seems in today's money, in 1914 this evening would have cost just about a month's wages for an ordinary worker in the engineering industry.[4]

Or look at the illusion of rapid growth in earnings created by inflation. The mid-1970s were the heyday for the growth of pay in Britain. In 1975 alone average earnings rose by 30%. They had risen by 20% the year before and rose by another 20% in 1976. In the four years from 1974–7 average earnings just about doubled, making it seem as though people were a lot better off. The trouble is that prices just about doubled as well. The end result was that, in real terms, pay was just 2% higher.

Or take, for example, the widespread public disquiet at how much public servants are currently paid. In 1995, the salary of John Major as Prime Minister was £82,003 a year, which sounds handsome compared to the £4022 paid to the Duke of Wellington in 1830. Admittedly the Duke also enjoyed a 'pension' of £13,168, so his total payment from the state was just over £17,000 per annum. But in terms of today's money, that translates into £743,000 a year, more than eight times Mr Major's income.[5] This is a pretty large discrepancy by anyone's standards, but considering the huge rise in real incomes over the years, it is enormous.

Another interesting way of looking at the issue is to compare the Prime Minister's salary with the earnings of ordinary people. In 1914, the Prime Minister's salary was worth 84 times the earnings of an engineering worker. In 1994 it was worth only 5½ times.[6]

The Causes of Insecurity

People ought to be enjoying the transfer of power from producers to consumers which I described in Chapter 2. In fact, as we move into the zero era people are far from euphoric, not least because they feel insecure and uncertain. Undoubtedly, some of these feelings correspond to real factors which have brought genuine losses – in particular, reduced employment prospects and reduced employment security across the industrial west. But much of the feeling of hurt is down to *confusion and lack of understanding*, and a good deal of this is directly caused by the collapse of inflation.

Outside the Germanic countries, people had got used to inflation and, in a way, found it comfortable. Everywhere there are signs that people were taken in by its illusions and feel worse off without them. If pay rises at 4% a year and prices by 2% then they are just as well off as when pay rose by 10% and prices by 8%, but they don't feel it that way. Similarly, people miss the large increases in the value of their homes, even though, if they are going to remain in them, they are no worse off in real terms. And investors miss routine double-digit interest rates on their deposits.

These feelings of loss, insecurity and confusion are the problems of transition to the new regime without inflation. In time, they will fade as people adjust. But the insecurity relating to the underlying conditions in the economy will not fade. It is a permanent feature of the newly competitive world.

Both sorts of feeling are responsible for creating the mood of anxiety among consumers – 'the joyless recovery', and the lack of a 'feel-good factor' so remarked on by commentators in 1994–6. They constitute one of the major difficulties confronting business in the zero era.

6

The Challenge for Business

When there is inflation in the economy at large, price increasing is easier for everyone, for a host of reasons. The techniques learned then, like the techniques learned in skiing, tennis, swimming, or anything else by doing it first under easy conditions, can be employed later when inflation in the economy at large has slowed down. Thus, there as elsewhere, inflation begets inflation.

W.D. Slawson[1]

COMPANIES AND THEIR FINANCES ARE THE CRUCIBLE FOR ALL THE powerful forces I have described as being let loose on the economy from persistent high inflation – money illusion, distorted decisions, consumer confusion and financial market over-reaction. They are also the focus of the new forces operating in a world without inflation, including consumer wariness and low interest rates. And, of course, they will be in the front line when the general price level starts to fall.

The result is that on top of the issues presented by the technological revolution, organisational change and competition from the dynamic countries, the death of inflation presents business with wholly new challenges. It is in the response of business to these challenges that my optimism about the future will be proved justified or ill-founded.

There are three main areas where the changed inflationary environment can make a major contribution to prosperity – persuading firms to opt for a lower margin, high volume strategy; encouraging a higher level of investment; and improving the quality of decisions taken by management. In all these areas there are gains to be had for both companies themselves and society as a whole.

But I do not mean to suggest that everyone is bound to be a winner in the new world. Many companies will founder as a direct result of the changed environment, often because they have failed to perceive the radical changes necessary to survive and prosper without inflation. And the financial services industry may have a particularly hard time.

The Effect of Price Sensitivity

In Chapter 2 I pointed out that the collapse of inflation has gone hand in hand with consumers' increased sensitivity to prices. This has important consequences for the macroeconomy. But it also has powerful implications for individual businesses. Because constantly rising prices are the order of the day in an inflationary environment, this means that sellers can try it on with a price increase. If they have gone too far, all they have to do is wait for the general price level to catch up. In any case, the limited price sensitivity of consumers will mean that the loss of volume will probably not be too severe, and the power of the marketing and advertising departments can usually be relied on to shift what would otherwise be unsold stock. Time is on the side of the inflationary price rise.

All this is turned upside down in a world of low inflation. Of course, other factors besides price, such as quality, design and levels of service, still matter, but price now matters more than it used to. If the price is raised too high, there will now be a significant volume response. It won't do for sellers simply to wait for a rise in all other prices to bail them out. Consumers' increased price sensitivity should now encourage sellers, in their own interests, to opt for a strategy of higher sales volumes and lower unit margins.

One sign of consumers' new attitudes is the threat to brands which have been established for decades. In 1993, the US tobacco company Philip Morris stunned the industry and the financial markets by slashing the price of Marlboro cigarettes in the face of weak sales. And on both sides of the Atlantic, branded goods from cereals to cola have been under pressure from retailers' own labels and from discount stores. Meanwhile, established European retailers themselves are under pressure from discount stores such as Germany's Aldi and Denmark's Netto. Already these take about 25% of the food market in Germany. In the rest of Europe the share is much smaller, but everywhere it is growing.[2]

The power of retail price competition is being felt in surprising quarters. In November 1995 Guinness admitted that the growing power of supermarkets was damaging the ability of drinks producers to dictate prices. It had not been able to raise the prices of its spirits brands even by 1% that year. Stockmarket analyst Andrew Holland said:

Spirits bosses are wringing their hands in horror. They keep saying they will be able to increase prices without being able to demonstrate it.[3]

Apparently, not even an increase in Guinness's huge marketing budget (which runs to £300 million a year) could alter the situation.

This is part of a general trend. The power to manipulate consumers by advertising seems to be slipping. As Peter Brabeck, Nestlé's chief marketing strategist put it:

People today don't just act because someone tells them something.[4]

The increased price sensitivity of consumers under conditions of low inflation has recently received ringing endorsement from a surprising quarter – Argentina. Traditionally a country of endemically high inflation to which the populace had become inured, Argentina has recently undergone a dramatic stabilisation plan which brought inflation down to zero in 1996. According to the *Financial Times*[5] this, combined with the associated recession, has led to a transformation in Argentina's price sensitivity – with dramatic effects on business behaviour.

After half a century of rampant inflation, most Argentines' sense of relative value was heavily distorted, to the extent that 'How much is that?' was a phrase seldom heard in Buenos Aires. But now things are different. Last year the US discount retailer Walmart opened its first store there and it was bombarded with bargain hunters, keen to see whether it could beat the prices of its rivals in Argentina, the French Carrefours and the Chilean firm Jumbo. The phrase 'price war' entered conversation.

The *Financial Times* reports other dramatic effects. Car-makers, which for years have sold overpriced cars to a captive market, have slashed the price of new cars by up to 40%; rents have dropped by almost a quarter; leaflets offering discounts on items such as haircuts and restaurant meals 'litter the pavements'. Even wages have been falling in some sectors.

And there has been a significant effect on efficiency, the flipside of which is a collapse of small businesses and increased unemployment. Increased price sensitivity means low margins, and low margins mean that small, inefficient producers cannot survive. According to Carlos Paciarotti, a director of the Disco supermarket chain, in the old days in Argentina:

Anyone could be a butcher, grocer, or a baker.

But not any more. Over the last four years, tens of thousands of small shopkeepers have been put out of business.

These effects are not restricted to countries, such as Argentina, with turbulent recent histories. Recent UK experience clearly reveals the effects of consumers' increased price sensitivity. When UK retail spending is broken down into its component parts, it is evident that in 1993–4 those sections of retailing which adopted a strategy of low prices did so well in volume terms that their sales values (and presumably profits) rose. Those who did not heed this lesson lost out.

Interestingly, this was *not* true in the recovery of the early 1980s, nor in the boom period at the end of the 1980s. In other words, because the consumers of the 1990s have become more price sensitive, it now pays for producers and retailers to be competitive on price.

In Britain, this realisation has led to frequent outbreaks of price wars, often in surprising quarters. Areas of retailing which have recently discovered the power of price in Britain include clothing and footwear outlets, newspapers, insurance and supermarkets. As it launched a campaign of lower prices in September 1995, the supermarket group Somerfield pointed to the results of five months of research which showed that customers were still demanding low prices. Somerfield's marketing director said:

In these uncertain times, today's family wants value for money.[6]

The demand for newspapers had always been thought to be insensitive to price but the price war in 1994 proved this wrong. A 7p differential and a one-day-only lower price of 10p boosted sales of *The Sun* to almost 4 million and opened a record lead over its rivals. Meanwhile, sales of *The Times* rose by nearly 30% after the price was cut to 20p.

Increase price sensitivity, combined with competitive markets, forces marked changes in pricing behaviour. Even the sale of books in Britain, which had been governed for nearly 100 years by the 'net book agreement', a sort of cartel, is now going to be governed by normal competitive forces as supermarkets set out to offer best-selling books at about 50% of their 'full' price. Meanwhile, the package holiday trade, long the home of market illusions, is constantly being brought face to face with economic reality. In late 1995, the big high street travel agents were offering to cut 10% off prices in the following year's brochures before they were even on the streets.

Instead of openly cutting their prices, many retailers of both goods and services have resorted to discounts, special offers, tokens, gifts and other forms of disguised price reduction. Presumably this is because they regard the current 'value sensitivity' in the market as temporary and/or wish to protect the image of their posted price as the 'real price'. As time goes on, they will learn that the demand for value is permanent, and it may make more sense to consolidate the discounts and special offers in the posted price.

At the level of the individual business, the result is to turn cost-plus pricing on its head. Rather than starting with their costs and adding a reasonable profit to reach the price they must charge to customers, businesses now have to start with the price customers will pay and work back to the costs they can afford. It is not cost-plus but price-minus.

At General Motors' Cadillac division, for instance, they now begin by setting a target price for a new model. 'Then, you say your profit is so much, and you back down into the cost. We never used to do it that way,' says Janet Eckhoff, director of marketing and product strategy.[7]

Some Go Up, Some Go Down

Under inflationary conditions, business at least knows that the price of just about everything always goes up. It is simply a matter of when and by how much. The necessary movement in relative prices is accomplished by some prices going up by less than others. In a world of broadly stable prices, however, this would not be true; some prices would trend up while some would trend down and others would fluctuate. But knowing which would be which presents a real business challenge.

With labour costs still rising overall, it would be the labour-intensive goods and services whose prices would rise. This would represent a repeat of the experience that we are used to, for in the era of persistent inflation it has tended to be the labour-intensive goods, and more especially services, whose prices have risen most.

But this time there should be a difference. Whereas the post-war period was characterised by chronic labour shortages, including shortages even of unskilled labour, because of both technological changes and competition from the east, the period we are now in looks likely to see a surplus of unskilled labour and a widening of income differentials, as I have argued in Chapter 2. Accordingly, the price of goods and services heavily dependent on unskilled labour may remain constant or even fall. The costs of eating out and various sorts of domestic help, for instance, which have tended to rise sharply over the last 30 years, may now not rise much at all.

By contrast, goods and services relying heavily on highly skilled labour will rise in price. Private school fees, medical costs, legal charges are all likely to continue to rise, even in the brave new world where there is no inflation overall.

The goods which are likely to fall in price are those where productivity growth and technical progress lower the costs of production, or those which are increasingly provided by low cost producers in the east. The obvious candidates for this group are cars, consumer durables, electrical goods, basic clothes. By contrast, designer clothes will surely continue to rise in price, reflecting the scarce specialist skills of the top designers!

Commodity Prices Still on the Up?

What about commodity prices? Would they tend to rise in relation to other prices? It is difficult to be sure. Periodically we hear scare stories from experts suggesting that some or all commodities are getting scarce and may well soon run out. In the 1970s, the Club of Rome predicted that the world would have to accept much lower economic growth or it would soon face the exhaustion of many key commodities. In practice, not only has a shortage of commodities not inhibited growth but the real price of most commodities has not risen. The real price of oil, supposedly one of the greatest danger spots for the industrial world, has *fallen* considerably since the early 1980s.

Nevertheless, with strong growth in the dynamic countries of the east, the demand for commodities of all sorts will rise – oil, metals, chemicals, food and fibres. With limited supply, the result would be rising commodity prices to be paid by east and west alike. Indeed, it is because they recognise this danger and do not recognise the other disinflationary forces which I analysed above that many commentators see eastern development as an inflationary force for the west.

So rising commodity prices pose a threat, but how serious a danger is this? Eastern growth is, in many cases, highly resource intensive. Old-fashioned, smokestack, metal-bashing industry is alive and well and living in many of the dynamic countries.

In the west, though, economic activity has become much less resource intensive. This is partly because price changes and environmental concerns have made people economise (as in the case of oil), and partly because the west has allowed the east to take over some of its resource-intensive activity. But the most important reason is that as the west has got richer, more and more of its economic activity is taken up with activities which naturally use few raw materials. The service sector, particularly financial services, uses few raw materials compared to the great manufacturing enterprises whose growth dominated economic development for most of the early part of the twentieth century. The result is that although the absolute quantity of raw materials demanded by the west as growth proceeds continues to rise, it now rises by less than the growth of GDP.

Accordingly, the west is nowhere near as exposed to the movement of commodity prices as it used to be. If the price of oil were to rise in the same proportion as it did in the 1970s, for instance, the adverse effects would be nowhere as serious now as they were then. Quite simply, extremely important though it still is, oil is not as important as it was. As they develop further, the dynamic economies will themselves reach this stage, when further expansion is based on services rather than manufacturing. Indeed, Hong Kong and Singapore are already there. Moreover, there is enormous scope for economies in the use of energy. The widespread use of computer-controlled mechanisms will allow fine tuning of fuel demands.

How far commodity prices are driven up both by continued western demand and by eastern development will also depend upon how far it is possible to increase commodity production in line with increasing demands. In fact, there are good prospects of big increases in supply. Technological improvements are having a big impact on the production even of commodities. Only a few years ago, for instance, it was impossible to drill for oil in the North Atlantic.

Moreover, whereas the development of Japan and then, subsequently, the Asian Tigers has involved countries which, by and large, are not resource rich (Singapore, Hong Kong and Taiwan, for example), the new wave of development is bringing along countries which *are* resource rich (e.g. Indonesia).

Furthermore, as and when the ex-Soviet Union and the former eastern Europe recover from their present travails, they will bring massive resource-producing capacity with them. One of the major sufferers from turmoil and dislocation in Russia has been oil production. If the energy extraction industries in Russia were properly established along modern western lines, then it would be possible to secure substantial increases in the output of oil, coal and gas. In the former Soviet republics of Kazakhstan and Azerbaijan, most of the leading western oil companies are vying with each other (and with the Russians) to get oil out of what look likely to be some of the world's largest oil fields.[8]

An End to Exchange Rate Instability?

One possible compensation for business managers grappling with pricing policy could come from the end of damaging currency fluctuations. After all, large and frequent currency changes only emerged in the 1970s, at the same time as the upsurge of inflation. So will the demise of inflation put an end to them?

The answer depends partly on how far the new non-inflationary environment is shared internationally. If it is widely shared, then exchange rate changes can become much smaller because there is no doubt that differential inflation rates have been the main reason behind secular trends in exchange rates, such as the long decline of sterling against the deutschmark. And indeed, the reduction in inflation in the 1980s did generally reduce the inflation differentials between countries, as formerly high inflation countries like Italy, France and Britain tended to converge on low inflation countries such as Germany.

This might be taken to offer support for the idea of greater stability of exchange rates, whether across the EU, or even more widely across the industrial world as a whole – a sort of new international monetary system based on fixed exchange rates. The implication would be that companies would find it easier to manage their exposures to currency differences – and banks harder to make money from their foreign exchange operations.

But exchange rate changes are unlikely to disappear, even in a world without inflation. For they are useful for reacting to *real* events, such as German reunification, which have a differential impact across different countries. Such events will still occur, even if all countries' inflation experience is broadly similar. Indeed, as I discuss in Chapter 9, the absence of an inflationary threat would make currency devaluation a more feasible policy for countries facing adverse shocks.

On a wider canvass, one of the messages of this book is that however much the western world converges on low inflation, the fast developing east will still be likely to experience a serious inflationary problem. Where this is confined to pure development inflation, then there is no reason why trade competitiveness should be impaired and no need for the currency to fall. High inflation may even be consistent with a strong currency. Moreover, letting the currency be strong is just about the only way development inflation can be suppressed.

Where inflation in the east accelerates beyond this stage, however, then it will be necessary for the eastern currency to depreciate against the leading western currencies. And, of course, western companies will be doing an increasing proportion of their business with eastern counterparts so what is happening to eastern currencies will be of increasing importance.

Furthermore, as I have tried to emphasise throughout this book, even in the west, the new world is not likely to be one of heavenly equilibrium. The price level may fluctuate, and at different times and to different degrees in different countries. Some countries' financial systems will be better able to cope with a period of falling prices than others. In particular, countries with heavily indebted governments will find things especially difficult when prices start to fall. And all this will be happening in an atmosphere of confusion and uncertainty when no one will be sure exactly what is going on. There are likely to be major exchange rate consequences.

So the end of inflation in the west will not simply put an end to exchange rate changes, and the business headaches caused by having to manage currency exposures will continue. But at least foreign exchange traders, and their employers, can rest easily in their beds.

A World of Falling Prices

No inflation sounds like good news for the economic world as a whole, even though many businesspeople and managers might complain that it will make life tougher for them. This does *not* mean, though, that things are even better if prices start to fall. In fact, a world of falling prices is very similar in its effects to a world of continual inflation, only with the signs reversed. If everyone *knew* that prices were going to fall by 3% a year, every year, *and all arrangements were adjusted to this*, then price deflation would make next to no difference.

But as with inflation, people would *not* know by how much prices were going to fall, and indeed everything would not be free to fall in price. Some prices would fall freely and others would be sticky.

As I argued in Chapter 1, interest rates would be a particular problem because they could not go negative. So once you get beyond small rates of price deflation, the problem of high real rates of interest looms up again. And precisely because individuals and companies cannot be adequately penalised for holding financial assets by the imposition of negative interest rates, there is an incentive to postpone spending money and to save it instead. People will still have to spend on the ordinary expenses of living – food, transport, clothing, entertainment. But consumer durables would be a different matter. If you can defer a purchase then you will find it cheaper when you come to buy it later.

This may not really seem like a completely new phenomenon because consumers have had a fair amount of experience of it already in the sphere of high-tech goods. Videos, camcorders, faxes, computers and mobile phones have all come down in price substantially and there is already something of a tendency for consumers to defer purchases of such items, in order to benefit not only from lower prices, but also better quality or higher specifications later on. But in the market for high-tech goods this tendency is at least partly offset by fashion consciousness and cachet. Although a mobile phone might be cheaper in two years' time, it would lend you added status to have one *today*. The same sort of consideration would not apply with the more established consumer durables in a world of general price deflation.

Moreover, the tendency to defer purchases would not extend only to consumers. Companies would be subject to the same incentive structure. In a regime of falling prices, if they defer purchases of machinery or buildings, or even of shares in another company, they will find them cheaper when they eventually come to buy them. And since inventories depreciate in value, it will pay to hold as few of them as possible.

So just when higher spending is needed to reestablish stability of the price level, there is a systematic tendency towards lower spending.

Although small rates of deflation may be perfectly tolerable, just as were small rates of inflation, the business reaction to anything more than minimal price falls is likely to be one of extreme fear, bordering on panic. For quite apart from the element of surprise and the contrast with the recent past, falling prices without volume rises carry the possibility of disaster. Real interest rates rise, real income and wealth are transferred from borrowers to lenders; heavily indebted companies are imperilled; financial institutions look shaky; even governments see their financial standing deteriorating.

The reaction of companies is likely to be to retrench and to seek further cost reductions, including reductions in rates of pay, just as they did in the depression of the 1930s. This would surely be met by resistance from employees. Accordingly, the onset of deflation might lead to industrial strife and conflict, just as the upsurge of inflation did in the 1970s. Nor is this surprising. For just like inflation, a period of deflation would represent a struggle over real income shares in conditions of profound uncertainty and anxiety.

Recognising the Importance of Price

These changes sharply increase the importance and status of pricing policy within firms. It used to be possible to raise prices on a regular
timetable – 'the January price rise', more or less regardless of the market.
Not any more. Nor is it any longer a safe option to test the market by
pushing prices up, because time is no longer on the side of the attempt
to raise prices. If the market will not bear the increased prices, the seller
may be forced into an embarrassing (and damaging) price reduction.

Moreover, it is now vital for businesses to know which sort of cate-
gory they are in with regard to the long-term trend of product prices. Is
their product the sort whose price can go on rising even in a world of
general price stability, or is it the sort whose price should fall over time?
It is vital for firms to get this right. If a business thinks that it is in the
former group, and that effectively it can go on behaving much as before,
but in fact it is in the latter group, then it will find itself in serious trouble. Sales will slip, marketing and advertising bills will rise, unsold
stocks will mount.

These warning bells are ringing especially clearly for the car industry.
The costs of car production fall with higher output, but the industry puts
enormous effort (and expense) into differentiating one product from
another. The product itself is old and is no longer at the cutting edge of
image definition and status projection (as it once was). Meanwhile, the
rapidly developing low cost countries are becoming more and more
capable of supplying cars to the developed west. In short, in a western
world without inflation, this is a product whose price should fall. But try
convincing the heads of the world's car giants of this.

Without inflation, the *annual wage round* takes on a new complex-
ion. The general assumption that wages go up for everyone at least
once a year is closely related to the experience of continual inflation.
In a world of zero inflation, businesses will have to consider a different system, perhaps involving seniority payments as well as the usual
combination of merit and promotion awards.

The sharp change in the inflationary environment requires a different
approach to budgeting and corporate planning. If inflation is going to be
zero then the broad mass of companies will need to start off assuming that
their product prices will be static, whatever the marketing people may

say. For some, as I argued above, even in 'normal' times budgets need to be made on the assumption of falling prices. And as a contingency, all need to do their sums on the basis of a fall in the general price level.

Most importantly, budgets and plans need to be consistent with regard to the future rate of inflation. The demise of inflation means not only product prices (on average) not going up, but also wages hardly rising, sustained low interest rates and asset prices not rising by much. To see and embody in the corporate plan one part of the non-inflationary world but not the whole could spell disaster.

Interest Rates and Investment

Inflation has caused particularly serious problems for the assessment, and financing, of investments. Its demise will bring big advantages in this area for both companies and the wider economy.

The tendency for interest rates to rise to reflect inflation means that the cash flow of any project on which money is borrowed is transformed, even if the real interest rate is the same as it would have been without inflation.

If you borrow money for a fixed period, you pay interest during the life of the loan and pay back the capital either gradually or in one go at the end. Once inflation enters the system, however, and nominal interest rates reflect inflation, then the time profile of repayments changes. That part of the interest payments which compensates for inflation in fact represents a part-repayment of capital, to compensate for the diminished real value of the capital repayments in the future. So the burden of financing projects is greater in the early years than it would be without inflation and with correspondingly lower interest rates. It is exactly the same phenomenon as the redistribution of the real value of mortgage payments over time, which I discussed in Chapter 5.

Large, sophisticated companies can now find ways round this difficulty. They can finance themselves in different ways, relying more on retained earnings or equity, extending the length of loans, or reshaping the repayment scheduling, or borrowing more money from other sources during the course of a loan, effectively to finance the payment of interest.

But small companies cannot readily do this. Even if they understand the process at work and therefore fully comprehend that the *real* cost of borrowing is nowhere near as high as the nominal rate they are having to pay, being able to act on this realisation is not so easy. Small companies often face a battle for survival, caught between an anxious bank manager on the one hand and a ticking clock on the other. The cost of finance for their borrowed money directly enters the costs of current production. To take on an added burden to finance an investment project at double-digit interest rates can be really frightening.

It is all very well saying that interest rates are 15% because inflation is expected to be 12%, and that means that businesses should be able to raise their prices by 12% a year. In the meantime, though, they have to *pay* the interest. If things go wrong, the bank manager may call in the loan.

The upshot is that even if inflation does not end up raising real interest rates, it will act to deter real investment, especially by the small company sector. On top of this, of course, inflation *has* tended to raise real interest rates, both short and long, and this has discouraged investment, for companies both large and small.

How Far into the Future?

The adverse effects of inflation on real investment may have gone further. For one of the effects of the fogginess about money values that occurs during inflation is the shortening of people's time horizons. Businesses tend to regard the far future as purely uncertain and instead concentrate more on the here and now. This is clearly documented in the case of very high inflation. For a start, when inflation really lets rip, the inflation rate itself is no longer referred to in terms of a rate per year but rather per month, or even in really extreme cases per day. But this effect also extends to the length of agreements and contracts. Indeed, with very high inflation, long-term financial markets disappear altogether.

In ordinary, moderate inflation nothing as serious as this happens, but the effects are similar in type. For instance, the market for 30-year bonds and 30-year fixed-rate mortgages in the US virtually disappeared in the 1970s.

This issue of time horizons could prove to be of enormous importance to the world of business. It is striking that the successful, dynamic economies of the Far East seem to have a sharply different attitude to time from the view common in the west. Chinese culture is traditionally long-sighted, partly because it places so much emphasis on the life of the family and the community, stretching on beyond the life of the individual.

Something similar is seen in other eastern cultures. In Japan, as well as the life of the family and the community, there is the life of the company, stretching on beyond the individual. The effects of this ethos on corporate decision making are reinforced, of course, by the absence of many of the short-term competitive forces which threaten corporate survival, never mind prosperity, in the west. And recently, it has been reinforced also by low interest rates.

The west cannot hope to ape the east's cultural background. Even so, it has to be recognised that it has not always been as short-sighted as it appears to have been over recent decades. The culture of Victorian England, for instance, was decidedly long-sighted. Doubtless this too had its non-economic components in the shape of the period's confidence and optimism and sense of stability. But prolonged low interest rates surely made a big difference.

This is where low inflation in the west could make a major contribution now. If companies (and governments) discount projects at real rates of return of 8, 10 or even 12%, it is little wonder that investment rates are low. Moreover, the longer lived the project, the more sensitive it is to the rate of interest used for discounting.

A particularly invidious practice has grown up of using high discount rates as a way of allowing for risk. If the company thinks that the appropriate risk-free rate of discount to use is, say, 15%, it may add 5%, making 20%, to allow for risk. But because longer-lived projects are particularly sensitive to discount rates, this position weighs particularly strongly against them, irrespective of whether they are riskier than projects with a shorter life.

Accordingly, the death of inflation should help to encourage companies to invest, to invest in longer-term projects, and generally to operate on longer time horizons, provided that interest rates do indeed come down fully to reflect the new reality, and provided that companies take full advantage. But here we come face to face with a paradox.

Problems of Transition

During the process of disinflation, some of the distortions caused by inflation may get worse. In particular, as I argued in Chapter 4, the financial markets have taken their time in adjusting to low inflation. The result is to keep real rates of interest high, and in some cases even to *raise* them, even though nominal rates have in general been falling. Indeed, without some sort of shock to bring financial markets to a rapid adjustment, this state of affairs could last for years after inflation has in practice been killed off completely, thereby perpetuating high real interest rates and *discouraging* investment.

But this problem of transition is not confined to financial markets. As inflation falls, industrial and commercial companies can be left expecting too much. This can be seen clearly in the case of companies which insist on looking for rates of return on investment prospects which only make sense on the assumption of continued high inflation. In Britain in 1994, the Bank of England bemoaned the fact that many companies were evidently still looking for rates of return of 20% or more when inflation was currently below 3% and the yield on long gilts was well below 10%.

Companies clearly had not adjusted their target or hurdle rates of return, which were defined in nominal terms, to the new lower level of long-term interest rates, let alone to the underlying change in the inflation environment which went beyond what the bond markets recognised. In the process, they were effectively setting much higher real return requirements than they had in the past. Quite why they behaved in this way is a good question. Were they simply operating on habit? Were they so cautious about the future that they consciously chose to impose tighter criteria than before? Did they understand what they were doing? Whatever the reason, the result was that they turned down prospective investments which should have been made.

A Distorting Mirror

Inflation has distorted the allocation of resources by bending incentives and creating confusion. Accordingly, its demise should improve business decision making and the allocation of resources.

Serious problems have been created by the interaction of inflation with the tax system which, in most western countries, was constructed on the assumption of an economy with little or no inflation and has been little modified since. Indeed it can be argued that in the US, inflation raised the effective tax rate on equity capital and in the process deterred real investment in plant and machinery.[9]

Moreover, inflation has played havoc with the activities of companies in the most basic sense – the measurement of their profitability and balance sheet strength. Inflation seriously distorts company accounts which are compiled, as virtually all are, under the *historical cost convention*, that is to say, the recording of all transactions in terms of the prices paid at the time, regardless of subsequent changes to the value of money caused by inflation. Various attempts have been made by the accountancy profession to devise a satisfactory method of inflation accounting and some companies today present their accounts under both the historical cost convention and a form of inflation accounting. But since the rate of inflation has fallen, the impetus to create a widely recognised and generally employed system of inflation accounting has dissipated and companies and accountants have decided to make do with the historical cost method, warts and all. Even so, the distortions that remain are significant, and the death of inflation would remove the serious effects of inflation on company accounts.

The most important problem concerns fixed assets and depreciation. The amount allowed in the accounts each year for depreciation reflects the original cost of the equipment. But under inflationary conditions, the cost of such equipment generally rises and its replacement cost, at the end of its life, will be correspondingly higher.

The amount allowed for depreciation should therefore rise with the general level of prices. The fact that it does not means that company profits are overstated. Correspondingly, companies pay more corporation tax than they should. According to one leading accountant's estimates, if you properly accounted for depreciation to take account of the effect of inflation, ICI's apparent retained profits over the period 1972–91 of £4.9 billion would be transformed into retained *losses* of £4.5 billion.[10]

Inflation, however, does not work on company accounts in only one direction. It is customary for companies to value land and buildings at cost, even though, under inflation, their value would tend to rise. Equally, inflation also affects the liability side of balance sheets by reducing the real value of debt. Adjusting for this effect as well as the effect of inflation in relation to three leading US companies in 1979, during the heyday of inflation, produced some startling results. According to Professor Stanley Fischer, whereas AT&T's reported profits were substantially increased by this procedure, Exxon's were slightly lowered, and General Motors' were sharply reduced.[11]

Accordingly, even though inflation has not recently posed such intense problems for company accounts as it did in the 1970s, a world in which the general level of prices was stable would undoubtedly improve the accuracy and worth of company accounts. But a regime of completely stable prices hardly looks on the cards. And sustained *deflation* would surely cause problems as serious as those under inflation.

A world in which the price level fluctuated, although at least having the property of limiting and then correcting distortions, might perhaps cause still greater confusion, as one sort of distortion was succeeded by its opposite.

Profits Up or Down?

What would a regime of price stability imply for company profits? On a very simple view, the answer is nothing at all. That is to say, the absence of inflation would mean that profits in money terms would rise less fast than in an inflationary world, so that at any given point they would be lower in money terms. But this would be of no significance. In real terms they would be the same. In fact, things are unlikely to be quite that simple.

In the past, sharply differing views have been expressed on the desirability or otherwise of inflation for companies. On the plus side has been the idea that a regime of constantly rising prices allows sellers to get away with more and 'oils the wheels' of commerce, helping to ensure the flexibility of relative prices, while simultaneously bolstering confidence through rising asset values, rising selling prices and increasing (nominal) profit levels. It is not unheard of for an industrialist to add: 'If only wage inflation could be suppressed, then rising prices would be fine!'

On the debit side, there have been worries that companies are slow to adapt their pricing behaviour to higher costs and that any pick-up in inflation is liable to leave profits squeezed. Moreover, the interaction of the tax system with inflation may lead to an overstatement of company profits and excessive tax payments. Where does the balance lie?

The logic of increased price sensitivity is that unit margins, particularly at the retail level, may tend to be lower but levels of capacity utilisation will be higher in the absence of inflation. Because of this voluntary strategy by sellers, as well as the other factors helping to keep inflation down, even at lower levels of unemployment the monetary authorities will be able to run the economy at higher levels of demand. The result is that the rate of return should increase, even though unit margins are lower.

Meanwhile, lower interest rates would have an impact on the shape of company profit and loss accounts. For those companies with extensive borrowings, the deductions from trading profits for interest payments would be much smaller. In fact, if real interest rates were unchanged, provided the accounts made full and proper recognition of inflation, the real profitability of the business would be unchanged.

But I have argued that the absence of inflation is likely to lead to lower real interest rates, both short and long. In that case, the real returns due to shareholders would be higher. As a result of lower real interest rates and lower nominal long rates, companies might start to borrow more long-term fixed-interest money. They might use this both to finance increased investment and to substitute for equity, with the result that gearing ratios would rise.

There is an important caveat to all this. A regime of stable prices matched by lower long-term interest rates which recognised this would be conducive to long-term fixed-interest funding, but if companies feared a period of falling long-term prices this would worry them, and discourage them from long-term fixed-rate borrowing, even if the apparent real rate of interest were the same.

The death of inflation may sharply alter the pattern of relative strength between firms. Some will doubtless fail to see the heightened importance of pricing strategy and will suffer against rivals who do perceive it. Balance sheet status will also play a major role. Firms which borrowed heavily at fixed rates of interest that only make sense if inflation

continues will now shoulder a heavy burden. Equally, firms whose assets
are heavily loaded with land and buildings may now find that they do
not do as well. The worst position to be in would be to have a high level
of fixed-interest debt funding holdings of land and buildings.

Industries Under Pressure

Most of these factors will affect the position of particular companies
within a sector, rather than the fate of one industry against another. But
you can argue that three large sectors are set to do *relatively* badly in the
new environment – housing, retailing and other consumer-related businesses, and retail financial services.

I discussed the *housing market* in detail in Chapter 3. In the zero era,
real house prices will be lower and housing turnover will be lower than
the market is used to. Even though there will of course be a continuing
need for new housing to reflect demographic pressures and replacement
demand, the result is a continuing squeeze on most of the businesses
connected with the housing market.

There are two powerful forces acting against *consumer spending* and a
third which will make it more difficult to make money in consumer-
related businesses. First, there is the argument that the combined effect
of technological change and eastern competition will be to reduce the
share of pay in national income, a process for which there is definite
supporting evidence in the UK.

Secondly, whatever their incomes, consumers might reasonably
decide to save more in the light of more uncertain times, and the lack
of anticipated appreciation in the price of their homes. Thirdly, when
they spend their money they will continue to be extremely price sensitive and value conscious, thereby making it more difficult for sellers to
make money at any given volume of spending.

Over and above this, there are likely to be big shifts within the consumer sector. The increasing inequality of incomes observed in so many
western countries will increase the profitability of catering for up-
market spending, while the lower level of mortgage payments may
prompt higher spending by younger couples with families.

The pressure on *financial services* is related to the illusions created by inflation. Financial intermediaries are usually rewarded in the form of a percentage spread between buying and selling prices, or the difference between two interest rates. This is a real amount. Something like it will have to be paid come what may, but it is so much easier to palm it off on the client in a system of high inflation and high interest rates.

Think about the initial charge when buying units in an investment or unit trust. Say the charge is 5%. That is a pretty hefty amount whatever happens, but at least in a world of high inflation the investor may be able to 'pay' for it easily out of one year's returns. Suppose that the nominal return in your first year is 15% but inflation is 10%. You can say to yourself that the initial charge was easily covered by the returns. In fact this would be wrong, because you need 10% just to make up for inflation. You are only making 5% real and that has been completely swallowed up by the initial charge.

Or consider the commissions on insurance and pension policies. It is the same story. Nor does this point apply only to initial charges. The managers of pension monies or other funds charge an annual fee which is typically in the region of 1½–2½% which is taken from the fund. With much lower nominal returns, this deduction will come to be seen as very substantial. Indeed, on occasion it will be sufficient to make the annual return on the fund, net of expenses, negative.

The same point applies to banks. A deposit-taking institution makes its money by paying less on its deposits than it charges on its loans. Similarly, it pays less on its less competitive deposits than it would have to for money market funding. Consider the deposit which normally pays about 3% below official interest rates. If official rates are 3% then it will pay nothing at all. This is unlikely to be readily accepted by bank customers.

Or think about mortgage rates. These are usually 1–2% above the official level of interest rates. Now 1 or 2% can seem neither here nor there when the general level of interest rates is 10 or 12%, but when the general level of rates is very low these same margins will seem enormous. Suppose the general level of interest rates were 3%. Mortgages might then be offered at 5%. This seems a pretty low level, but it would be seen as almost *double* the market rate of interest.

The upshot is that the onset of the very low interest rates which are bound to be associated with low inflation will bring the margins and commissions in the financial services industry into much sharper focus.

This is likely to lead to increased consumer sensitivity and, as a result, more intense competition and lower margins.

Management More Difficult

At very high rates of inflation, management becomes more difficult as business leaders have another major factor to manage, namely the position of the business in the inflationary process. But at more moderate rates, inflation may make management easier because it provides an extra lever – the power to deceive. Those deceived may be customers, workers, shareholders, or indeed the managers themselves.

How often have we heard managements pat themselves on the back for achieving 'record profits'? Yet with inflation proceeding continually, even if the business carries on performing at exactly the same level in real terms, each year should produce 'record profits' in nominal terms. Anything less than this implies a deterioration from the previous year. To produce 'record profits' in real terms, of course, the nominal profit level has to increase faster than the rate of inflation from the last *real* record level. Accordingly, inflation provides a temptation for managements to set their sights too low.

In relations with workers, under inflationary conditions, managements were at least able to reward their workforce once a year with a substantial pay rise, say in January, which made them much better off than they were in December. Without inflation, by contrast, managements are only able to give small pay rises, or indeed none at all. Workers do not enjoy their January boost. (Nor, of course, do they endure the slow decline thereafter, but that is another matter.)

The end of inflation lays out the bare facts for all to see. Illusion is no longer a management tool. At the same time, the substantial real changes in the world of business and finance associated with inflation's demise impose enormous burdens on business leaders.

This will put a premium on good management. Almost anyone can preside over a profitable business chugging along in stable conditions. It takes real skill, however, to perceive the nature of sharp changes in the external environment and adapt a business successfully to cope with them. This is the challenge that business now faces.

Part III

Deflating Economics and Reflating Economies

7

Rise and Fall:
The History of Inflation
and Interest Rates

Inflation is the form of taxation which the public find hardest to evade and even the weakest government can enforce when it can enforce nothing else.

John Maynard Keynes[1]

The economic stalactite of inflated demand has met a sociological stalagmite of upthrusting claims; and when stalactite and stalagmite meet and fuse in an icy kiss ... nobody on earth can be quite sure where the one ends and the other begins.

Sir Dennis Robertson[2]

W E ARE PASSING THROUGH A PERIOD WHEN THE DEGREE OF change is so profound that past and future seem divided as if by a chasm. It is as though they were in different worlds. But with regard to *inflation*, what is happening to separate us from the recent past is reuniting us with the bulk of our history.

From the first beginnings of a monetary economy in ancient times, the spectre of inflation has always been there. But the history of inflation is in many ways the history of the *absence* of inflation, a history of extensive periods of *fluctuating* prices resulting in long-run price stability, interspersed with occasional bursts of inflation. Before modern times, there were some long periods of rising prices, but only at moderate rates. Equally, in the last few centuries, there are many examples of short periods of very rapid inflation – known to economists as hyperinflation – usually associated with wars or the aftermath of wars.

But there is nothing in the whole of human history quite like the sustained peacetime inflation of the last 50 years. Understanding why this inflation developed in the first place is critical to understanding why it is now collapsing.

From Classical Beginnings to Spanish Gold

For monetary systems using coins made of precious metal, such as gold, the main inflationary risk was always systematic debasement by the issuers of the currency, that is to say, a reduction in the precious metal content of the coins below their official value. There is evidence of the use of plated coins as far back as classical Greece, as shown by a section of Aristophanes' *The Frogs* which must be about the earliest expression of Gresham's Law (that bad money drives out good):

> The noble silver drachma, that of old
> We were so proud of, and the recent gold,
> Coins that rang true, clean stamped and worth their weight
> Throughout the world, have ceased to circulate.
> Instead, the purses of Athenian shoppers
> Are full of shoddy silver-plated coppers.
> Just so, when men are needed by the nation,
> The best have been withdrawn from circulation.[3]

In the monetary system later introduced throughout the Roman world by the Emperor Augustus (44BC to 14AD), using gold, silver and copper, the face values of coins were at first closely related to the value of the metallic content. Subsequently, however, as public spending increased beyond the capacity of the tax system to finance it, the silver *denarius* was debased. For about 200 years, the pace of this debasement was supportable, but under the Emperor Gallienius (253–68) all restraint was abandoned. It has been suggested that over the third century, money may have fallen to a fiftieth of its value at the beginning. Under the Emperor Diocletian there was even an attempt to impose a wage and price freeze throughout the Roman Empire.[4]

Even so, there does not appear to be any evidence of rapid annual rates of inflation. Indeed, the average annual rate of inflation seems to have been only 3–4% over the third century as a whole, which is a mere bagatelle compared to the rates of inflation which have been generated in modern times by the printing of paper money.

The first country to use paper money seems to have been China. After Marco Polo visited it (or at least claimed to) in 1271–95 he remarked:

All these pieces of paper are issued with as much solemnity and authority as if they were pure silver or gold.[5]

Moreover, China had early experience of quite serious inflation. From 1190 to 1240, the supply of paper money increased more than 6 times and the price level more than 20 times, or at an annual rate of more than 6%.[6]

In Europe, the invention of paper money had to wait for several centuries during which the money supply continued to consist mainly of coins minted from precious metals, but there was plenty of scope for the generation of inflation through debasement, by reducing the weight of the coins, or clipping or shaving them, or 'crying up' their value, that is to say, decreeing their worth to be greater than their precious metal content warranted.

Our knowledge of monetary affairs during the Dark Ages is limited, but we do know that the founder of the modern monetary system in western Europe was Pepin the Short (715–68), father of Charlemagne, who decreed that a *livre* (pound) of silver was to be divided into 240 *denarii* (pennies). The Byzantine gold *solidus* was currently worth about twelve *denarii*, so a sum of twelve pennies was known as a *solidus*, *sou* or *shilling*. This Carolingian system of pounds, shillings and pence spread throughout Europe, including the various Anglo-Saxon kingdoms in England. It remained the basis of English money until decimalisation in 1971.

In continental Europe, the break-up of the Carolingian Empire was followed by a fragmentation of monetary authorities and a debasement of the coinage. In England, though, the silver content of the coins held up fairly well. In the 1696 recoinage, 66 shillings worth of coins were struck from a pound of silver, instead of the 20 which the original relationship would have allowed. That meant that the pound had lost two-thirds of its silver content over eight centuries, but this gave an average rate of depreciation of only 0.13% per annum.

In the sixteenth century, most of Europe underwent a pronounced inflation which, although its origins may well have been mainly monetary, was not caused by debasement (although a separate problem was created by debasement in England under Henry VIII). The explanation lay with the arrival of large quantities of Spanish gold from the New World. But increases in the money supply seem far from the whole story, for in large parts of Europe the origins of the inflation predated the gold influx. Moreover, we know that in England prices rose considerably faster than the change in the quantity and composition of coins would suggest. The pressure of increased population on a limited food supply seems also to have played a part.[7]

Historians refer to the 'Great Tudor Inflation', meaning the long period of continuously rising prices, leading to a large cumulative increase in the price level over the period as a whole. Even so, the average annual inflation rate in England and France in this period seems to have been between 2 and 3%. The inflation rate was fastest in the place where Spanish gold entered the system – Andalusia. Between 1550 and 1600, prices there rose by a total of 500%, equivalent to an average annual rate of almost 8%.[8]

The Evolution of the Gold Standard

Although the integrity of English coinage was restored under Elizabeth I, by the late seventeenth century monetary affairs were again in turmoil, but not because of mismanagement or debasement by the authorities. Silver coins were losing their value because they were being clipped by many of their users and the clippings melted down and sold for their metallic value. Meanwhile, the Royal Mint was issuing new full-weight coins with milled edges to prevent clipping and these two sorts of silver coin were circulating in tandem, along with the gold guinea.

But foreigners demanded payment in the new, heavy coins, leaving the smaller, lighter weight coins in domestic use. This lowering of the silver content of the coins resulted in rising prices (which were adjusted to the *silver* value of the coins). Meanwhile, the gold guinea, which was originally worth 20 silver shillings, rose to 30 shillings in 1695.

This operation of virtually three separate currencies caused enormous complications for trade and commerce and many contemporary observers were concerned that the increase in uncertainty and transaction costs was reducing the level of economic activity.

What should be done? There ensued a dispute which involved, among others, Sir Christopher Wren, John Locke and Sir Isaac Newton. Newton argued that there should be a reduction in the silver content of the pound, effectively recognising the inflation that had already occurred. If instead the silver content of the pound were restored to its official level, he argued, prices would have to fall or production would be cut.

John Locke, by contrast, argued for the maintenance of the old silver value and for a recoinage of the clipped money. His arguments were a remarkable combination of the view that money is 'neutral', that is to say, changing the quantity does not affect anything real, and the idea that unanticipated changes cause damaging distortions. He wrote:

> The having the Species of our Coin One-fifth bigger, or One-fifth less than they are at present, would be neither good nor harm to England, if they had always been so... The Harm comes by the change, which unreasonably and unjustly gives away and transfers Mens properties, disorders Trade, Puzzels Accounts, and needs a new Arithmetick to cost up Reckonings, and keep Accounts in; besides a thousand other Inconveniences.[9]

William III took Locke's advice, kept the official content of the pound unchanged but renewed the currency with heavy silver coins with milled edges. In other words, he took the deflationary option. And the result, as Newton had predicted, was depressed business conditions and a period of falling prices, proving that the great man's genius extended even into the realm of economics.

Newton subsequently became Master of the Mint and was involved in the gradual switch from the use of silver to gold. In 1711 he fixed the pound at £3 17s 9d per ounce of gold. With two suspensions – during the Napoleonic Wars, continuing up to 1821, and during the First World War, continuing up to 1925 – the pound was still at this rate when the link to gold was finally abandoned in 1931, for reasons which I shall review in a moment.[10]

Long-run Price Stability

The Gold Standard provided Britain with two centuries of monetary stability. But its success needs to be put in a longer-term context. The British economic historians, Henry Phelps-Brown and Sheila Hopkins, constructed a price index going back to 1264.[11] I have spliced recent price data onto it, thereby bringing it up to date, as shown in Figure 7.1. As I have presented it, the figure reveals next to no detail from early periods. But that is for a good reason; changes in the price level in the early centuries are insignificant compared with the explosion of prices after the Second World War.

This historical record shows long periods of overall price stability, stretching over hundreds of years. The price level seems to have been more or less the same at the beginning of the sixteenth century as it was at the beginning of the fourteenth century. Moreover, after the long period of quite high inflation in the sixteenth century, there was a very long period of overall price stability which remained to the very eve of

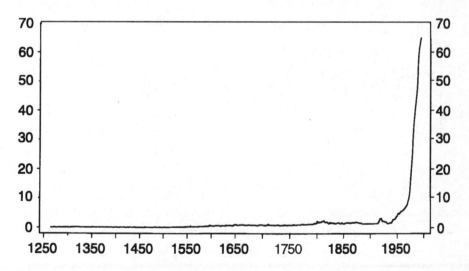

Source: E.H. Phelps-Brown & S.V. Hopkins, quoted in 'Seven Centuries of the Prices of Consumables', *Economica*, November 1956; updated with data from Datastream

Figure 7.1   UK price level 1264–1995 (1264=1000)

our own era. Indeed, in 1932, prices in Britain were slightly *lower* than they had been in 1795. Of the total increase in the price level from 1264 to 1995, less than 3% of it occurred in the 676 years up to 1940. More than 97% of it occurred in the 55 years after 1940.

In these periods of long-run price stability, the price level was any-thing but stable from year to year. On the contrary, prices fluctuated and they were just as likely to fall as they were to rise. This is brought out clearly in Figure 7.2, which shows the annual inflation rate in Britain going back to 1700. Notice how the downward spikes (indicat-ing falling prices) were just as common and just as severe as the upward spikes – until the post-war period. During the last 60 years, alone in the whole of history, prices only ever went up.

This bout of inflation since the Second World War has seen a cumula-tive rise in prices greater than in any other previous period, including the great Tudor inflation of the sixteenth century. Two Bank of England econ-omists have studied inflation over the 300 years from the Bank's founda-tion in 1694 to 1994. They point out that the index of prices tripled between 1694 and 1948, but rose almost twentyfold from 1948 to 1994.[12]

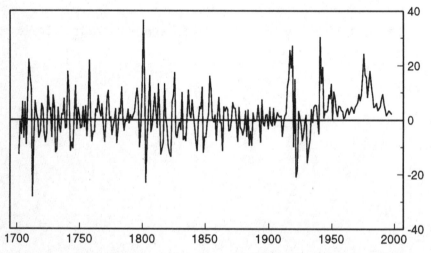

Source: E.H. Phelps-Brown & S.V. Hopkins, quoted in 'Seven Centuries of the Prices of Consumables', *Economica*, November 1956; updated with data from Datastream

Figure 7.2   UK inflation, %, 1700–1996

There are many striking examples of individual prices which reveal the contrast between the stability of the past and the rapid inflation of recent years. For instance, in 1694 when the Public Carriage Office started awarding licences to 'Hackney Carriages', or cabs as we would call them, the basic fare was set at one shilling (i.e. 5p) per mile. More than 200 years later it was still at this same rate. In 1995, however, it stood at £1.25 per mile, i.e. 25 times the original rate.[13]

Striking though this British evidence is, it is unusual only in the length of the historical record. Other countries show a broadly similar pattern. For the US, the contrast between the era of fluctuating prices and the era of perpetual inflation is clearly brought out in Figure 7.3, which like Figure 7.1 for Britain shows the overall level of prices. And just as in Britain, the pre-war experience was of prices fluctuating, leaving no pronounced upward trend – until the years after the Second World War. The same is broadly true for France and Germany.

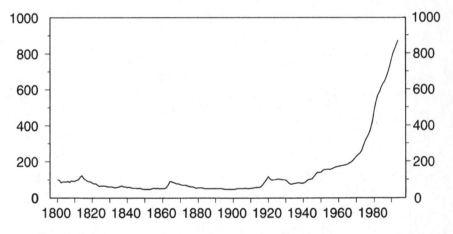

Source: *Historical Statistics of the United States*, US Bureau of the Census 1975, Bureau of Labor Statistics

Figure 7.3   US price level, 1800–1995 (1800=100)

Hyperinflation

For all the gnashing of teeth about Britain's inflationary tendencies, it has never experienced really serious inflation in the way that many other countries have. We do not usually think of the US as a country of very high inflation, but in fact in its early history it experienced two bouts of serious inflation. The first was at the founding of the country, during the American War of Independence (1775–83), which was largely financed by the issue of paper money. In Philadelphia, prices rose by over 1000% over the two years 1779–80.

The second was during the Civil War when the rebel South financed itself largely by printing money. Figures for the eastern part of the Confederacy show prices at the end of 1865 standing at more than 90 times their level at the beginning of 1861.

In France there was also early experience of very high inflation associated with the combination of revolution and war. Again, this was similarly due to the excessive printing of paper money, in this case known as *Assignats*. If we measure prices against a base of 100 in 1790, then by May 1796 they stood at 38,850.

The world's most spectacular experiences with inflation, however, came in the twentieth century. During the First World War, there was substantial resort to the printing of paper money. But the really high inflations emerged not during the war, but rather after it. Between 1919 and 1925, five countries suffered hyperinflation – Austria, Hungary, Poland, Russia and Germany. The rates of price rises in these countries from the beginning of the hyperinflation to the end were, respectively, 14,000, 23,000, 2.5 million, 4 million and 1000 million.

The best known hyperinflationary episode is Germany in 1922–3 when the average monthly increase in prices was 322%. Staggering though this is, it is dwarfed by the equivalent figure for the *second* Hungarian inflation of 1945–6 – 19,800% *per month*.[14] There was also a hyperinflationary episode in Greece (1943–4) and a long major inflation in China from 1937 to 1949 which, at its peak, saw monthly rates of price rise in excess of 50%.

In both Germany and Japan, the end of the Second World War also brought bouts of violent inflation. More recently, there have been bursts of very rapid inflation in several Latin American countries, as well as in Ghana, Israel, Indonesia, Turkey, Russia and various other former members of the Soviet Union.

In every one of these cases, the money supply expanded enormously, yet this was not the root cause of the inflation but rather the symptom of a deeper problem. The proximate cause was generally a huge budget deficit which the authorities chose (or were obliged) to finance by printing notes.

But even this does not quite reach the root of the matter. The huge deficits have typically been brought about by distinctly real events which have given rise to deep political crisis. The unifying theme running through all these inflationary episodes is the coincidence of weak governments and bad times, often as a result of war or its aftermath. In Europe, each country which has endured hyperinflation had either suffered defeat in the war or had undergone a complete change of political regime, or both.

The position of Austria after the First World War is an interesting example. It had been the centre of a huge empire with 50 million inhabitants. It was now reduced to a tiny country with 6½ million inhabitants. Its sources of food were cut off and its trading relationships fractured. And it now had to absorb a vast influx of unwanted bureaucrats from former imperial territories. Its response was to run massive budget deficits, with more than half of all expenditure covered by new issues of paper money.[15] But saying that it could have avoided inflation by controlling the money supply simply misses the point.

Depression and Falling Prices

Although various European countries experienced bouts of hyperinflation in the 1920s, most of the developed world, including much of Europe, underwent price *deflation* at some point in the inter-war period. But when the Great Depression struck the world in the early 1930s, although prices and wages did fall and on occasion by a considerable amount, the decline was nowhere near enough to absorb the impact of the drop in aggregate demand, with the result that output fell sharply and unemployment soared.

From the perspective of recent inflation, the degree of downward wage and price flexibility demonstrated in the US in the depression of 1929–33 looks remarkable, but by the standards of the time, given the scale of the economic contraction, it was remarkable for the opposite reason. In the contraction of demand which followed the First World War prices fell sharply. From the first quarter of 1920 to the third quarter of

1921, about 85% of the drop in nominal demand was absorbed by lower prices and only about 15% by lower output.

In the Great Depression, by contrast, during the period of maximum spending decline, in the year to the second quarter of 1932, 67% of the decline was absorbed by a drop in real output and only 33% by lower prices.[16]

From a recent perspective, the degree to which prices and wages fell in Britain during the inter-war period also looks remarkable. But contemporary observers saw it differently. During the 1920s and 1930s, many distinguished commentators made much of what they saw as a sharp decline in downward wage and price flexibility.[17] And in continental Europe it was a similar story, with prices in Germany being particularly sluggish.[18]

The forces which prevented pay and prices from falling freely effectively killed off the Gold Standard. Downturns in demand would now produce unacceptable rises in unemployment. Defenders of the old regime, including much of the economics profession, might say that unemployment was 'voluntary', or inevitable, or structural, or that the problem was too high a level of wages, but in the teeth of the Great Depression this cut little ice with the ordinary person. And the proponents of the old wisdom were lambasted by various iconoclastic economists, the most prominent of whom was John Maynard Keynes.

When, more or less throughout the industrial world, a revival of demand in the mid- and late 1930s, subsequently compounded by the onset of war, brought very much lower unemployment, Keynes looked to have been vindicated. In the way of these things, his once heretical views now became established as the intellectual orthodoxy for the next 30 to 40 years.

Inflation After 1945

The attenuated fall of money wages and prices in the face of weak demand in the 1930s foreshadowed the subsequent emergence of perpetual inflation. Whatever stopped prices and wages from falling when demand was weak could readily cause prices to rise when demand was only a little stronger. Moreover, in conditions where some parts of the economy were experiencing very strong demand and others weak demand, price rises in the first would not be offset by price falls in the second. This would cause the overall price level to edge up.

So it proved. After the Second World War, inflation became ingrained as the norm everywhere in the industrial world. During the Korean War there was a brief inflationary upsurge, which took inflation in the US above 9% in 1951. After this, however, the rate of inflation subsided. In the 1950s as a whole, inflation averaged 2% in the US, just over 1% in Germany and just over 4% in Britain. And it remained quite low until the late 1960s.

What makes the first 25 years after the war so remarkable from a current perspective is that low inflation was not bought at the expense of high unemployment or slow growth. Quite the opposite. Growth was rapid and sustained, and unemployment was maintained at unprecedentedly low levels.[19] In the US, it fell throughout the 1960s. In many ways, these years look like a golden age.

But by the late 1960s, the warning bells were already ringing for the regime of strong growth accompanied by steady, low inflation. In a number of European countries, there were severe civil disturbances and labour unrest in 1968. In France, the *Protocole de Grenelle* between the unions and the government allowed a jump in pay in manufacturing. In Britain, the devaluation of the pound in 1967 unleashed inflationary pressures, and the long-running problem with industrial relations reared its head in a bout of wage militancy in 1969. And in Italy there was unrest and wage militancy in the 'hot autumn of 1969'. In most of the industrial world, the 'trade-off' between inflation and unemployment seemed to be deteriorating.

The Collapse of the International Monetary System

Then in the early 1970s, three partly related shocks nearly brought the industrial world to its knees. The first was the collapse, in 1971, of the fixed exchange rate system (Bretton Woods) which had operated since the end of the war. The world staggered towards a new system of floating exchange rates.[20]

In many countries, the end of fixed exchange rates was thought to remove an unnecessary shackle on domestic economic policy. Governments would now be able to concentrate on boosting demand and cutting unemployment. In the US, the authorities no longer had to worry about the drain of gold from US reserves which had been a growing feature in the dying days of dollar convertibility under the fixed link. In Britain, when the pound was floated in 1972, the government felt able to 'go for growth', unrestrained by worries about the balance of payments.

Moreover, the collapse of the external restraint posed by fixed exchange rates meant that governments and central bankers were operating with no nominal anchors at all. For the collapse came before the widespread adoption of monetary targets.

Furthermore, given that in modern economies there was an asymmetry between upward and downward movements of the price level, those countries whose currencies appreciated would not benefit from disinflation to the same extent that the countries whose currencies depreciated would suffer from inflation. And the collapse of the fixed exchange rate regime and of the old international economic order probably helped to exacerbate the inflammation of inflationary expectations, and thereby worsened the inflationary response to two other shocks which quickly rocked the system.

The Commodity and Oil Price Explosions of 1972–3

In 1972–3 there was an upsurge of commodity prices, which then fed back into the inflationary process in the developed economies. Measured by *The Economist* Commodity Price Index, in dollar terms, non-oil commodity prices rose by nearly 30% in 1972, by more than 60% in 1973 and by more than 20% in 1974.

Yet for all the potential importance of the rise in commodity prices in causing inflation in the early 1970s, it probably does not constitute a wholly *independent* explanation for the inflationary upsurge in the early 1970s. For although the commodity price explosion was perceived in the west as a supply shock, and although it was partly associated with the effects on food production of bad weather in the US and elsewhere, it was also partly a result of the rapid increase in world *demand* and industrial production.

The same cannot be said, however, of the much more important shock which appeared in late 1973 – the dramatic hike in oil prices. It is difficult to exaggerate the impact that this had on costs, prices, expectations and economic management. For the industrial west, it was comparable, in economic terms, to the outbreak of war. As Figure 7.4 brings out, the west had been used to remarkable stability in oil prices for a very long time – until these prices went through the roof in 1973.

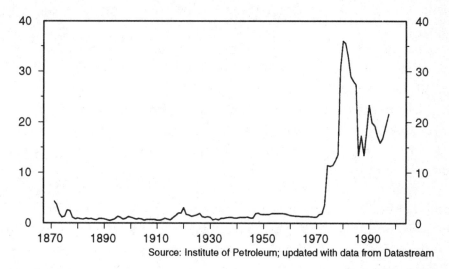

Source: Institute of Petroleum; updated with data from Datastream

Figure 7.4   Level of oil prices, US$ per barrel, 1870–1996

According to one viewpoint, the increase in oil prices was simply another manifestation of the worldwide boom, and as such is of no particular importance analytically. In practice, though, it is difficult to sustain this view. For a start, the magnitude of the rise in oil prices – six-fold from 1972 to 1974 – cannot plausibly be pinned on an increase in demand for oil, not least given the history of the oil price since the end of the war and the way in which the price was increased, as a result of production cutbacks instituted by the producer cartel, OPEC, in the wake of the Arab–Israeli conflict.

Nevertheless, there is still an important question to ask – why should the rise in oil prices (or indeed the earlier increase in non-oil commodity prices) have produced an upsurge in inflation rather than simply a shift in relative prices? After all, monetarist economists would argue that as long as the money supply was held constant, a rise in some prices would be off-set by a fall in others. There are several reasons why this did not happen.

The importance of the commodity in question and the ubiquity of its use throughout the industrial world, combined with the sheer size of the price increase, meant that the rise in oil prices effected a substantial worsening in the terms of trade for industrial countries which was bound to imply a substantial fall in their real incomes, the brunt of which would have to fall on consumers. In the circumstances, the only way the overall price level could be held constant was for wages to fall in *nominal* terms. In practice, however, in most countries workers were unprepared to accept the falls in their *real* wages implied by higher oil prices, let alone falls in nominal wages.

Indeed, what workers would have had to accept in order to prevent inflation was more demanding than what was expected of them in the early 1930s. At that time prices were falling, with the result that real incomes were rising. Even then, as we saw above, workers were extremely resistant to pay cuts. After 1973, far from accepting cuts in nominal incomes, workers pushed pay up. A struggle over relative real incomes occurred as governments, companies and groups of workers fought to preserve their share of a diminished cake.

Moreover, the very visibility and ubiquity of the price rises caused by the oil price hike led people to increase their inflationary expectations, thereby exacerbating the inflation itself. It cannot be emphasised enough how shocking the upsurge of inflation was at the time. The US CPI, which had risen by only 3.4% in 1972, rose by 8.8% in 1973 and 12.2% in 1974.

The oil shock presented policy-makers with an acute policy dilemma. For it was a double-edged blow. To the oil-consuming countries (which meant most of the industrial west) the rise in the oil price was both *inflationary* of prices and *deflationary* of real demand. The higher prices paid for oil reduced real incomes and therefore tended to reduce consumption. Yet the oil producers were unlikely to spend their new-found riches. Accordingly, there would be a slump in demand which would cause higher unemployment. Should the world's monetary authorities respond to the higher inflation and tighten policy, thereby worsening the upward pressure on unemployment? Or should they respond to the upward pressure on unemployment by easing policy and hence risking higher inflation?

Under the weight of the prevailing (Keynesian) orthodoxy of the time, which emphasised the overriding importance of combating unemployment and downplayed the significance of inflation, most governments chose the latter course. Even so, they soon discovered that they still had to endure a large rise in unemployment, alongside very high inflation.[21] The scene was set for the subsequent resistance to inflation through the imposition of very high short-term interest rates. But before I discuss that, interest rates themselves have a long history worthy of close attention.

Interest Rates Ancient and Modern

Just as with inflation, the evidence on interest rates in ancient times is pretty sparse. We do, however, have Homer as an authority; but alas I am referring to the American financial historian, *Sidney* Homer. He has put together a long historical record stretching back to ancient times which contains many instances of very high interest rates, but usually reflecting the extremely poor credit of the borrower or an immediate need for funds in straitened circumstances.

Homer tells us that in the fourth century BC, Demosthenes permitted a client to defer paying his legal fee, but added 12% per annum interest, which was precisely the top of the range of normal rates in Athens at the time. (This only goes to show that lawyers have not changed much over the last two millennia.) Homer also notes:

> when Caesar's friend, the noble Brutus, attempted to charge the City of
> Salamis 48% for a loan, he shocked his contemporary, Cicero... Money
> in Rome was in fact then offered at as low as 4% per annum.[22]

But in modern conditions of organised financial markets, at least for borrowers of good standing, Homer's story is predominantly of very low interest rates. Just as with inflation, the longest detailed history comes from England, and for the last 300 years it is very detailed indeed. In the closing years of the seventeenth century, the Whig government of William III was having to pay dearly for money because of the risk that the Stuarts would be reestablished and would repudiate William's debts.

At the same time, the provinces of Holland were borrowing at 3–4%.

Not many decades later, the British government was able to borrow at 'Dutch' rates. In 1749 Henry Pelham, the Chancellor of the Exchequer, converted a number of outstanding debt issues into an issue of '3% consolidated annuities', the celebrated 'consols'. The long life of this stock provides us with a consistent history of long-term interest rates in Britain and, as Figure 7.5 shows, it is quite an extraordinary history. During the Napoleonic wars, when the survival of the country was at stake, the market rates of interest on consols rose, reaching a crisis point in 1797 and 1798. This crisis level of long-term interest rates was 6.3%. A rate this high was to seem impossibly *low* during the quarter-century after 1970.

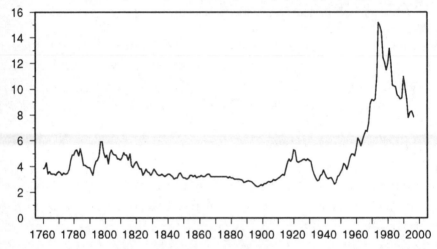

Source: *The Economist*, One Hundred Years of Economic Statistics; updated with data from Datastream

Figure 7.5   *UK 2.5% consol yields, annual average %, 1760–1996*

After the Napoleonic crisis, interest rates were in almost continuous decline throughout the nineteenth century, culminating in Chancellor Goschen's conversion of 3% consols into 2½% consols in 1888. At the high point for consols (in terms of prices) in 1896–8, they paid only 2¼%.

In the twentieth century, interest rate history has been dominated by inflation and inflationary risk. Interest rates began rising in Britain from the beginning of the century and continued rising until just after the First World War. Even so, in 1920, consols paid just over 5¼%. The 1920s brought a slight decline from this peak and then a plateau in rates, followed by a sharp fall in the 1930s after Britain abandoned the Gold Standard. In the mid-1930s, consols were again paying less than 3%. After the war, as the government sought to maintain a policy of low interest rates in order to stave off a repeat of the Great Depression, consol rates fell even further, with the price briefly getting within spitting distance of 100, the stock's nominal value, where it would give an interest rate of 2½%.

But thereafter it was downhill all the way, although the really big decline did not set in until 1968. In 1967, consols stood at 40, where they paid 6¼%. By 1974, however, at the height of Britain's inflationary and financial crisis, they fell to less than 14, where they paid an interest rate of more than 18%. In late December 1995, they stood at 32, paying 8%.

The history of *short-term* interest rates is just as striking. Bank Rate, the rate at which the Bank of England would lend to the banking system and thus the basis of all private sector short-term interest rates, began the twentieth century at 3%, subsequently falling to a low of 2½%. It reached a peak of 10% in 1914, but then subsequently retreated to its normal range of 3–7% until after Britain came off the Gold Standard in 1931. It was then reduced to 2% in 1932 and, with the exception of a brief period in 1939 when it was raised to 4%, it remained at the 2% level until 1951.

This rate may seem incredibly low, but in fact Bank Rate was designed to be a penal rate, standing above normal market rates. Indeed, open market rates of discount on short-term bills stood at less than 1% from 1933 to 1938. After the war, they were again below 1% until 1951. Thereafter, short-term interest rates began their steady climb which culminated in a high of 13% for Bank Rate in 1973–4, subsequently exceeded when official rates reached 17% in 1979.

The American Story

For US long interest rates, the broad trends were similar to the British experience – at their high points during the Napoleonic wars and at their lowest in the closing years of the century, achieving a low of close to 3% and averaging 3½% for one decade.

In the twentieth century, rates on American bonds, shown in Figure 7.6, followed the by now familiar pattern – rising to a peak at the time of the First World War, falling in the 1930s, reaching a trough just after the end of the Second World War at less than 2¼%, and then rising

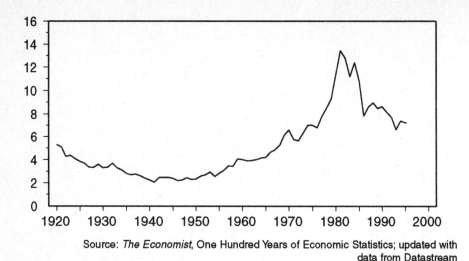

Source: *The Economist*, One Hundred Years of Economic Statistics; updated with
data from Datastream

Figure 7.6   *US long bond yields (30-year), annual average %, 1920–96*

more or less without interruption to the 1970s.

For those of us still fixated by the high interest rates of the last 20 years, the earlier history of American *short* rates, shown in Figure 7.7, is striking. Having averaged just under 4% in the 1920s, Treasury Bills averaged 0.6% in the 1930s. In 1938 and 1939 they yielded a mere 0.01%. In the 1950s they averaged 2% and even in the 1960s they averaged only 4%. After that, of course, there occurred the inexorable rise to double-digit rates.

I need not rehearse the same history for European interest rates. They tell a similar story, except that Germany's interest rate history bears the mark of its own more extraordinary economic and political history. The hyperinflation of the early 1920s was accompanied by massive rates of interest. At one point, the Berlin Stock Exchange quoted a rate of interest on call loans of over 10,000%. And in Germany, in contrast to other leading countries, the international financial crisis of 1930–32 brought extremely high long-term interest rates. Subsequently, under Hitler, long rates were lowish but nowhere near the extra-low levels seen in the US or Britain.

After the war, German rates were kept up by inflation, although Germany's comparatively good inflation performance enabled it to operate with lower interest rates than most other countries. The crisis of the mid-1970s also saw German rates at a peak, but well short of the levels reached in Britain and America.

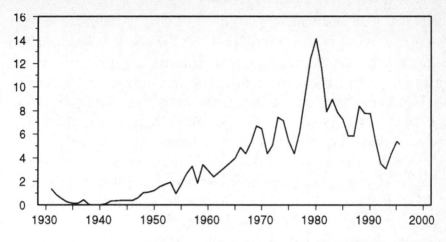

Source: *The Economist*, One Hundred Years of Economic Statistics; updated with data from Datastream

Figure 7.7   US 3-month Treasury Bill yields, annual average %, 1930–96

The Switch to Anti-inflation at All Costs

It is now time to return to the story of interest rates and inflation from the late 1970s onwards. The two can easily be taken together, because they are inextricably interlinked. When a second oil price shock in 1979 threatened to produce similar results to the 1973–4 experience, the prevailing reaction of governments and central banks throughout the western world was now very different. Having experienced the rapid inflation of the mid-1970s, this time round the response more or less everywhere was to try to resist the inflationary upsurge by the use of high real short-term interest rates.

With inflation initially very high, this meant very high nominal short rates. In the US, the Federal Reserve under Paul Volcker drove interest rates up to 17% at times during 1980, and even to 19% in 1981. In the UK, the newly elected Conservative government under Margaret Thatcher drove base rates up to 17% in November 1979. Moreover, this tough policy stance was maintained, even though the world endured a deep recession.

Furthermore, *long* interest rates (yields) rose sharply as well since investors were reluctant to buy bonds. It is as though, having been caught by the high inflation of the 1970s for which they were unprepared, and having thereby been rewarded with negligible or even negative real returns, bond investors now set out to make up for lost time.

This change of policy compared to the first oil price shock, and the preparedness to accept serious recession and unemployment as its consequence, marked a turning point in the history of inflation in the post-war period. It reflected a profound change in the intellectual climate, as well as a marked change in society's attitude towards inflation and unemployment.

The intellectual change had begun with Milton Friedman in the US. In a classic article published in 1968,[23] he had argued that there is no trade-off between inflation and unemployment, that is to say, there is nothing to be gained from accepting a higher rate of inflation. Any attempt to do this will result in *accelerating* inflation. (This is the essence of the *natural rate* theory, which I discuss in Chapter 8.)

At first, this new approach fell on stony ground in the still Keynesian-dominated academic and policy establishments in the US and Britain. But all this changed with the advent of very high inflation in the 1970s. Monetary authorities everywhere came to fear financial instability. In Britain, the economy seemed on the brink of hyperinflation when, in August 1975, inflation rose to a peak of nearly 27%.

Meanwhile, all the Keynesian establishment could offer in response to the upsurge of inflation was prices and incomes policies, which were by now widely perceived as both distortionary and ineffective. These events seemed to confirm the correctness of Friedman's vision of the relation between inflation and unemployment, and the academic view began to shift accordingly.

Among the public at large, there was a corresponding change. Without knowing anything of inflation/unemployment trade-offs, many people experienced alarm at the high inflation and instability of the 1970s. This was reflected electorally in a marked shift to the right which brought in conservative administrations in the US, Britain and elsewhere. When, despite the serious recession and unemployment produced by anti-inflationary policy, these conservative administrations were subsequently reelected, the change of voter preferences was apparently confirmed.

The policy revolution spread further. In the early 1980s, under President Mitterand, France tried to resist the tide and carried on with a policy directed towards maintaining high employment. But eventually it buckled in the face of the strain. Indeed, its *volte face* was nothing less than extraordinary, for having tried to go it alone in pursuit of the old orthodoxy, it later decided, in the shape of the *franc fort* policy, to try to be more German than the Germans in pursuit of the new orthodoxy. The result was inflation in France running below that in Germany, but also unemployment stuck at very high levels.

In Australia and New Zealand, *Labour* governments espoused the new orthodoxy. In New Zealand, the tenure of the central bank governor was even explicitly tied to his success in meeting the objective of low inflation.

In reaction to the new, tough policy regime inflation did start to fall, but the unemployment performance continued to be dreadful almost everywhere. Both short and long interest rates also fell, but long rates remained high by historical standards. Investors took a great deal of convincing that inflation was going to stay low. Accordingly, they exacted a premium to compensate them for the risk that inflation would turn out to be higher than a central forecast would suggest.

Another boom at the end of the 1980s saw a short-term uptick in inflation, again resisted by high interest rates. For those countries which were members of the European Exchange Rate Mechanism (ERM), real interest rates were kept up by the peg to German nominal interest rates, which themselves were kept high in order to bear down on the high rates of inflation which followed the boom of the late 1980s and the excesses of German reunification. France was the most extreme case, with real interest rates at one point approaching 10%.

But this bout of high interest rates did bring inflation down again. Real interest rates, though, stayed high well into the 1990s, except in the US where, at the beginning of the decade, the Federal Reserve pursued a policy of trying to revive the economy (and recapitalising the US banking system) through persistently low short rates, so low that in real terms they were effectively zero.

In 1993 bond markets rose dramatically throughout the world as markets sensed the dramatic change in the inflation regime. At the peak, the rates were as low as 5.7% on US long bonds and 6.3% on their British equivalents. But then 1994 saw a sharp reversal – the 'bond market crash' – in reaction to a large rise in commodity prices, signs of strong economic growth and small increases in short-term interest rates. Bond prices plummeted and long-term interest rates soared. The prices of bonds now suggested that market participants believed there would be a return to significantly higher inflation and interest rates, in short that a return to the 'bad old days' was in store.

In the event, the markets were proved wrong. Despite good growth in the US and elsewhere, and in the teeth of the big rise in commodity prices, inflation stayed low more or less everywhere. And in 1995–6, short-term interest rates in the main countries were reduced. After the experience of 1993–4, in the bond markets a feeling of caution remained, but long-term interest rates still fell steeply. It had all been a false alarm. The optimism about inflation prospects which had over-taken markets in 1993 had been justified after all. The western world real-ly did look as though it was moving to a new inflationary environment.

A Peculiar Phase in History

In reality, it was moving *back* to an environment which used to be famil-iar. In the wider sweep of history, the long period of perpetually rising prices experienced throughout the west since the Second World War, and which we have all taken for granted, is an aberration. It was caused by the interaction between micro structural factors and macroeconomic policy. The distinguished British economist Sir John Hicks summed up the dominant ethos of the first quarter-century after the war when he said that the world had replaced the Gold Standard with a *Labour* Standard.[24] What he meant was that, whereas under the Gold Standard economic policy was dominated by the need to maintain a certain fixed link to gold, it was now dominated by the need to maintain unemployment at a low level. What had destroyed the Gold Standard was the unacceptably high unemployment costs of deflation in conditions where pay and prices had become institutionalised and subject to producer power. But in the crises of the 1970s these self-same conditions then destroyed the Labour Standard, by producing unacceptably high rates of inflation.

What makes the future look so different now is that these structural forces which destroyed both the Gold Standard and the Labour Standard are collapsing, with dramatic consequences for both the world economy and the world of economics.

8

The Need for a Rethink by Economists

Inflation is always and everywhere a monetary phenomenon.

Milton Friedman[1]

Inflation is a monetary phenomenon in the same way that shooting people is a ballistic phenomenon.

Henry Wallich[2]

IF YOU LISTENED TO MOST PROFESSIONAL ECONOMISTS, YOU WOULD think that despite all their doubts and uncertainties about other parts of the subject, they had the causes of inflation all sewn up. The trouble is that they have had them all sewn up before.

For all the heavyweight, theoretical articles on the role of the money supply, and all the binloads of computer printout on the statistical relationships, it was primarily the emergence of high inflation in the early 1970s, and, in particular, its persistence despite what seemed high rates of unemployment, which killed off the old Keynesian orthodoxy that had dominated both theoretical economics and practical policy making since the war. The people who had espoused Keynesian thinking simply had no answer to this new state of affairs. It was natural, therefore, that both thinkers and practitioners should turn to those who did profess to have an answer – the monetarists. Could the *death* of inflation bring about the downfall of the new orthodoxy?

This orthodoxy consists of a mixture of monetarism – the doctrine that inflation is always caused by increases in the money supply – and belief in the so-called natural rate of unemployment – that is to say, that there is only one level of unemployment at which inflation is stable. In its extreme form, monetarism finds no room for the historical and institutional factors which I have stressed in this book. The natural rate approach explicitly does make way for structural and institutional factors to affect the natural rate of unemployment, but has little to say about them. Meanwhile, it rejects the idea that they can have a direct bearing on the rate of inflation.

Both these approaches are riddled with dogma and have difficulty in dealing with the facts of recent experience. Not for the first time, economists badly need a rethink. In what follows, I try to explain the failings of the current theoretical orthodoxy and to outline a different approach, without resort to the pyrotechnics of economic theory. I have endeavoured to make inherently difficult material comprehensible to the non-economist. Even so, many a general reader may reasonably feel they would need to wrap their head in a hot towel to understand it all. They should rest assured that neither I nor, I hope, the economists whose ideas I here discuss would be offended if they chose to skip this chapter and pass on to Chapter 9, where economic theory is kept firmly in its place and centre stage is given over to the practical problems – and opportunities – confronting our political leaders in the zero era.

Theory Without History

Given any economic problem, economists feel an urge to find a single and complete answer – *the* answer – which will apply in all circumstances. This naturally leads them to downgrade the importance of institutions and historical processes, which is dangerous. But the prize is great – a law or fundamental relation to which economists can adhere come what may, use as a foundation for other theoretical developments, or wave in the face of those who disparage economics compared to the physical sciences. In my view, monetarism represents just such a temptation and economists have fallen for it – and paid the penalty.

Monetarism gives us a powerful explanation for the world's inflationary experience in the post-war period. Freed from the constraints of the Gold Standard, and backed up by an intellectual climate in which it was widely believed that monetary control and even low inflation itself did not matter and that 'full employment' was all important, governments have persistently inflated the money supply, effectively 'print-ing money', and the result has been 'too much money chasing too few goods'. Moreover, this provides a link with the inflations of the past, and with the hyperinflations of recent memory and current experience, which always involve massive increases in the money supply.

So we have an explanation, not just of a particular phenomenon at a particular time, but rather of the inflationary experience in general – what the physicists might well call a grand unifying theory. This is what makes monetarism so powerful and so attractive.

Money in Hyperinflation

Much of the monetarists' evidence about the role and importance of money comes from the world's various experiences with hyper-inflation, which I briefly reviewed in Chapter 7. And there is no doubt that monetary expansion plays a dominant role in hyperinflation.

Even with very high rates of inflation, however, changes in mone-tary growth are far from the be-all and end-all. In his classic study of seven hyperinflations, Philip Cagan[3] found that in each case, in addi-tion to the massive increases in money supply, there were substantial declines in the demand for money (in real terms) such that the rise in prices substantially exceeded the rise in the money supply.

Indeed, from the beginning of the second Hungarian hyperinflation to the end (which Cagan dates from August 1945 to July 1946), the rise in prices was no less than 320 times the rise in the money supply. The German experience in 1923 was less spectacular, but still pretty impres-sive. The rise in prices was 40% greater than the rise in money supply. So even in conditions of hyperinflation, therefore, changes in the demand for money play a major role alongside changes in the supply.

To the monetarist, creeping inflations are really the same as hyper-inflations, differing only in degree. Yet there are some substantial differences which go beyond mere questions of magnitude. First, in hyperinflations it is plain to all that the process is fed by excessive mon-etary expansion. Accordingly, a change which *credibly* promises to stop this expansion has a marked effect on expectations and behaviour. And for this reason, most hyperinflations have been ended quickly.

This was notably *not* the case when the British government first rigidly followed the dictates of money supply targets in 1979. Excessive monetary expansion was not the sole or root cause of the British inflationary problem. The causes were much more complex. The public at large, if not the government's economic officials and advisers, implicitly understood this very well. Accordingly, the government could go on publishing monetary targets until it was blue in the face, but this would not do anything to undermine the widespread conviction that inflation would continue more or less as before. And the process of reducing inflation was therefore slow and painful.

Secondly, as I pointed out in Chapter 7, in hyperinflations the reason for excessive monetary expansion is almost always a huge budget deficit which the government is unwilling or unable to finance in the ordinary way by borrowing in the capital markets. Rather than cut the deficit, it prints money or borrows the money from the central bank, which amounts to something very similar.

This fairly describes the recent situation in modern Russia, Turkey and a host of other countries. Clearly, this sort of inflation bears close comparison to the debasement of the coinage by the medieval monarchs, and with similar results. It also bears more than a passing resemblance to the distribution of dollar bills by helicopter, a method of monetary expansion not used anywhere in practice (to the best of my knowledge) but which once made an appearance in the theoretical work of Milton Friedman.

It is very striking, however, that developed and mature economies do not normally suffer from such inflation. When they *do* occasionally succumb, as I pointed out in Chapter 7, there is nearly always a distinctly *real* phenomenon – such as a war, a revolution, or a sharp political change – at the root of it.

Not All Monetary Expansions Are the Same

Western post-war inflation is quite different in type from hyperinflation. On the whole, governments in the developed west did not cause inflation by deliberately choosing to print notes because they could not otherwise make ends meet.[4] The idea that inflation was the direct result of an attempt to raise revenue puts governments too much in the driving seat of events. In the 1970s especially, governments and their economic policies were the unwilling victims of what was going on in the world, and were puzzled and bewildered like everyone else.

So in this important sense, the modern, moderate inflation in the west is not a direct descendant of the inflation created by the debasements of ancient monarchs, or a tame continuation of the same phenomenon which produced hyperinflation in several European countries after both the First and Second World Wars. It is different.

It is striking, for example, that the upsurge of inflation in Britain in the late 1980s occurred when the public accounts were in *surplus*, so that, far from issuing new debt, the government was actually buying it back. Moreover, this was also the case when inflation flared up in Britain at the end of the 1960s. In virtually all cases of moderate inflation in the west, the literal printing of money or government borrowing from the central bank has played a minor role.

Rather, if expansion of the money supply is still the prime culprit for moderate, post-war inflation, it must be on the commercial banks and their lending to the private sector that we must pin the immediate blame and, behind them, the businesses and consumers who seek to borrow money from them. And if governments and central banks are still to be held *ultimately* responsible for this inflation, it must be through their encouragement of, or connivance at, the lending behaviour of the banks, by failing to set interest rates high enough, presumably for fear of the consequences in terms of lost output and lost votes. But once this is the mechanism through which the money supply increases, interpreting the evidence becomes a lot more difficult.

Traditional monetary theory teaches that the money supply can be thought of as set outside the system (exogenously) by an act of policy. Accordingly, if you observe a strong link between money and income (or prices), the causation inevitably runs from money to income and not the other way round.[5]

But in a modern monetary system 'the money supply' is determined by a series of different factors, none of which is under the *direct* control of the authorities – the lending criteria of the banks, the demand for credit in the economy as a whole, the attractions of bank credit compared to other forms of finance. Accordingly, in a modern monetary system, even if you observe a strong correlation between changes in the money supply and changes in national income or the price level, this does not necessarily tell you much. You do not know whether a change in the money supply is the *cause* of events in the economy or a *response* to them.

The Econometric Battle

This is where heavy-duty econometrics comes into play. The distinguished economists Milton Friedman and Anna Schwartz produced epic studies of the monetary history of the US and the UK[6] which they claimed supported monetarist conclusions. In their wake, many other economists devoted much of their professional life to investigating the links between money and prices in the data. So monetary economics became largely a battle between econometricians. And what a battle! As Podolski put it:

> Rarely have such varied data purporting to proxy the same concept – 'money' – been subjected to such persistent torture, with such ingenious and innovative devices.[7]

Friedman and Schwartz's work was immensely detailed and meticulous. They were careful to give due weight to the idea that the level of nominal income might influence the level of the money supply as well as the other way round. It was simply that from their investigations they were able to conclude that the *predominant* influence ran from money to prices rather than the other way round.

But when it came to their less guarded pronouncements, let alone to the pronouncements by other monetarists, the balance of this message was lost. Friedman dismissed non-monetary influences on inflation with the assertion: 'Inflation is always and everywhere a monetary phenomenon.' Yet if the level of nominal income (and prices) sometimes determined the money supply and not the other way round then there was room for real forces to have a role in the determination of monetary variables.

This slippage from careful analysis to strident slogan was nothing new. Schumpeter said:

In the nineteenth century as well as in the twenties and thirties of the twentieth a rigid quantity theory, one that attributed to M [meaning the money supply] an altogether unjustifiable role in economic therapy, had a way of suddenly emerging from more careful formulations.[8]

Moreover, Friedman and Schwartz's conclusion that money was the predominant causative influence was far from incontrovertible. Indeed, their empirical work came in for strong criticism.[9] Their approach to the definition of money was to adopt whichever definition produced the best statistical results and then to use this definition to test the various monetarist projections against the data. This struck many observers as odd, and some indeed thought it unscientific. W.E. Mason pointed out:

An empirical definition of money designed to validate a monetary hypothesis precludes empirical invalidation.[10]

Monetarism in Practice

Whatever the academic evidence on the interaction between money and prices over long periods, the practical experience of relying on measures of money supply as a guide to macroeconomic policy has not been good.

In the UK, when the Conservative government of Margaret Thatcher was elected in 1979, it put control of the money supply at the forefront of its economic policy. It even published in 1980 a plan for the growth of the money supply stretching over several years into the future. Its chosen monetary target was Sterling M3, a broad measure of the money supply roughly equivalent to the total of sterling bank deposits. This was chosen on the basis of the apparently close links between this measure of the money supply and UK nominal income over long periods.

Yet as the authorities sought to control Sterling M3 by the imposition of very high interest rates in the period 1979–81, something strange happened. Sterling M3 kept growing rapidly but, contrary to the monetarists' predictions, the economy was plunged into deep recession and inflation fell.

At the time this caused considerable puzzlement, but all is clear now.

By the imposition of high interest rates and the concomitant high exchange rate, the authorities had succeeded in producing an old-fashioned recession. *This* reduced inflation, even though monetary growth continued at high levels. Indeed, rapid monetary growth was an *expression* of the deflationary policy as people were persuaded by the high interest rates to keep a significant part of their savings in bank deposits. Evidently, the previously observed tight relationship between Sterling M3 and nominal income had broken down.

For a time, it was possible to argue that this was a one-off phenomenon applying to one measure of the money supply at one particular juncture. But subsequent experience proved this wrong. It soon became clear that it was impossible to adopt (or construct) a monetary measure which could be relied on.

The story was broadly similar in the US. Financial innovation had shifted monetary behaviour so that it was impossible now to identify relationships on which the Federal Reserve could rely.[11] And the contrasting picture presented by different money supply measures continues to pose serious problems of interpretation. In October 1995 anyone wanting to read the monetary runes had to chose between M2 which had recently been growing at an annualised rate of 6%, thereby pointing to a resurgent economy, and M1, a narrower measure, which had just posted its fifth straight month of negative 12-month growth – suggesting the looming threat of recession. What on earth is a good monetarist to do?

It is tempting to think that Germany is an exception to these developments because of the Bundesbank's steadfast championing of the money supply. From its actions, it is clear that the Bundesbank is staunchly anti-inflationary and it often advances belief in some sort of monetarism as part of this. But it wants to bolster anti-inflationary psychology. The idea that inflation depends solely on the rate of monetary growth and that this rate, in turn, is perfectly under the Bundesbank's control is helpful to it.

In reality the Bundesbank is more flexible and more eclectic than its reputation acknowledges. In recent years, its record in hitting its monetary targets has not been good. Nor has this simply been an accident. In 1993–4 it consciously chose to reduce interest rates despite the fact that the money supply was overshooting its target. It made the judgement that the money supply was giving a misleading signal.

A Historical Perspective on Monetarism

The monetarists' beliefs about money are paradoxical given their beliefs about the non-monetary economy. Monetarism is usually (though by no means necessarily) associated with a belief in the effective functioning of free markets and the dynamism of free enterprise. It is common for monetarists to believe, wearing their pro free enterprise hat, that the private sector is dynamic and ever changing with the result that, among other things, it is difficult, if not impossible, for governments to improve on free market performance by intervention and regulation, not only in the micro sphere, but even in the sphere of macro policy. Yet amidst this stormy sea of ever-changing dynamic adjustment and uncertainty there is supposedly one rock of stability – money.

Since money itself is a socioeconomic institution, this presumption of stability is odd. You would think that money also would be subject to dynamic adjustment and unpredictable change. Indeed, that is exactly what the historical record tells us has happened. From the gradual transition from barter to using some good such as cattle as a means of exchange, to the widespread use of the precious metals, to the stamping of these metals by merchants and monarchs, to the goldsmiths' discovery that they could lend out the gold deposited with them, to the evolution of banks, to the development of paper money, to the proliferation of money substitutes, and now 'plastic money', and soon electronic money – the monetary system has been evolving in a process of continuous change.

In the light of these changes, why should people have a stable demand for money? The answer, supposedly, is because 'money' has unique properties. How strange it is, therefore, that it proves to be so difficult to define money clearly in theory or to identify it satisfactorily in practice!

When confronted with the evident failure of monetary targets in the early 1980s, the initial response of both monetarist theorists and monetary practitioners was to think they had focused on the 'wrong' definition of money and to embark on a search for the 'right' one. As a result, monetary measures proliferated and eventually a fashion even grew up for using weighted average measures of different monetary aggregates ('Divisia money').

The idea was that central banks or forecasters or investors could use any of these various monetary measures, or indeed any combination of them, as a guide to economic and market developments, or as a basis for policy, regardless of how these definitions corresponded to the money of theoretical models, their likely substitution relationships or their exo-geneity. Yet this *à la carte* monetarism left a funny taste in the mouth. For the original idea behind monetarism had been the *uniqueness* of money. This hardly squared with the user being invited to pick and choose from a wide variety of different monetary measures, according to taste.

Some economists, though, held firm to the original idea of mone-tarism and insisted that only a single definition of money would do. The trouble was that they could not agree between themselves on what that definition should be. One amusing aspect of this was the venom with which supporters of one monetary measure now attacked support-ers of another. In Britain, some supporters of the narrow money mea-sure M0 (consisting mainly of notes and coin) argued that this was the only measure which properly corresponded to the money of theoretical models. Broad money (M3 or M4), by contrast, was a hotch-potch of financial assets whose total size was influenced by financial flows and the competitive position of banks within the financial system.

The supporters of broad money countered by saying that notes and coin were easily substitutable with bank deposits and that no *causative* role could possibly be ascribed to them. The supply of narrow money was determined by the demand for it.[12]

The irony is that both sides in this dispute were right in their criticisms. But this left monetarism without a leg to stand on.

Monetarism's Enduring Appeal

Despite its obvious problems, monetarism still has enormous appeal both inside and outside the academic world. Why is this?

First, like all the best myths, there is a significant element of truth in it. There are innumerable examples, notably in the history of hyper-inflation, of inflation directly caused by excessive monetary growth. Moreover, even where the underlying cause is not monetary but real, it may often find expression in an increase in the money supply. So it is always right, when thinking about inflation, to look at what is happening to monetary variables. The trick is to recognise this yet not to think it is the end of the story. Many people appear to find this difficult.

This ties in with a second reason – monetarism's simplicity. It is extremely attractive to believe that the answer lies simply with the money supply. Moreover, the plasticity of monetary definitions enables the idea to be stretched to fit the facts.

The attractions are increased by simple confusion. Many people confuse the *stock* of money with the *flow* of expenditure in money terms. They believe that the flow of expenditure in money terms *must* have a close bearing on the behaviour of prices. Of course it must, but that is non-controversial. It leaves open, however, the vital question of the *relationship* between the stock of money and the flow of expenditure in money terms. They are not the same. Indeed, monetarism is a set of propositions about precisely this stock/flow relationship, principally that the ratio of the flow of money expenditure to the money stock ('velocity') is stable and predictable.

For professional economists, monetarism's simplicity and certainty enables them to believe in a fundamental law or rule of economics, which thereby lends status to the subject, and saves them from the messy world of historical analysis and institutional studies. Moreover, it enables non-monetary specialists to get on with their own part of the subject, confident that when it comes to the monetary aspect, or to the integration of their specialist topic with the rest of economics, they can latch it on to an edifice that itself has secure foundations. If they were instead to believe that the edifice of monetary economics is built on shifting sands, then this would cause profound insecurity, and not a little difficulty.

Furthermore, the way the debate about monetarism has been conducted has suited the trend of modern economics. As I noted above, this has been a battle of econometricians. One of Milton Friedman's great successes was to change the language of debate. In McCloskey's words:

crude experiments and big books won the day, by their very crudeness and bigness.[13]

You could question the logic or plausibility of the monetarist position, but you would then be referred back to the 'decisive results' produced by Friedman and Schwartz in one or other of their tomes. Unless the distinguished critics of monetarism, such as James Tobin or Lord Kaldor,[14] undertook a similarly gigantic study, their criticisms were liable to be palmed off as lightweight or unsubstantiated. It was rather as though in order to be entitled to entertain serious doubts about the capacity of Gipsy Rose Lee to foretell the future, you first had to undergo an intensive three-year course in astrological theory.

Moreover, with every piece of evidence that ran counter to the monetarist canon, it was possible for someone else to show that with a different specification, different lag structure, slightly different periods or whatever, the monetarist result emerged.

Now, long after monetarism has passed its high-water mark, it lingers on as the conventional wisdom, partly because a whole generation of economists, journalists, bank officials and market practitioners have been trained in Friedmanite economics, and partly because so many economists have poured so much intellectual capital into it that they cannot bear to write it off.

Curves and Menus

In the 1960s and early 1970s, economists attempted to bypass theoretical controversies about inflation, including the semi-theological disputes over monetarism, and rely simply on *measuring* the relationship between inflation and unemployment. For a brief while, this seemed to solve the problem. In 1958, the economist A.W. Phillips 'discovered' that over the period 1861–1957 in the UK[15] the rates of unemployment and wage inflation were closely related. High unemployment was associated with low inflation. Low unemployment was associated with high inflation. When described graphically, this relationship became known as the Phillips Curve. Other economists soon 'discovered' a similar relationship for other countries.

For a time, the Phillips Curve appeared to offer governments a menu of policy choice. They could choose lower unemployment, if they liked, but they would have to put up with higher inflation. They could choose lower inflation, if they liked, but they would have to put up with higher unemployment. Accordingly, the explanation for the last 60 years having been characterised by persistent inflation would be very simple – governments and central banks have chosen to operate with very low rates of unemployment. If they had chosen higher rates, then we could have experienced price stability or even falling prices.

Unfortunately, although the answer provided by the Phillips Curve was for a time beguiling, it proved to be a chimera. Soon after economists thought they had the inflation problem licked, the Phillips relationship started to break down. Indeed, by the mid-1970s the Phillips Curve seemed to shift around so much that it soon appeared that there was no reliable relationship at all between inflation and unemployment.

How Many Angels Can Dance on the Head of a Pin?

From the naive hopes of the Phillips Curve, economists now retreated into a sort of militant agnosticism. After believing, a few years previously, that a bit less unemployment could be bought at the expense of a bit more inflation, according to a menu of policy choice which they, the economists, could provide, the professors of the dismal science performed an extraordinary *volte face*. They now took the view that there was only one level of unemployment at which inflation would be constant. At any other level, inflation would be either accelerating or decelerating without limit. This unique level they dubbed the *natural* rate of unemployment or, more clumsily, the non-accelerating inflation rate of unemployment, or NAIRU for short.

Even though it is often regarded as a necessary truth, valid in all circumstances, the natural rate idea is simply another theoretical construct and should be treated accordingly. Its role and contribution have been to debunk the idea of a stable trade-off between inflation and unemployment, as posited by the Phillips Curve, and to emphasise the role played by inflationary expectations. As such it has been tremendously useful. But it is not the last word on the relationship between inflation and unemployment.

In some interpretations, the theory can be made virtually into a tautology. 'If the inflation rate is accelerating then the actual level of unemployment must be below the natural rate. If it is decelerating, then it must be above it.' 'If inflation is now accelerating at the same level of unemployment at which it was recently decelerating then the natural rate must have increased.' To anyone who asks what the natural rate *is*, the reply is, 'there's no way of knowing; look at what is happening to inflation.'

This is more than vaguely reminiscent of the debates between medieval schoolmen about how many angels could dance on the head of a pin. Yet for the natural rate idea to be able to explain anything about economic behaviour, it must be more than a tautology – it must be capable of being disproved, or rendered inapplicable, by the facts.

And the facts make it seem a pretty extraordinary creed. For in practice, far from accelerating without limit, there are plenty of examples of inflation persisting at roughly the same level for long periods. So, while the natural rate theory emphasises the infinite possibilities for vertical movement in the inflation/unemployment relationship, in practice there seems to have been a good deal of *lateral* movement, that is to say, roughly similar inflation rates have occurred with wildly different unemployment rates.

How can this be reconciled with the natural rate idea? One possibility is that the natural rate has been shifting about a lot. Yet it seems highly improbable that it could have shifted quite so conveniently as to offset the tendency for inflation to fall at higher unemployment rates – unless there is a systematic tendency for the natural rate to rise as the actual rate rises above the old natural rate. This is precisely what may happen as workers left unemployed lose skills and motivation and cease to be attractive to employers. It even has a special name – *hysteresis*.

But if the level of the natural rate is in practice shifting about quite so much, and especially if it is following the actual level of unemployment, then the *concept* of the natural rate ceases to be of much practical relevance.

Explaining Twenty Years of Non-acceleration

Even though for some countries there are those who claim that the natural rate has been a good predictor of inflation in recent years, the most serious problem for the natural rate theory surely lies with the post-war historical record for most of the industrial world, which I briefly discussed in Chapter 7. According to the theory, as long as unemployment is below the natural rate, there will be a tendency for inflation to accelerate. Yet for at least 20 years after the Second World War (and longer in some countries) inflation did *not* accelerate. Why not?[16]

The natural rate theory gives an extraordinary answer. Its central idea is that, given the current state of technology and institutions, there is one level of the real wage at which the demand and supply of labour will be equated, and at that rate such unemployment that exists is 'voluntary'. But unanticipated changes in inflation may deceive workers into accepting or refusing jobs by deluding them about the real value of money wages.

According to this theory, the apparently large variations in the actual rate of unemployment compared to the natural rate are entirely due to *persistent illusion* about the true real value of current money wages. Thus the explanation for 20 years of non-acceleration after the war is that it took people a long time to adjust to the experience of persistent inflation.

But it is difficult to believe that it took wage and price setters *twenty years* to realise that inflation was occurring and accordingly that they should incorporate prospective inflation into their wage and price fixings. This implies that they were constantly surprised by inflation, which seems scarcely credible.

Yet all the problems of reconciliation with the facts deal the NAIRU idea only glancing blows. After all, economists are notorious for not allowing the facts to interfere with a good theory. It is as *theory* that the NAIRU idea must be challenged.

A Different Theoretical Approach

A more convincing theoretical story about the relations between unemployment and inflation emerges from the Keynesian analysis of unemployment and wage flexibility in the decidedly non-inflationary conditions of the 1930s. Why didn't real wages fall in reaction to the high level of unemployment, sufficient to encourage businesses to reemploy people and reflate the economy?

The Keynesian answer is that once aggregate demand has fallen, each group of workers is not facing the same set of options as before. For their employers can only restore the old level of output and employment if they can sell the same quantity against the backdrop of lower general demand in the economy. But they can only do that at lower prices. They can only afford to accept lower prices if wages are lower, that is to say, *lower than they were before the downswing in demand*. In severe cases, there might be no level of wages which could do the trick.

Accordingly, the absence of wage cuts in the face of a slump is not altogether surprising. It is not necessarily due to trade union wage fixing, nor to people misperceiving the situation and failing to understand the real value of current money wages. Nor, indeed, are excessive wages at the root of the problem. The problem is simply a lack of effective demand, about which any individual employer or group of workers can do nothing. This is a story in which a systemic failure puts businesses, individuals and unions in a nigh-on impossible situation.[17]

But in this story, when demand revives, employment can rise, and an increased supply of labour will be forthcoming (even despite lower real wages). There is an asymmetry in the aggregate labour supply function – opposition to real wage cuts when demand is low and/or falling, but willingness to supply more labour even at lower real wages as demand rises. Yet this behaviour makes perfect sense, because the choices facing both employers and employees in the two situations are not the same.

Now transfer this same vision to a world of inflation. Prices and wages are going up together, but the same reasoning applies. Suppose that demand falls and unemployment rises. People have the option of taking pay increases below the rate of inflation to boost employment and if, in general, they do this, then the rate of inflation will fall. But they do not. This prompts the judgement of natural rate economists that the economy is still running with unemployment at or below the natural rate or that expectations are proving stubborn. Yet when demand revives employment increases without pay rising any faster.

If you plotted the inflation and unemployment results of this behaviour, you would get a sort of horizontal Phillips Curve, with widely differing unemployment experiences at the same rate of inflation – the exact opposite of the natural rate view of the world, and in line with much of our experience in the post-war period.

A 'Natural' Death?

The explanation which the natural rate theory provides for the inflation of the last 60 years is at once blissfully simple and hopelessly
unilluminating – the economy has been run with unemployment below
the natural rate. The trouble is that this is about as close to a non-
explanation as an explanation can get. It is all very well saying that the
answer lies in changes in the natural rate, due to a variety of institutional factors, but in that case the big story lies with these institutional
factors, on which the natural rate approach has no light to shed.[18]

In short, it is not so much that the natural rate theory is wrong, but
rather that it misses the point. Remarkably, nearly 30 years after it was
first propounded, this concept still dominates both theory and policy,
immobilising thought and action alike.

The Output Gap

More recently, another theoretical construct has emerged to take a
leading role in the way that people think about inflation – the output
gap. But this is really the natural rate idea in another guise, although it
is often employed more crudely.[19] It posits that the degree of inflationary pressure is linked to how close the economy is to its 'potential' output, which is calculated by extrapolating the economy's previously
realised levels of output.[20]

But as a guide to inflation prospects, the output gap suffers from
three serious defects. First, the idea that capacity utilisation (or the
natural rate) can give a full picture of inflationary pressures flies in the
face of the structural and institutional forces I have outlined in this
book. Increased price sensitivity by consumers has given producers the
incentive to keep prices low and to aim for higher volumes. This means
that far from being in conflict, low inflation and high capacity utilisation may be two sides of the same coin.

Secondly, the output gap approach implicitly assumes that the point
of 'capacity utilisation' at which inflation begins is unchanged over
time. This is akin to assuming that the natural rate of unemployment is
constant. In practice, though, we know that the natural rate can

change to an enormous extent.

This simple idea has the power to make a nonsense of output gap calculations. In the 1950s, unemployment in the UK averaged less than
1½%. At its peak in the mid-1980s it ran at more than 11%, and at the
end of 1996 it was below 7%. Arguably, unemployment at its peak was
above the natural rate but even so, there were times in the 1980s when
the behaviour of inflation seemed consistent with the natural rate of
unemployment being as high as 10%. So in the last 30 years, there may
have been a rise in the natural rate of almost 10%. In principle, we could
now be witnessing a reduction in the natural rate of similar proportions.

Thirdly, the output gap calculates the sustainable long-term growth
rate by reference to the *realised* growth rate over some past period.
Accordingly, if the economy grew at an average rate of 2¼% per annum
over the last 20 or 30 years, it is appropriate to assume that its sustainable growth rate now is 2¼%.

At a broadbrush level, this may be an appropriate first approximation. But when it comes to the estimation of output gaps and the risk
of inflation, discrepancies of ½% or even ¼% make a big difference. If
the sustainable growth rate increased by ¼% four years ago, then 'full
capacity' is already 1% further away now than we thought *and* when full
capacity is reached, the economy can grow by ¼% per annum faster
than we thought, before engendering inflation.

And the idea that future sustainable growth rates will be the same as
average realised rates over the last 20 to 30 years, even to within ¼%, is
pretty odd. The sustainable growth rate of Germany in the 1950s was not
the average of its realised growth rates over the previous 30 years. Nor was
its sustainable growth rate the same in the 1970s as it was in the 1950s.

When you reflect on the size and nature of the changes that have
happened to western economies over the last 15 years, the idea that the
sustainable growth rate now is appropriately measured by the past
realised growth rate seems even more bizarre. The western economies
have seen a dramatic rise in the share of services, the collapse of union
power, a large rise in international trade and the opening up of new,
dynamic economies, wholesale privatisation, demanning on a massive
scale and the information technology revolution.

Is it not likely that these changes, which have probably reduced the
'natural rate of unemployment', have also probably raised the sustain-

able rate of growth? But if we cannot be sure of the sustainable growth rate then we cannot be sure of the size of the 'output gap'.

The idea of the output gap represents another attempt in economics to put measurement before thought. Economies are not machines and do not work like machines. There are good reasons for believing that over recent years, the assortment of structural factors which influence inflation have changed in a favourable direction, just as they deteriorated in the 1970s. As a result, calculations of the output gap are likely to produce conclusions that are much too pessimistic about the outlook for inflation.

A Historical Approach to the Causation of Inflation

The upshot is that economists' attempt to find a general explanation for inflation which can bypass history and institutions has failed. If we are to understand our inflationary experience, we have to delve into the historical processes that have brought us to where we are. We have to ask the very historical and institutional questions which conventional theory has attempted to sidestep.

To be sure, there is no philosopher's stone which gives all the answers to our questions about inflation. There is, however, one very general, all-embracing framework which has some appeal – inflation is caused by the struggle between different groups within society over their share of national income.

Classic monetary inflation fits nicely into this framework. Governments cause inflation when they try to secure more of the national income than they are willing or able to finance openly through taxation. But their power to create inflation by monetary expansion is not immutable, nor is it exclusive. Indeed, it can be argued to be a feature of a particular stage in monetary history, albeit a pretty long one. After all, in primitive societies which use some commodity, such as cowrie shells or cattle, as money, there is no state-created inflation, if indeed there is any sort of entity which can meaningfully be called a state. But there is money.

State-produced monetary inflation emerges once the sovereign is able to issue money (first coins, later notes) which have a greater value in exchange than their intrinsic value. Because of their power to issue this money, which is legally bound to be accepted as means of payment, they can expropriate resources from the private sector. In relatively undeveloped societies, indeed, they are the only entities which can do this. The sources of inflation are then restricted to government debasement of the coinage, natural disasters, or an influx of precious metals.

Once a metallic standard is replaced by paper money, then the power of governments to create inflation is increased enormously. But simultaneously, without the anchor provided by a metallic standard, the power of the private banking system to increase the money supply is unleashed. The possibility of a credit inflation opens up, where it is not competition for resources between the public and private sector which causes the inflation, but rather competition between different parts of the private sector. In an inflation driven by private credit creation, borrowers lay claim to more resources than are currently available without others in society giving up some of their claims.

In the modern developed world, though, the power of the state to create inflation by monetary expansion is gradually being circumscribed. First, there is the increased self-discipline of governments and central banks who, in normal circumstances, now believe that there is no economic advantage to be had from allowing higher inflation, and see positive virtue in having low, or no, inflation. In this they are supported both by public opinion and by the current intellectual orthodoxy.[21]

Secondly, in the advanced countries of the west, the increased power of financial markets is imposing an external discipline. Financial markets are now so sophisticated and so integrated internationally that the slightest whiff of higher inflation sees money market and bond market interest rates rising and the currency falling. Higher bond yields themselves may serve to depress economic activity but, more to the point, if the government is borrowing from the financial markets, the increase in interest rates makes its financial predicament worse. Indeed, depending on the level and structure of borrowing and the degree of financial market response, it may readily end up a net loser as a result of the attempted inflation.

Thirdly, the advances of technology are bringing closer the time when money is virtually entirely electronic, with next to no role for notes and coin. At this point, governments' incentive to create inflation by printing money in order to benefit from the 'inflation tax' will have been sharply reduced.

Is Paper Money the Real Culprit?

It is all too easy to think that the problems of restraining governments are restricted to a paper money system. But I pointed out in Chapter 7 that simply setting out with a monetary system based on precious metals was not enough to prevent inflation. In earlier times, the sovereign power had to refrain from debasing the coinage and, once paper money had been 'discovered', had to keep to the original declared parity of the national currency in terms of the precious metal, and indeed to keep to a metallic standard at all. This required both understanding and self-discipline.

In addition, the system required either some form of management or a good deal of luck. Under the Gold Standard, failure of the supply of gold to respond to increasing demands created by economic growth created deflationary pressure, while large influxes of gold created inflationary pressure. Indeed, during the US's adherence to the Standard from 1879 to 1914, although annual inflation rates were low, the cumulative loss of purchasing power of the dollar was 40%. And if the world had been on a gold standard over the last 25 years, periodic disturbances in the gold market might have caused severe difficulties.

Nevertheless, there were long periods of successful operation of a metallic standard in England, and for many countries the Gold Standard worked well in the nineteenth century. Given that governments had the option to devalue or abandon the metallic standard and print notes with gay abandon, why didn't they?

There are, I think, three (related) answers. First, they realised that if they proceeded in this way they would create inflation and thereby bring distortions to the economy, without actually increasing real wealth or production. (This is the view so clearly reflected by Locke in the passage I quote in Chapter 7.) Secondly, they saw no economic purpose in abandoning the standard as it seemed to work perfectly well, without undue strain. Thirdly, in normal times they had no need of the printing press, or what modern economists have referred to as the 'inflation tax'. They could finance their expenditure perfectly well through normal taxation.

This history has clear lessons about the role of governments in causing inflation. It is not sufficient to explain inflation solely in terms of the inherent tendency of governments to inflate the money supply under a paper standard. During the long periods of price stability under a metallic standard, success was not automatic. Governments still had to exercise self-restraint. The common theme linking most inflationary episodes in both the earlier metallic era and the more recent period of paper money is the coincidence of *weak* governments and bad times. This coincidence has led governments to abandon self-restraint.

For most of the last 25 years, the managed paper money system has not worked well, but there have recently been major changes, which are moving towards establishing these same three conditions which sustained effective use of a metallic standard. Perhaps the real historical significance of these changes is that, after several decades of failure, we have now found a way to manage a paper money system, by imposing and self-imposing the appropriate restraints.

The Advent of Producer Power

The sort of inflation we have experienced in the post-war period reflects a further stage in historical development – the upsurge of producer power, which led to battles between producer groups for shares of the cake, battles in which the role of monetary factors was secondary.

In the largely agricultural society of previous eras, the power of producers to affect the *general* price level was limited. Small units of production and poor communication made collusive behaviour difficult. The result was that there was no persistent inflationary pressure arising from producer groups. And when circumstances demanded that prices and wages should fall, they fell almost as easily as, on other occasions, they rose.

But industrialisation changed all this. In the new world, the price of industrial output was something to be *decided* by the producers. Goods were highly differentiated one from another. The nature of massproduction technology limited the number of firms which could viably operate in an industry, so there was a tendency towards industrial concentration. Meanwhile, groups of workers also acquired producer power. The conditions of mass production favoured mass organisation of labour into unionised groups, mirroring the cartelisation of employers.

The structural tension between services and manufacturing which, I have argued, played a major role in the tendency toward rising prices in the post-war period can be usefully analysed within this framework. It can be described as the attempt by both labour and capital employed in manufacturing to bag all of the benefits of increased productivity. Inflation is the mechanism through which this cornering of the benefits was resisted by other groups, and the real income gains spread throughout society. What I have called 'development inflation' in the dynamic economies can be seen in a similar way.

The increases in oil prices in 1973 and 1979 can also be seen within this framework. They represented the exercise of producer power on an international scale. They imposed a substantial real income loss (corresponding to OPEC's gain) on all of the industrial countries which were not self-sufficient in energy. This unleashed a struggle within society over who should bear the loss.

Is the oil price experience sufficiently *sui generis* to be described as a one-off? No. It surely bears comparison with the end of rationing after the Second World War, with the destruction or diversion of productive capacity which happens in most wars, with the failure of harvests or with the pressure of increased population on limited productive capacity. All of these are real phenomena which have monetary consequences.

Indeed, for the established countries of the industrial west, the development of the new industrial world can be viewed as a series of oil price hikes in reverse. Whereas the oil price rises of the 1970s combined a fall in real income for the west with a sharp rise in the price level, so the current process of industrial development in the east combines an increase in real income with a *reduction* in the price level in the west. Just as the influence of the oil price rise was to promote higher inflation, so the process of industrial development will promote lower inflation.

A similar comparison can be made for many of the technological and organisational changes sweeping through western businesses. And perhaps we can think of the influence of the silicon chip, just like oil in the 1970s, as so pervasive that it is felt on the price of just about everything.

This point can be generalised. Before the natural rate framework became widely accepted, many economists argued that the inflationary character of the post-war world and the acute inflationary problems of the 1970s had their roots in real, structural phenomena which acted directly on the price level. With the triumph of the natural rate approach, this view was either rejected outright, or only grudgingly accepted as a partial explanation by incorporation into the rag-bag of factors which might have raised the natural rate of unemployment.

Now so many of the inflationary forces to which these older economists referred are in the process of fading out or even going into reverse. The period when producer power (including the power of organised labour) was a major inflationary source can be regarded as a phase in economic development – the phase beyond the largely agricultural and before the intensively competitive and largely service-based economy, the phase when mass-production manufacturing was the dominant force in the economy.

The Importance of Costs and Prices

There are two related reasons why conventional theory has neglected the implied scope for real, structural factors affecting the general level of costs and prices to have a role in determining inflation. First, for real factors to affect the general price level they must be of sufficient size to affect all prices. In a competitive economy without strong linkages between pay and prices in different sectors, there are comparatively few forces which qualify.

Secondly, whatever the size of the effect of real forces on the price level, they are dwarfed by the potential size of the effects of monetary expansion. This means that very high rates of inflation *have* to be analysed in monetary terms (even if the root causes go beyond the money supply). But once inflation has been reduced to very low levels, as it is now in most of the west, then real factors can have a significant effect on inflation. Indeed at this point, economists would do well to stop talking about *inflation* at all, and to think instead about *changes to the price level*.

In this respect, a parallel could be drawn between economics and physics. Modern developments in physics have not proved Newtonian mechanics 'wrong' but have rather revealed limitations to the conditions under which they apply. At the subatomic level, to explain the behaviour of particles, physicists replace Newtonian mechanics with quantum mechanics, while the laws of Newtonian mechanics continue to apply above the atomic level. This does not invalidate Newtonian mechanics, but it does undermine its claim to complete generality.

But for economics, adopting the idea that changes in the money supply are not always in the driving seat for changes in the price level leaves a major theoretical problem. If there is no determinate relationship running from the money supply to the price level, what is it that determines the price level?

I think it is helpful to see it as determined by an interactive process between important price and cost factors at the micro level and the various aggregate demand and asset price factors which are usually reflected in the various measures of the money supply. A sharp change in any of these factors can set off a chain reaction in the others. In an important sense, the price level is what it is because of what it has recently been. Theory must make way for history.

Where does this leave the fundamental issues about the causation of inflation which have obsessed economists for so long? Inflation will still be caused when aggregate demand runs at too high a level relative to aggregate supply, but there is no unique link between money supply and aggregate demand or inflation, and across wide variations in the rate of unemployment there will be no systematic relation between the level of demand and the rate of inflation. Moreover, when inflation first appears or accelerates this does not necessarily mean that this is the point where there is no more supply capacity. It can easily be the result of a supply shock which reverberates through the system.

But in current circumstances supply shocks are predominantly favourable. Moreover, the factors which in the old days propelled costs up relentlessly and which, in the past, could only be suppressed by substantial excess capacity and high unemployment, are now held in check by competitive forces. Furthermore, the effect of increased price sensitivity in forcing firms to opt for lower unit margins and higher volumes itself improves the relationship between output and price changes.

The upshot is that, although there is still a limit to how strongly we should allow demand to press on capacity, we can now run the economy at higher levels of demand than previously thought feasible without engendering higher inflation.

The Changeover Point

At the moment, the change in the general price level is being driven by two opposing forces – on the one hand, the continuing process of cost and price rises produced by the struggle for income shares, inherited from the past, together with the fast-fading remnants of inflationary culture; and on the other, by the cost and price *reductions* originating from technological advances, the organisational revolution within companies, the development of the dynamic east and the intensification of the competitive climate. We are in a phase somewhat akin to the position of a river at the point where it meets the sea, and fresh water and salt water confront each other.

But this is an unequal struggle. One influence is dissipating while the other is burgeoning. The problems of perpetual inflation are yesterday's story; the problems of a fluctuating price level are tomorrow's.

9

What Should the Politicians Do Now?

Economic ideas move in circles; stand in one place long enough and you will see the same old ideas come round again.

Sir Dennis Robertson[1]

EVERY GENERATION OF ECONOMIC THINKERS HAS A SEARING experience which colours attitudes for a lifetime. For the generation which influenced the economic management of the industrial west in the early post-war years, the searing experience was the Great Depression of the 1930s.

So great was the impact of the Depression that they continued to be obsessed with maintaining very low levels of unemployment even when the challenge of high inflation emerged right under their noses. With the benefit of hindsight, they not only downplayed the seriousness of the inflation danger, but by the 1970s were aiming for levels of unemployment which were unrealistic in the changed circumstances of the time.

Germany was an exception. There, inflation, recession and financial disaster were seen as closely intertwined, not only because of the inter-war experience, but also because of the burst of inflation after the end of the Second World War. All along, the Bundesbank was keen to stress the importance of stability, alive to the seriousness of the inflation danger, and scornful of Anglo-Saxon insouciance. Throughout the 1960s and early 1970s, the German approach to this issue struck the economic policy establishment in the US and Britain as quaint, if not bizarre. But then things changed.

The searing experience for today's generation of economic thinkers and policy-makers is surely not the Depression of the 1930s, nor indeed any depression, but rather the inflation and instability of the 1970s.

The prevailing orthodoxy is that a repeat of this inflationary upsurge must be avoided, almost at all costs. This orthodoxy is now so deeply ingrained that, like its predecessor, it looks likely to be with us until well past its sell-by date. Indeed, it may well continue to dominate until a new generation, marked by a different searing experience, rises to take positions of power and influence in economic policy.

The change of attitude with regard to inflation was so profound that after the 1970s the new policy orthodoxy not only held that inflation brought no benefits and that high inflation could deteriorate into financial disaster, but also that even fairly modest inflation was an unmitigated catastrophe. For the policy-maker, it seems, the source of all evil was now not money, but inflation. Whereas their equivalents just a few years previously had explicitly been prepared to tolerate a little bit of inflation in order to secure low unemployment, ministers, officials and central bankers now chanted the mantra 'inflation creates unemployment'. It was commonly believed that inflation was responsible for low growth rates, as well as microeconomic inefficiencies.

Like all revolutions, this one surely went too far. In the rush to purge the previous tolerance of inflation, every macroeconomic ill under the sun was now blamed on inflation.

It is particularly ironic that the new orthodoxy has taken such a firm grip at just the time when, as I have argued in this book, the inflationary impulses are fading, to be replaced by powerful anti-inflationary forces. Indeed, it is this combination of anti-inflationary forces and anti-inflationary policy which is likely to produce zero inflation in the years ahead and, I think, a real chance at some point of price deflation.

Plus Ça Change

It is sometimes suggested that the apparent changes in the inflation environment are the temporary product of a particular political conjuncture and that a shift in the political pendulum could see a return to more inflationary policies.

I do not believe that the forces which I have analysed in this book are much, if at all, dependent on which particular political party is in power. Indeed, over the last 10 years, across the industrial world, governments of widely different political hues have pursued broadly similar policies. In western democracies, the real differences between major political parties at any one time are much smaller than is commonly supposed, and much smaller than the differences between what *all* parties believe at one time and what they all believe at other times.

It is the tide of ideas which makes the difference. It sweeps over politicians of every democratic party. Consider two big questions in political economy over the last 50 years – redistributive taxation and the role of the state both in owning economic enterprises and in providing social security and a healthcare system. Parties wrangle about their differences with each other over these questions. But just think about the differences between what they are all thinking and doing now and what they all thought and did 30 years ago.

Even so, it has to be admitted that the tide of ideas, and the groundswell of political pressures welling up from below, could turn against both anti-inflationary policy at the macro level and market efficiency reforms at the micro level. If this does happen, it is likely to be in reaction to the high levels of unemployment in many western countries.

I have to admit that there are some dangers to my thesis here, and I am particularly concerned about the risk of protectionism. (More on this below.) Even so, there are several reasons for believing that these dangers can be avoided. For a start, the tide of ideas does not change abruptly without warning. It is driven partly by the natural movement of the generations. And the tide still seems to be running in favour of budgetary discipline and competitive forces. In continental Europe the view that high rates of unemployment are due primarily to overregulation and excessive taxes is only now gaining ground. It looks to have a long way to run. And the influence of ideas is reinforced by technology. Governments simply have less and less power to resist competitive forces and are less able to pursue inflationary policies to advantage.

Political pressures are also influenced by generational factors, and the ageing of the population in many western democracies is building a powerful constituency against inflation. Nor is it only a matter of numbers; self-confidence and group identity also count for a good deal. In the United States 'grey power' is already a potent political force.

Furthermore, precisely because of the structural, micro changes which I have stressed in this book, there is room for many of the western world's

monetary authorities to aim for higher growth and lower unemployment, *without* setting off an inflationary upsurge.

A Further Turn of the Screw

Cynics and inflation hawks already sense an imminent change of
course, not so much towards economic expansion as such, but rather
towards greater toleration of inflation. Accordingly, they are warning of
inflationary risks ahead. But I think that the signs point in exactly the
opposite direction. As the central banks have 'succeeded' in reducing
inflation so they have set their sights on still lower levels. At the international conference on inflation targets organised by the Bank of
England and held in early 1995, there was interest in the idea of target
levels for *price stability*, in relation to which the currently employed targets for low inflation could be regarded as merely a staging post.

Ever since the mid-1970s, the prime difficulty facing macro policy-
makers has been the containment and then reduction of inflation. The collapse of this enemy leaves them a bit like the west's defence establishment
after the collapse of the Soviet Union and the end of the Cold War – still
possessing all the old equipment, but not quite sure where to point it.

The great danger facing the world now is that the policy-makers will
insist on policies which are too tight, and in particular that they will
impose short-term interest rates which are too high. This danger is all
the greater because interest rates which seem dangerously low by reference to the last 20 years are in fact dangerously *high* in a world without
inflation. It is the years before the persistent inflation of the post-war
period which provide the clues to the future. But it is the years immediately after the inflationary explosion of the 1970s which inform the
thoughts and fears of policy-makers.

Thus the US Federal Reserve, followed by the Bank of England, pursued a policy of raising interest rates in 1994–5, in advance of the supposed upsurge of inflationary pressures which was just around the corner.
The markets concluded that this was another version of the typical post-
war boom and assumed that interest rates would have to rise to 9 or 10%
or beyond. In the event, nothing of the sort happened. The cyclical rise
in inflation was extremely modest and growth slackened markedly in

reaction to interest rates which by recent standards seemed very low –
6% in the US and 6¾% in the UK.

The role of the Bank of England in this episode was instructive.
Charged with the job of monitoring and advising on progress towards
meeting the government's inflation target, the Bank concentrated
every effort on the inflationary risks ahead. For much of 1995, its
Governor seemed to be at loggerheads with the Chancellor of the
Exchequer, pressing for a rate rise in May when the economy was starting to weaken, and subsequently failing to endorse rate reductions
when the economy looked dangerously weak. The Bank appeared to be
obsessed with the danger that policy would be too loose, but scarcely
aware of the danger that it could be too tight.

This was not a uniquely British phenomenon. At the meeting of the
Group of Seven in October 1995, the Finance Ministers and central
bank Governors were evidently in smug mood and felt able to give
themselves a pat on the back. The communiqué stated:

> The ministers and central bank governors agreed that in most countries
> the conditions for continued growth and employment gains are in place
> and inflation is well under control.[2]

At the time, Japan had still not convincingly beaten off the *deflation*
threat, throughout most of Europe unemployment was frighteningly
high and the pace of economic growth had turned down in both North
America and Europe. It was the same old story – as far as the central
banks were concerned, only inflation control really mattered.

It's Tougher at the Bottom

Why was the response of the economy to higher interest rates so much
stronger than the authorities and the markets had expected? It was
because individuals and companies were reacting to the here and now.
Companies saw that they could not raise prices, even though their costs
had risen. The competition was simply too great and the customers would
not wear it. Meanwhile, the customers were not about to step up their
spending by borrowing more at the supposedly 'low' level of interest rates

of 6% plus, because they feared *higher* rates and because their earnings were hardly rising at all, their jobs were insecure and the value of their main asset, their home, was steady or falling. In short, they were reacting to the realisation that things were different.

The financial markets, meanwhile, were continuing on the assumption that things were just the same. The power of conventional expectations kept them locked onto autopilot. So much so, indeed, that in 1994–5 they were obsessed with the supposed danger that the recent sharp rise in commodity prices would cause an inflationary upsurge, just as it did in 1973. Meanwhile, the monetary authorities, obsessed by the modern nostrum that the financial markets always know best, assumed that they were right.

Apparently, the markets had not noticed that commodities, including oil, are nowhere near as important to western economies as they were, and even if they were as important, western workforces are in no position to protect themselves against the consequences by pushing pay up sharply.

If things continue like this and both the authorities and the markets fail to acknowledge the extent to which things have changed, then we could be facing a real disaster. What is to be done?

Ending the Pessimistic Tendency

The first necessary change is one of attitude and perspective. Markets and monetary authorities are locked in a state of pessimism about our economic potential, a state of mind which surely has its roots in the disastrous 1970s. The logic of the enormous changes taking place in technology, organisational efficiency and the scope for international trade, never mind the reduction of inflation itself, is that our sustainable rate of growth should be higher. Rather than constraining economic performance to the average of the last 10 or 20 years, monetary authorities should be raising their sights.

Moreover, it should now be possible to run our economies at a higher level of demand without engendering inflationary pressure. For a time, therefore, with the possible exception of the US, the west should be aiming at *unsustainable* rates of growth, rates of growth which will eat into the margin of unused capacity, including surplus supplies of labour.

This does not mean, however, that we can or should risk a 'dash for growth'. The *speed* with which economies are expanded will be critical. The aim should be to reexpand slowly, thereby allowing cost reductions from technological and efficiency improvements and eastern development to offset the inflationary effects from land shortage, shortage of particular sorts of labour and upward pressure on commodity prices, while giving time to draw in more labour from the large groups of people unemployed, partly employed, or hovering on the margins of the labour force. By contrast, 'a dash for growth' would risk setting up inflationary pressures which overwhelmed the power of these anti-inflationary forces and reignited inflationary expectations.

Nor does it mean that we can dispense with structural and market reforms. Indeed, it is these reforms, coupled with autonomous, competitive pressures, which make it possible for economies to operate at higher levels of demand without engendering inflationary pressure. Those countries which have not proceeded far down this route, including most of continental Europe, will not be able to expand as fast as those, such as the US, the UK and New Zealand, which have.

The importance of realising our growth potential does not derive solely from the benefits which would otherwise be forgone. There is a serious danger that if we do not achieve the high rates of growth, high levels of output and employment, accompanied by next to no inflation, which I have argued are within our grasp, then we could slip into a world which is altogether uglier than the one we face now. For there are big losers from the process of technological change and integration with the dynamic countries in east Asia and elsewhere. If these losers are left to fester then there could be untold political and economic consequences.

The most prominent danger is an outbreak of serious social unrest. At the end of 1995 and again with the lorry drivers' strike at the end of 1996, there were clear warnings of the simmering dangers in France, but the potential problems are not confined to France alone; they stretch across the developed world. And they carry a serious economic risk, namely that in order to forestall social unrest, or in reaction to it, politicians will lurch towards protectionist trade policies in an attempt to shut out the apparently job-threatening development of the dynamic countries. In the process, the west would risk the reemergence of inflation, as well as blocking off one of the sources of enhanced prosperity.

The way to stave off this danger is to make sure that the west realis-es the economic potential made possible by both eastern development and technological advance, rather than seeing the effects expressed in even higher levels of unemployment. That way, the group of losers will be smaller, there will be a constituency of obvious gainers to offset the losers, and it will be easier for the winners to afford to cushion the effects on the losers.

Are Central Banks Now Alive to the Danger?

I have so far been fairly critical of the world's central banks, and in par-ticular of their reaction to apparent signs of higher inflation in 1994. But how have things changed more recently? Are there signs that cen-tral banks have taken on board the importance of structural changes for the inflation environment? And are they now alive to the chances (and dangers) of deflation?

Fortunately, the answer is, at least partly, yes. In 1994 and 1995, while the first edition of this book was being prepared, the idea that many countries faced a much improved trade-off between inflation and unemployment (or, if you like, the natural rate of unemployment had fallen markedly), and the idea that deflation was a serious threat, both met with widespread derision.

But subsequent events have gradually brought about a change of view. The persistence of the US recovery, accompanied by even lower levels of unemployment, but without higher inflation, challenged the pessimistic view about capacity limits. Meanwhile, the experience of negative infla-tion in Japan and Sweden challenged the widespread complacency about the supposedly inviolable status of the number zero. Then in June 1996, a few months after the first edition of this book was published, something remarkable appeared, and from an unexpected source – the Bank for International Settlements (BIS). This Basle-based institution, which acts as the central banks' central bank, is not given to hyperbole. But in its June 1996 annual report[3], it made a striking statement:

the forces bearing on the price level are now more balanced than they have been for some decades. Thus, it is perhaps the right historical moment to recall the advice of Keynes and Wicksell in the early 1920s. Reacting against the vagaries of the gold standard, which allowed the price level to drift for extended periods in either direction, they concluded that it was appropriate as well as feasible for central banks to resist both inflation and deflation. At a time of rapid social and economic change, with attendant implications for social order and relative prices, it is all the more important that price stability be pursued as an anchor for rational and forward-looking decisions on all fronts.

To the layman that may not sound impressive, but in central bank-speak it was a bombshell. At the BIS, at least, the penny had dropped. In fact, central bank thinking was changing in some other surprising quarters. Clearly alive to the structural difficulties facing Germany, and increasingly confident that inflation would remain low despite strong growth of the money supply, M3, the Bundesbank not only lowered interest rates sharply in 1995 and continued edging them down, but in 1996 actively sought to encourage the deutschmark lower against the dollar in order to improve German competitiveness.

Facing similar circumstances, in the closing months of 1996 the Swiss National Bank also presided over a much weaker Swiss franc, coincident with Swiss three-month interest rates falling to $1\frac{1}{4}$%. For in Switzerland the mood about the economy was gloomy and some people were actively talking about the danger of deflation.

Meanwhile, at the international level a serious debate began among central bankers concerning the appropriate objectives of monetary policy. Should central banks aim for inflation at zero or 2–3%? What were the dangers of deflation and what risks did deflation carry?

That this debate was taking place in 1995 and 1996 speaks volumes about the change in the inflationary environment. For so long after the inflationary upsurge of the 1970s, central banks (and others) could justifiably push such issues into the background as being questions of academic interest only. However elegantly it might be dressed up, the underlying reality of their policy with regard to inflation was stark and simple – 'just get it down'. Turning to consider differing definitions of price stability, or debating whether zero, 2 or 3% inflation was best, as participants did at a recent central bankers' conference – the economic symposium of the Kansas City Federal Reserve held at Jackson Hole, Wyoming in

September 1996 – was an indication that this phase had now drawn to a close. Even central bankers apparently now believed that, if inflation had not yet stopped dead in its tracks, it had at least shifted down several gears.

There appears to have been a clear division of opinion at Jackson Hole.[4] One camp believed that there was merit in trying to maintain inflation at some very low, but always positive, number, say 1–3%. Their reasoning mirrored several of the arguments in this book: measured inflation overstates true inflation; getting inflation lower will involve significant real costs and yet it is by no means obvious, once you have got inflation as low as 1–3%, that there are large gains to be had from getting it still lower; indeed, there could be substantial losses even after the investment in reducing inflation is over, for a little inflation 'oils the wheels', while the prospect of *deflation*, which is much more likely if central banks are aiming for zero inflation, poses serious dangers, particularly since interest rates cannot be negative.

The opposite position, not surprisingly, revolved around challenges to these self-same arguments, as well as the abiding belief that, from the point of view of maintaining public confidence in the value of money and all the valuable structural and institutional features which spring from it, there is something special about zero.

Opportunistic Disinflation

An interesting compromise has emerged between these two views on inflation policy, namely the idea of 'opportunistic disinflation'. Instead of the policy-makers trying to get inflation a degree or two lower when the economy is strong and/or there are powerful upward cost pressures, and thereby swimming against the tide, the advocates of opportunistic disinflation suggest that in this phase of the cycle they should simply aim to hold the line on inflation. But when the cycle turns down, they should take the opportunity to allow inflation to fall a notch or two further.

The idea is that the costs of reducing inflation are not uniform over the cycle. The policy authorities should work with the grain of the economy rather than against it. If they take this approach, it is argued, a cost/benefit analysis of the investment in even lower inflation may look favourable.

I find this idea of opportunistic disinflation attractive, not least because it chimes in with the notion of the policy authorities having to work in an economic environment over which they have only limited control, as opposed to the notion that the current inflation rate is whatever it is because that is what the central bank explicitly chose it to be. Thinking that the Federal Reserve may well follow this approach, some US economists believe that the US is 'one recession away from price stability'. That is to say that, as long as the Fed manages to hold the current level of inflation while the economy continues to grow on track, even though no one knows when the next recession will be, there will be one some time and, when it strikes, the rate of inflation can readily be expected to fall by 2 or 3%, thereby producing price stability.

Yet although I find the idea of opportunistic disinflation attractive, it has to be said that it leaves many of the key questions unanswered, in particular the points raised at Jackson Hole about the difficulties of functioning without any inflation at all, or even with conditions of deflation, and the problems this may cause for the operation of monetary policy.

I suspect, however, that opportunistic disinflation does hint at the way in which the inflation debate is likely to move over the next few years. If the US and other major countries come to experience just about zero inflation, apparently as the result of events outside anybody's control, rather than being chosen by the policy authorities, this might well shift the debate about what rate of inflation was desirable. Once it was already in place, zero inflation might be seen to be more desirable and efforts might even then be expended to retain it which were not expended to achieve it in the first place.

This raises important questions about deflation. If, having reached something like price stability, a major industrial country such as the United States looked set to experience a period of falling prices, would the policy authorities panic and seek to prevent or reverse such an outcome? I think the answer is, not necessarily. After all, if you are aiming to achieve and preserve price stability, then given that there are bound to be periods in which the price level is driven up by either demand or cost pressures, there have to be periods when prices fall.

The Policy that Dare not Speak its Name

This was also the implicit message in a paper presented at Jackson Hole by Professor Mervyn King, the Bank of England's Chief Economist.[5]

He argued that central banks' objective should now be to achieve and maintain *price stability* over the medium term. True, the fact that official, measured inflation overstated true inflation meant that the objective in terms of official or measured inflation was some sustained small rate of increase, say 2% per annum, but this was a mere statistical distortion. If the true rate of inflation is distorted upwards by 2% per annum, then 2% measured inflation represents price stability.

Yet how would central banks sustain this low rate of inflation, effectively amounting to price stability in the event of a major adverse shock, such as the two oil price hikes of the 1970s? They could seek, of course, to contain the immediate inflationary impact by imposing very high interest rates. But this could have catastrophic consequences, if indeed it would be possible at all. More feasibly, the authorities could allow a once-and-for-all rise in the price level (above the 2% level corresponding to the mis-measurement factor). This would produce a temporarily higher rate of inflation, but if they were trying to achieve price stability they could and should resist any second-round effects – which is easier said than done.

Nevertheless, this would still not produce average annual inflation at 2% over the medium term (i.e. effective price stability) because the inflation rate would be 2% when things were going according to plan and 2% plus when the economy was hit by an adverse cost shock or particularly strong demand. In other words, the price level would continue to be subject to an upward ratchet, and there would continue to be an upwardly biased risk to the rate of inflation. Furthermore, because the authorities embraced a policy regime embodying this asymmetry, the financial markets might well suspect that when push came to shove, the 2% target for inflation in normal times was also upwardly flexible. Accordingly, the markets would continue to embody a considerable risk premium in long-term rates of interest. Thus one of the prospective gains from achieving a very low rate of inflation would be lost.

There are two ways out of this problem and they both end up in the same place. The first is for the authorities to determine that, once the inflation rate has been driven up beyond 2%, they will deliberately try to force it down below 2% to make up for the period spent above 2%.

The second approach is for the authorities to live with the fact that a burst of inflation above 2% has raised the average rate and that the price level is no longer on track, but when the next *favourable* shock occurs they will allow measured inflation to fall below 2%, and be happy with it standing below 2% until the average rate is down to 2% and the price level is back on its target path.

In either case, the result is that there is no longer a sharp asymmetry of risk. As long as they believe that the authorities will adhere to this regime, the markets can have confidence that over the medium term, the price level will on average rise by 2% per annum, regardless of shocks. Accordingly, they do not need to embody a substantial risk premium in long-term rates of interest.

Sounds simple, doesn't it? But the rub is that following such a policy certainly means sometimes allowing, or forcing, measured inflation to fall below 2%, which already amounts, *ex hypothesi*, to effective price deflation. And if there has previously been a substantial burst of inflation above 2%, then the authorities may need to force/allow a period of measured inflation below zero, that is to say price deflation.

The idea of encouraging or tolerating price deflation is still such a taboo subject that central bankers and economists feel that they cannot raise it in polite society. But we may be closer to its being adopted as official policy than you might think on the basis of current practice and official policy pronouncements.

Continuing Debate – and Success – at the Fed

The theoretical and policy issues raised by the striking behaviour of inflation over recent years have nowhere been under closer scrutiny than at the US Federal Reserve. There appears to have been an intense internal debate there about many of the issues discussed in this book. In particular, there has been a disagreement between those who have been loyal to the old relationships and concepts – notably the natural rate of unemployment, and who have consequently seen the danger of higher inflation round the corner – and those who have been persuaded that major structural changes have rendered concepts like the natural rate of unemployment of limited relevance.

Having raised interest rates pre-emptively in February 1994, to fend off the supposed danger of higher inflation, the Fed must have been struck by what a feeble creature the inflationary demon proved to be. Subsequently, the Fed's actions appear to have been strongly influenced by this experience, as it first reduced interest rates and then unexpectedly held them steady against insistent market calls for higher rates, notably in September 1996. At the same time unemployment first fell through several key levels which had been thought likely to trigger higher inflation, and was then sustained at a low level, without triggering more than a murmur from inflation.

To be fair, by the beginning of 1997 there were some signs of higher inflation round the corner. Headline inflation had edged up. But this reflected higher prices for the (volatile and misleading) food and energy components of the index. Core inflation had actually fallen over the previous year. Some indices of labour costs indicated a firmer trend, but others did not. There was even talk that, because of the increase in the share of national income going to profits over recent years, there was scope for some pick-up in wage inflation which would not have a knock-on effect on price inflation.

Whether wage or price inflation would pick up decisively after all, and whether it would require higher interest rates to forestall or offset such a pick-up, remained in the balance. But by early 1997, the low-inflation school had so much credit in the bank that it could withstand an eventual rise in inflation and interest rates.

Indeed, the overall feeling in the US at the beginning of 1997, both among the public at large and among policy-makers, was one of satisfaction – mixed with surprise – that the US was in its sixth year of economic expansion, with unemployment running at 5.3%, while core inflation had actually fallen back to 2.6%.

This happy condition reflected great credit on the Federal Reserve, and in particular on its chairman, Alan Greenspan, who had managed monetary policy brilliantly. Greenspan had been particularly good in sensing the importance of the structural changes affecting the economy and in questioning the accuracy of changes in the US CPI as a measure of inflation. As he put it in a speech in December 1996[6]:

When industrial product was the centrepiece of the economy during the first two-thirds of this century, our overall price indexes served us well. Pricing a pound of electrolytic copper presented few definitional problems... But as the century draws to a close, the simple notion of price has turned decidedly ambiguous. What is the price of a unit of software or a legal opinion? How does one evaluate the price change of a cataract operation over a ten-year period when the nature of the procedure and its impact on the patient changes so radically?

Chairman Greenspan has expressed a clear view on what has accounted for quiescent wage inflation in the face of very tight labour markets – heightened job insecurity. This, he thinks, poses something of a threat for the future behaviour of wages because the effect of increased job insecurity is only a transitional phase, albeit one whose length is virtually impossible to foretell. Indeed, it was possible to see the stirrings of wage inflation at the end of 1996 as the first signs that the effects of job insecurity are now fading.

This may be right, but the pace of technological and organisational change in the US economy is now so rapid that I suspect that individuals and businesses will continue to feel insecure, even at current low levels of unemployment, for many years to come.

Debt and Danger

Central bankers may be waking up to the dangers posed by very low, or even negative, inflation, but what can and should governments do? Perhaps one of the most important tasks facing governments now is the need to prepare for a period of falling prices and forestall the worst dangers that would pose. They should minimise the extent of reliance on conventional long-term, fixed-interest debt and wherever possible replace it with short-term, floating-rate or index-linked debt.

Yet restructuring the debt can be at most a helpful extra. Governments' real task is to set the ratio of public debt to GDP on a sharply declining path. This is necessary to minimise the financial risks they will face when prices fall and to give them maximum flexibility to respond to a bout of deflation by employing expansionary fiscal policy if necessary.

But to try to achieve this by reductions in spending and borrowing now, when most of the industrial world is enjoying only modest growth, would, of course, risk plunging it into the first phase of falling prices, for which it is so ill prepared. The way forward is rather to combine sharp reductions in interest rates aimed at securing faster economic growth with continued fiscal restraint, thereby allowing budget deficits to fall in reaction to economic expansion. This would then help to reduce long-term interest rates, thus cutting the cost of financing the public deficit and encouraging an expansion in investment.

Wouldn't a period of very low interest rates set off another inflationary spiral? On the contrary. Even without fiscal retrenchment, low rates are possible, indeed necessary, because of the change in the inflationary environment – in the still relatively high-inflation countries, 6% now does the work of 15% a few years ago, and in the others, even 3% is no longer necessarily a low rate. But if interest rate reductions are also required to offset the effects of fiscal retrenchment, then rates will need to be lower still.

The EMU – and Other Birds of Paradise

At the beginning of 1997, most European governments were making strenuous efforts to reduce their budget deficits, not as part of a sensible, balanced economic policy, but rather in order to comply with the artificial timetable for progression towards European Monetary Union (EMU). But they had chosen a difficult time to proceed down this road, with demand weak and confidence fragile.

Moreover, the core countries continued to be hamstrung in their attempts to cut interest rates by the perceived need to keep in step with the Bundesbank, thereby keeping real interest rates high. This posed serious risks. If European growth were to weaken severely then, despite the efforts to reduce them, budget deficits would *rise*.

Meanwhile, the core countries of the EU and the EU central institutions remained at best lukewarm, and at worst downright hostile, to the forces of global competitive markets which, I have argued, promise so much. So, if it continues on this course, Europe looks set to end up with just about the worst policy mix – high budget deficits and high real interest rates and resistance to competitive markets.

The timing of the urge to form a single European currency is, in another sense, ironic. The snuffing out of inflationary psychology is making it possible for countries which devalue their currencies to sustain a real competitive advantage because the gains from a lower currency are not now automatically offset by higher inflation.

This was the established wisdom in economics before the onset of high inflation in the 1970s. Indeed, as one country after another seized competitive advantage after the collapse of the Gold Standard in 1931, the 1930s became a period of competitive devaluation. Accordingly, when the (Bretton Woods) fixed exchange rate system was put together for the post-war world, the desire by economists and officials to control the ability of countries to devalue was not because it was believed that devaluations did not work, but rather precisely because it was believed that they did.

This view of the world started to change after the devaluation of sterling and other currencies in 1967. After the inflationary explosion of the 1970s it was turned on its head. The conventional wisdom now held that it was impossible to change the competitive position of a country by changing its exchange rate; the price level would quickly adjust to reflect the change in the value of the currency. Accordingly, if members of the EU, by forming a single currency, forsook the ability to alter their exchange rates, they would be giving up something of little economic value.

So when several members of the European Exchange Rate Mechanism (ERM) either devalued or withdrew from the system in September 1992, the established view was that these countries would soon suffer such an increase in inflation that the initial competitive advantage would be wiped out. But this did not happen. In all the countries whose currencies fell, exports surged while inflation remained subdued.

Two bouts of currency turmoil mark out the boundaries of an era. Between 1967 and 1992 the susceptibility of inflation to upward shocks meant that currency depreciation appeared to be of little use. Now that inflation is tamed, however, changing the exchange rate is again a viable tool of economic management.

Accordingly, although it was ironic, it came as no surprise to learn

in 1995 that France was talking of the introduction of measures at the
EU level to counter the competitive gains of those countries which had
broken from the quasi-fixed link to the deutschmark. In the same vein,
there were proposals that EU members which did not join the European
single currency in 1999 should be obliged to maintain a semi-fixed
exchange rate link to the single currency.

We had come full circle. By 1997, the supporters of a single
European currency now argued in favour of ending currency changes in
Europe, not because the exchange rate was such an ineffective weapon
that it could easily be given up, but rather that it needed to be given up
precisely because it was so effective.

The Euro – Strong or Weak?

But what might be the effect on the inflation policies of European
countries of the transition to a single currency, the Euro?

If you listened to the propaganda, you would believe that the operation of a single currency across Europe would, *inter alia*, provide all
Europe with a currency as firm and reliable as the deutschmark, managed by a new, common European institution, the European Central
Bank (ECB), acting as a clone of the Bundesbank.

Since one of the main motivations for the French establishment in
joining the Euro is to escape from the dominance of the deutschmark
and the Bundesbank, this is deliciously ironic. Moreover, one of the
reasons for the Bundesbank having warmed somewhat to monetary
union is that even it, along with much of German business and the
German policy establishment, has seen the damage done to the
German economy from a strong deutschmark. So once the deutschmark
has been done away with, it is an open question as to how Euro monetary policy is operated, and whether the Euro proves to be a strong or a
weak currency.

I suspect that initially European macro policy would prove to be very
tough. For Germany to agree to go ahead with the Euro on schedule,
the German-inspired Stability Pact, which embodies tough restrictions
on the ability of member states to run budget deficits after the start of
monetary union, would have to be in place. This means that the Euro

would begin in the context of a strict fiscal policy across Europe.

As for the ECB, it would be well aware that the market would be watching its every move to see how soft it was compared to the Bundesbank. For its part, I expect it to try to take on the Bundesbank's mantle and to convince the markets that it is something like the Bundesbank by another name. Given that Europe will still be beset by all sorts of structural difficulties, making for weak demand and slow growth, the fact that both monetary and fiscal policy are likely to be tight adds up to a period of very slow growth. The chances are, therefore, that already low European inflation rates could fall even further.

There is, nevertheless, a big questionmark over how long European electorates would allow this state of affairs to continue. Pressure would surely build for a sharp change of policy. It is possible that this could take the form of a relaxation in the stance of monetary policy, with the result that the Euro is then perceived as a weak currency.

What effect could such a relaxation of policy have on European inflation performance? In most countries of Europe, it should be possible for economies to expand at a faster pace for some years without causing much of an effect on inflation. But there would be limits. Much would then depend on whether and how far Europe was prepared to go in making structural reforms to the labour market and welfare system. By this stage, the competitive challenge posed by the fast-growing countries of the east, including by this point eastern Europe, will have intensified. Unless Europe opts to put up protectionist barriers, structural reform offers the only realistic way forward, and there surely has to be a good chance that this is the path which Europe would choose.

Thinking the Unthinkable

But what if the single currency plan founders? While in many European capitals it is taboo even to contemplate this subject, it needs to be considered as a serious possibility. I should say that it is almost inconceivable that the Euro plan will be formally abandoned as such. If it fails to happen it will surely be through the announcement of a delay to the start date, which would then trigger a series of market and political reactions which would kill the project.

If this happened, how would it leave inflation in Europe? It would probably result in an interest rate war between European central banks as they tried to pass the parcel of currency uncompetitiveness between them. There would be currency turmoil and considerable uncertainty, but European growth would probably pick up. Markets would again focus on the deutschmark as the best store of value and drive it higher, intensifying disinflationary pressures in Germany.

Outside Germany, there would be some relief but it would prove to be only partial and temporary. The likelihood is that European central banks would seek to shadow the Bundesbank in some way or other. Meanwhile, competitive forces from around the world arguing for budget restraint and structural reform would still be there. The upshot is that, although there might be temporarily higher inflation in some of these countries, and even serious crises in the most delicately placed, in the end policies consistent with continued low inflation would probably prevail.

Too Cynical by Half

With or without the Euro, making the adjustments necessary to cope successfully and prosper without inflation presents enormous political problems. But perhaps the greatest barrier is one of perception. There are plenty of people who, professing a higher form of cynicism, reject any claim that the inflationary environment is fundamentally changed.

The Economist magazine, for example, has seen it all before. Only the gullible, it believes, will be taken in by the current signs of low inflation. The old demon still lurks round the corner, and we must all be constantly on our guard. In September 1995 is said that 'the more extreme version of the argument – that inflation has gone forever – verges on the economically illiterate.' [7]

The confidence of *The Economist* that nothing had changed was breathtaking, not least because it was pronouncing after a period when the economic establishment had got things spectacularly wrong, first by insisting that it was vital that Britain should stay in the ERM, and then by wrongly warning of a serious inflationary danger when Britain came out.

Yet why should we be surprised? Since when has the conventional wisdom in British economics been right? From the fear of depression after the war, to the desperate attempts to maintain unemployment at very low levels, to the intricate absurdities of incomes policies, to the obsession with monetary targets, then the supposed all-surpassing importance of ERM membership, the economic establishment has got all the big issues wrong.

Even the *concepts* have seemed all important at the time, only to fade into meaningless obscurity a few years later – inflationary and deflationary gaps, pay freezes, domestic credit expansion, fundamental disequilibrium on the balance of payments, the Phillips Curve. Where are they all now? Washed up on the intellectual shore, like so much flotsam and jetsam. The currently fashionable nostrums such as the 'output gap' and 'NAIRU' will doubtless join them after a few years.

A Reply to the Critics

The Economist's lofty disdain for the importance of the structural forces buffeting the western world's businesses and employees was reflected in much of the reaction to the first edition of this book. According to some critics, I had confused changes in particular prices, and therefore changes in the structure of relative prices, with changes to the general price level, i.e. inflation. While analysis of real forces of the sort with which I am concerned in this book is relevant to the former, it is supposedly irrelevant to the latter. Inflation is to be explained only by reference to the growth of the money supply. Thus, I am supposedly guilty of a gross theoretical error. Other critics have accused me of lacking any theoretical framework at all.

Needless to say, I reject both these charges. True, the theoretical framework behind this book is not thrust into the foreground. That is deliberate. I did not want to bludgeon the reader with pages of turgid prose discussing issues like the natural rate of unemployment or the output gap, or various arcane points of monetary theory.

Nevertheless, the theoretical framework behind the book should be clear enough from the beginning and I have tried to lay it out in Chapter 8. The real, structural forces on which I place so much emphasis, which may be collected together under the idea of more intense competition, affect the inflationary environment in three major ways:

○ They inhibit many sources of unfavourable cost and price shocks, notably wage push.
○ They provide a continuing supply of favourable cost and price shocks.
○ Relatedly, they allow unemployment to be lower without prompting a wage response.

It is a peculiarity of economics that the sophistication of its intellectual apparatus sometimes stands in the way of seeing the blindingly obvious. So it is with the impact of supply-side shocks to the price level, which economists are liable to dismiss as simply affecting the structure of relative prices. By implication, other prices move in the opposite direction – provided that the money supply remains unchanged (more on this in a moment).

But direct changes in the prices of significant parts of the economy palpably do not produce offsetting changes in the prices of others. On the contrary, if there is a direct effect on the others it is in the same direction as the original price shock. There are umpteen examples – the oil price rises of the 1970s and the near doubling of VAT in Britain in 1979 are two of the best known. The relative price change on which economists lavish their attention is achieved by different rates of price increase.

Similarly, when western industrial economies benefit from favourable price shocks, such as the availability of cheap imports from the east, the effect on the price level is not lost through offsetting price rises by other, domestically produced goods.

Money, Money, Money

How can the real structural factors which I emphasise affect inflation if they do not involve changes to the money supply? They can readily do so if the level of economic activity takes up the slack, or if the demand for money is flexible, as it is. But in fact, major supply-side influences on the price level probably *will* lead to a monetary response which validates the original shock. So there may well be a change in monetary growth to accompany the change in the inflation environment, but the line of causation runs from prices to money and not the other way round.

Some of my monetarist critics seem blissfully unaware of the idea that the money supply can respond to changes in the real economy. They somehow imagine that 'the money supply', whatever that is exactly in today's complex world, is set by the authorities at whatever level they choose and that everything else has to adjust. This is an intellectual relic from some half-ingested textbook of yesteryear. In the real world, if labour unions are less militant, for instance, with the result that the cost and price level is under less upward pressure, then the money supply is under less upward pressure as well.

In fact, far from being one of my flights of fancy, this is a very old idea. Indeed, it used to be the predominant view in the economics establishment of how the money supply behaved. That so many economic commentators seem to have lost touch with it altogether not only emphasises the triumph of Friedmanite monetarism but also betrays their superficial knowledge of Friedman's own work. For Friedman was well aware that some of the correlation between money and prices (and incomes) was due to connections running from prices to money, rather than from money to prices, and he said so. Not for the first time, many of the acolytes and converts have turned out to be much cruder and more extreme than the prophet himself.

Structure or Discipline?

A second strand of criticism is that, even if the various real forces which I emphasise do have the effects I describe, they can readily be overwhelmed by inflation which arises from purely the demand side (with or without an accompanying monetary expansion). Accordingly, the big story is not the structural changes but rather the switch by governments around the world to policies of demand restraint and financial probity.

I am, I feel, much more vulnerable to this criticism, although I think that it misses the mark. For I have not argued in the book that the state of demand is irrelevant to inflation. Far from it. Indeed, I have explicitly acknowledged that high inflations are in essence monetary phenomena (even if they have their roots in some real economic disturbance). Accordingly, I have acknowledged that countries which have made the transition from very high to moderate rates of inflation have not done so primarily through the force of structural change but because of the acceptance of tough monetary and fiscal policies.

But this is not the picture in the older economies of the industrial west. They have made the transition from moderate to very low inflation, and in some of them with surprisingly little cost in terms of output and employment forgone. The experience of the last six years is of several countries in the west enjoying surprisingly low inflation in relation to forces – strong demand, falling unemployment, rising commodity prices, devaluation – which were forecast to produce much higher inflation. And the record is of both markets and conventional economists getting it profoundly wrong. It is this which my book tries to address.

But there is another sense in which structural forces have a larger role in sustaining low inflation than is apparent at first sight. As I argued in Chapter 2, the structural forces which I emphasise have a crucial bearing on the operation of monetary and fiscal policy. For the world's financial markets are now globalised and highly competitive. Governments and central banks compete with each other in the international arena for the approval of the financial markets. And not getting it, or losing it, involves very real penalties in terms of the interest rate which has to be paid on government debt. So the power of the financial markets exercises some restraint on the temptation for politicians to operate too loose a macroeconomic policy. Far from being completely separate from the forces of globalisation and enhanced competition which I emphasise in this book, the more or less universal switch to 'tough and prudent' macroeconomic policy is itself partly a product of them.

Democracy and Paper Money

Nevertheless, there are those who argue that the policy of fiscal restraint and monetary prudence is merely a passing fad. There is a good reason, they say, why upsurges of excessive demand prompted by lax policy are to be expected as a matter of course, namely that democratic governments will regularly succumb to the temptation to gain popu-

larity. Bursts of inflation are simply the inevitable outcome of the interaction between democratic politics and paper money.

In my opinion, this view does not do justice to the workings of
democratic politics in advanced societies – and does a fair bit of violence to the facts. For the countries of the industrial west, at least, the
macroeconomic temptations facing politicians can easily be exaggerat-
ed. After the experience of the 1970s, inflation is not popular with the
voters, and the very high interest rates which go with it are decidedly
unpopular. Moreover, many of the voters are now fully aware of the way
the electoral cycle may affect what politicians offer in terms of expenditure increases and tax reductions. And they are cynical.

So it is by no means obvious that politicians win elections by dis-
tributing fiscal largesse or promising to do so. There are limits to what
they can do. Indeed, in some countries (e.g. Britain) elections can now
be lost by making promises to spend public money, and parties compete
with each other as to which can appear the more 'responsible'.

This is for good reasons. In a mature democracy, even if the voters
do not initially notice or understand what is going on, the opinion for-
mers do and they influence the voters. So the attractions for political
leaders of bribing the electorate are reduced. In the words of the British
Chancellor of the Exchequer, Kenneth Clarke, 'good economics are
good politics'. And just for the record, in the post-war period, the countries with the highest inflation are not the industrial democracies but
rather developing countries with only limited democracy, military dic-
tatorships and totalitarian regimes.

Keynes and After

In my view, the 'inevitable temptations' facing democratic politicians
were not even the prime reason for the west's prolonged experience
with moderately high but sustained inflation after the Second World
War. It was not a case of the politicians riding roughshod over their
officials and economic advisers and successfully hoodwinking the
electorate into welcoming what they, the politicians, knew to be
short-term palliatives with, at best, zero, and at worst, significantly
negative, long-term worth. The view that this is how things were

grossly underestimates the power of ideas.

The simple truth is that, far from being thrust on a critical economics profession, or rushed past serried ranks of sullen, admonitory officials, the polices of sustained expansion, low unemployment and the tolerance of continuous inflation were widely urged on the politicians by the bulk of both officialdom and the economics profession. Painful though it is for many to recall, or even to acknowledge, the policies which are now anathema were then the newly burnished, 'scientific', arrogant wisdom which they, the experts, dispensed to an often sceptical political class.

If there is a single explanation for the west's inflationary disaster in the first 40 years after the war, it is not the weakness and intellectual bankruptcy of democratic politicians, but rather the bankruptcy of a bastardised economic philosophy – 'Keynesianism' – which as the world economy moved on, not only failed to recognise the altered conditions, but was also a travesty of what the great man, Keynes himself, had thought and written. Moreover, in failing to adapt to the world as it changed, and seeking to preserve in aspic an outmoded approach to policy, it was sharply at odds with Keynes' own intellectual style, which was always to question the established view in seeking to understand an ever-changing current reality.

Deflation and Crystal Balls

Many of those critics who have liked this book a good deal have nevertheless baulked at deflation. They have thought that I overemphasise the deflationary danger. Some have even suggested that deflation in an advanced industrial country is incredible. Others have suggested that even if deflation began, the authorities would quickly put an end to it.

By contrast, I am sure that I have been right to point out the deflationary danger. There are now several countries in the developed west with inflation rates only just above zero, and that is without the 'benefit' of a really serious recession or a favourable price shock. As for the central banks stopping deflation in its tracks, I wish I could feel as confident about both their foresight and their power over events. It seems to me perfectly plausible to imagine central banks in the Japanese position, where they find that there is little more that they can do.

But I no longer feel that I need to defend myself on this point too strongly, after the BIS made such a clear statement (see the quote on page 220) on the dangers of deflation. If that is good enough for the BIS it is good enough for me.

I have to confess that there have been some critics who have become obsessed with the number zero – as in 'the zero era' – in the title. 'Why should inflation be exactly zero?' they ask. The answer, of course, is that there is no reason why inflation should be exactly zero. Indeed, in Chapter 1, I clearly described two different states of the world, one where inflation carried on year after year at some small positive number, say 0–3%, and another where the price level fluctuated, giving alternative periods of price inflation and price deflation. I said that either of these would be sufficiently close to zero inflation, and sufficiently different from what most of us had experienced and come to regard as normal, that I would refer to both as 'zero inflation', and that 'the zero era' could encompass both.

That still seems a perfectly reasonable shorthand to me. Relatedly, I should emphasise that the consequences of 'zero inflation' which I draw out in Part II of the book apply just as well, only less so, to inflation rates which are not quite zero, but are still very low.

I have also been criticised in some quarters for claiming to have a crystal ball. 'How can he pretend to know the future?' they ask. It is true that I make some bold statements in the book and that it makes predictions which may be proved wrong by events. I even warn the reader of this in the Preface.

But this susceptibility to being proved wrong does not alarm me. Too much of economists' output could not be proved wrong by events because effectively it is not saying anything. I believe that my view of the future is founded on sound analysis, and I strongly believe that it is both right and possible for economists to try to say something about the shape of the future, even if they cannot see its precise details, and even if they risk being wrong. What is the alternative? To leave the field to those who really do rely on crystal balls.

Raising Hackles at the Central Banks

When the first edition of this book appeared in April 1996, it raised something of a stir among central bankers. Herr Tietmeyer, President of the Bundesbank, criticised it, while in Britain, it registered a hat-trick at the Bank of England – the Governor, the Deputy Governor and the Chief Economist all made critical comments. Is the book's message really so unpalatable to central bankers?

I mentioned earlier in this chapter how several central banks had recently become less hawkish on interest rates and more aware of the dangers of demand turning out too weak. Nevertheless, they are still very touchy on the subject. Part of the reason, I suspect, is down to an unbalanced interpretation of the book. Some commentators have interpreted its message as being that if inflation is dead, then central banks and governments can relax their policies more or less without limit, without fear for the consequences. Indeed, on an extreme view, they can cut interest rates to zero and there will be no inflationary response.

As anyone who has read this book should be able to testify, that is a travesty of my views. But I can easily see how someone could fall into the trap of believing that this was the message, and if it were, I can readily imagine why central bankers should want to resist it strongly. In their position, so should I.

I do, of course, argue that many central banks can relax policy, that in nearly all countries the inflationary dangers are less than before, and moreover that there is now, for the first time since the 1930s, a realistic danger of deflation. These three points both challenge the prevailing monetarist orthodoxy and also call for a change of attitude by central banks. But this by no means amounts to the idea that they should throw caution to the winds.

Targets and Anchors

In particular, I am far from suggesting the abandonment of monetary discipline. All countries need some form of anchor for nominal values to keep the inflationary genie firmly in his bottle. Under the Gold Standard, the anchor was provided by a fixed link to a precious metal whose supply could not be manipulated, even by the authorities. In the early post-war period, for most countries in the developed world, with the important exception of the US, it was provided by the (almost) fixed exchange rate link to the dollar. More recently, in pursuit of the same objective, countries have used money supply targets, exchange rate links to the dollar or deutschmark, targets for the growth of the national income expressed in money terms (money GDP), or targets for inflation itself.

Circumstances in individual countries differ sufficiently, and change sufficiently, that in my view it is inappropriate in modern conditions to lay down a hard-and-fast rule for the form of nominal anchor to be employed by all countries at all times. With monetary aggregates still subject to substantial structural changes, for many countries inflation targets make very good sense, not least because they are comparatively easy for the public to understand. In Germany and Switzerland there is, nevertheless, a strong attachment to monetary targets, despite their vicissitudes, and for reasons of maintaining public confidence, it may make sense for the authorities there to continue to target the money supply.

For many smaller countries, a nominal exchange rate target, involving a tie to the dollar, deutschmark or the local currency's trade-weighted average value, may make perfect sense. This then hands back to the monetary authorities in Germany or the US the question of which nominal anchor to attach to.

In fact, the US Fed has recently managed the American economy remarkably well without adhering formally to any single nominal target, but rather using judgement to assess the messages coming from a variety of real and nominal variables. Yet underlying this process there seems to be something like an informal inflation target, albeit one qualified by simultaneous objectives for real growth. The bottom line is that, although the precise form can differ from country to country, *some* sort of nominal anchor there must be, even if it is an informal one.

Message Misaddressed?

I think some of the apparent hostility from central banks derives from a difference of perspective. Addressed to a central bank, the message that inflation is dead can readily be misinterpreted in the way described above. But the book's message is not addressed *primarily* to central banks but rather to investors, businesses, homebuyers, employees and consumers. To them, the message that inflation is dead is quite different. Indeed, as I have repeatedly argued in the book, a major part of the reason that they should behave on the assumption that inflation is dead is precisely because central banks and governments will not throw caution to the winds – for systematic reasons which I have tried to elaborate above.

I suspect that many central bankers would accept the book's message when put this way. Indeed, in the lecture which Professor Mervyn King of the Bank of England gave in October 1996, entitled 'Monetary Stability: Rhyme or Reason?',[8] he made several remarks which were supportive.

He began by posing a series of questions: 'Is inflation dead or merely dormant? If dead, was it killed by a wave of creative destruction resulting from intense competition in world markets, was it murdered by contract killers chosen by an electorate disillusioned by the inflationary excesses of the 1970s, or did it simply commit suicide as inflation itself undermined the factors that had led to a sharp acceleration of prices? If dormant, is inflation likely to return to haunt a future government?' Clearly, this book's central metaphor has struck a chord in the Bank even if its message has not.

In fact, King's conclusion was much more positive than that. Although his analysis of the causes of inflation was purely monetary, and although he insisted that we have not yet reached price stability, he went on to say:

> Both theory and history suggests that it (price stability) is within our grasp provided that we continue to pursue consistently a suitable inflation target.

And he gave powerful arguments as to why central banks and governments should pursue 'a suitable inflation target'. In other words, King's message to investors, businesses, homebuyers, employees and consumers, if not to other central bankers, is very close to the message of this book.

Central bankers will be very reluctant to say that inflation is dead, for fear of encouraging complacency which they fear will allow inflation to return, and their natural conservatism will mean that, whereas bad or unwelcome things are signposted well in advance, good things are only given full recognition once they are staring them (and everybody else) in the face. But even *they* are coming to recognise that the world has fundamentally changed and that the west's long inflationary nightmare is just about over.

Dead or Dormant?

Even those who do accept that the inflationary environment is fundamentally changed, however, may legitimately ask for how long inflation will remain down and out. The title of this book is *The Death of Inflation*. But is inflation to be thought of rather like Dracula – something which can be killed off, only to reappear a bit later?

Of course, inflationary impulses *may* reappear, even while the anti-inflationary forces described in this book remain in place. A war, nuclear accident or environmental disaster could cause an inflationary shock at some stage or other. Equally, there will doubtless continue to be countries, particularly in the dynamic east, which still experience persistent inflation, and some where this is the deliberate result of government policy, even as the vast bulk of countries in the west experience next to no inflation.

Nevertheless, the real, structural forces which I have stressed in this book are transforming the environment in which the authorities seek to hold fast to their monetary anchors. Just as in the 1970s intense inflationary forces operating in the world economy made the containment of inflation extremely difficult, so intense *anti*-inflationary forces at work in the west are now making it easier. The changes in economic structure and social psychology are rendering inflation more difficult to establish, easier to contain and less painful to reduce.

They also mean that shocks to the price level which can so readily have continuing consequences for the rate of inflation are now more likely to be downward shocks. This is the sense in which the current conditions in the real economy can be described as anti-inflationary. Together with the prevailing attitudes and priorities of the monetary authorities, this constitutes an anti-inflationary environment.

A Matter of Life and Death

As to how long this anti-inflationary environment might last, it is impossible to say anything precise. But we can say something, nevertheless. The conditions which make for both persistent inflation and price stability derive ultimately from an admixture of ideas and technology. The interaction between these creates the institutional framework in which inflation either thrives or founders. Both of these fundamental forces go through a sort of lifecycle, governed by the lifespan of the ideas themselves and the people who believe them, and the period – can we call it a life? – in which a particular technology or mode of production is dominant.

In this regard, we cannot know what the far future will bring. But we can see a little way ahead by observing the forces at work now. The life of the ideas which sustained the inflationary process in the postwar period, together with the life of the people who believed them and the institutions which they spawned, is drawing to a close. Moreover, the old technology is sputtering its way towards irrelevance. This is the sense in which it is right to speak not merely of the end, nor of the conquest, but rather of the *death* of inflation.

But as it dies, the new regime of zero inflation which is taking its place, though it carries serious risks, also promises a great deal. And it is emerging at the same time as, and partly because of, enormous changes in technology, trade and organisational structure which themselves promise major increases in prosperity.

The twentieth century, which began on a wave of industrial development and expansion which promised great material advance, was hit by four economic disasters – the First World War, the Great Depression, the Second World War and the Great Inflation of the 1970s. Only in the first 25 years after 1945 was the promise truly fulfilled.

As the twentieth century draws to a close, there is another period of great promise before us. Let us hope that our leaders are bold enough in their thoughts and actions to ensure that this promise is fulfilled.

Notes and References

Preface

1   J.M. Keynes, *Monetary Reform*, Harcourt Brace, New York, 1924, p. 88.

Chapter 1

1   J.M. Keynes, *The Economic Consequences of the Peace*, Macmillan, London, 1919.

2   I. Fisher, *The Purchasing Power of Money*, Macmillan, 1922.

3   The way out of the situation facing Japan almost certainly involved monetary financing of the deficit (printing money), including through massive sales of yen on the foreign exchanges to reduce the exchange rate. The combination of a lower yen and a higher money supply offered a solution, but shifting the exchange rate was easier said than done.

4   There is a useful survey of the issue of overrecording of inflation in Nicholas Oulton, 'Do UK Price Indexes Overstate Inflation?', *National Institute Economic Review*, No. 152, May 1995.

5   *Towards a More Accurate Measure of the Cost of Living*, Final Report to the Senate Finance Committee from the Advisory Committee to Study the Consumer Price Index, chaired by Michael J Boskin, published 4 December 1996 and alternatively known as the report of the Boskin Commission.

6   It was clear that there was a sharp break from previous experience in that whereas forecasts of inflation which relied on import prices and a measure of the output gap worked quite well throughout the 1980s, they severely overpredicted inflation after 1992. See Derek Morris and Adrian Cooper, 'Non-Inflationary Growth: Miracle or Mirage?', *The Business Economist*, Vol. 26, No. 3, 1995.

7   In the early 1990s, there was a revival of academic interest in the economics of debt deflation after the surge in indebtedness and subsequent sluggish growth performances in a number of countries.

    Indeed, Mervyn King found that for the G7 countries plus Australia, Norway and Sweden, between 1989 and 1992, the most severe recessions occurred in those countries which had experienced the largest increases in debt burdens. (See his 'Debt Deflation: Theory and Evidence', Presidential lecture delivered to the European Economic Association in Helsinki in August 1993.)

    The interest in debt deflation at around this time prompted a revival of interest in the classic studies by Irving Fisher, Booms and Depressions, Adelphi, New York, 1932, and Charles Kindleberger, Manias, Panics and Crashes, New York, Basic Books, 1978.

8   Figures quoted by Michael Prowse in the Financial Times, August 14 1995, p. 12.

9   Now there might plausibly be some reluctance to hold large amounts of cash for convenience and security reasons, and accordingly banks might be able to levy a small negative interest rate on deposits without prompting a stampede into cash. (Something of the order of ½–1%,

perhaps?) But it could only be small, not least because it would be open to other banks, or indeed non-banks, to start a 'new' business simply taking in cash to look after for safekeeping in return for a small fee. Once negative interest rates strayed beyond such a low level, they would indeed promote a stampede into either currency or such new 'currency deposits'.

There have been academic suggestions for a way round the difficulty in the shape of dated notes which lose value according to a set timescale, thus implying a negative interest rate. But there are no examples of a monetary system using such notes, and for good reason. Money is what it is because there has been a need for a financial instrument which is fixed in nominal value. Dated notes are effectively a form of bill or bond. Although bills of exchange do indeed circulate as wholesale media of exchange, the fact that they do not generally do so reflects an underlying reality of monetary economies.

It is also possible to imagine a system of taxes and controls designed to have the effect of mimicking a negative rate of interest even on notes. The central idea would be a tax on holdings of currency. But how could holdings of currency be verified? The fact that there has never been an effective system of mimicking negative interest rates on a sustained basis, despite umpteen deflationary episodes, speaks for itself.

10 There are a few special cases and qualifications. In 1978, for instance, amid a system of tight financial controls, the Swiss authorities managed to impose negative interest rates on foreigners depositing in Swiss francs in order to deter speculative buying of the franc. Some people were prepared to accept negative interest rates, that is to say, paying a commission for the pleasure of having their money looked after, because they hoped to offset this loss with a capital gain as the Swiss franc rose on the exchanges. But even this episode applied only to non-residents in special circumstances and did not last long.

Moreover, in the Great Depression in the US, there were instances of negative rates. Indeed, the prices of Treasury Bills at auction occasionally exceeded par, thereby giving a small negative yield. This can be explained by the fact that bank deposits were regarded as of uncertain security, while Treasury Bills were exempt from personal property taxes in some states. Moreover, from mid-1932 to mid-1942, most coupon-bearing US government securities bore negative nominal yields as they neared maturity. The reason is that holders of maturing bonds were given preferential treatment in the distribution of new issues. Accordingly, government bonds implicitly carried an option which was worth something. This was enough to justify a negative yield. (See S. Cecchetti, 'The Case of the Negative Nominal Interest Rates: New Estimates of the Term Structure of Interest Rates During the Great Depression', *Journal of Political Economy*, 1988, Vol. 96, No. 6.)

11 It is all very well if quality improvements in cars or high-tech consumer goods can be taken to offset the effects of increased prices for staple goods and services. But you cannot eat such quality improvements. For pensioners living on a fixed income it might be of little consolation to know that if they were to buy a new Mercedes all sorts of extras and improvements would be included, even though the price had not risen.

12 Andrew Haldane, 'Inflation Targets', *Bank of England Quarterly Bulletin*, August 1995, p. 257.

13 Economists interpret the objective of price stability as subtly different from the objective of zero inflation. If the policy-makers aim for zero inflation this means that if inflation turns out to be 2% in a particular period, then in the next period they still aim for zero, whereas if they adopt price stability as their objective then they would aim for minus 2%.

14 Advocates of such a system were attracted by the fact that it spread the benefits of rising productivity (and sometimes the pain of falling productivity) equally round the system. Those on fixed incomes shared in the general improvements (or deterioration) affecting society as a whole.

The productivity norm seems to have been taken for granted by the classical economists, but a dispute opened up in the 1870s over the desirability of the productivity norm versus price stability, coincident with the onset of a secular deflation which lasted until the mid-1890s. Some of the greatest names in economics at the time – Marshall, Robertson, Hawtrey, Pigou, Hayek, Haberler, Myrdal, Heckscher and Ohlin – were some time supporters of the productivity norm. This issue more or less disappeared from debate during the post-war years of continual inflation.

15 The argument was more than a mite arcane. Its essence was the idea that because currency (i.e. notes and coins) does not pay interest whereas other assets do, the public's desired holdings of currency are restricted, even though currency is virtually costless for society to produce. If, by contrast, prices were allowed to fall at the real rate of interest (perhaps 2–4% per annum) then currency would have a return, that is, the increase in its real value, and currency holdings would be optimised. See M. Friedman, 'The Optimum Quantity of Money', in M. Friedman (ed.), *The Optimum Quantity of Money and Other Essays*, Aldine, Chicago, 1969.

16 Even so, these supports for the price level cannot be relied on absolutely. After all, the current dominant intellectual trend in the west is towards dismantling large parts of the welfare state because of its cost. So if prices were falling and there was downward pressure on wages to which the state benefit system acted as some sort of inhibition, then there would be pressure to reduce state benefits in nominal terms, just as there was in the 1920s and 1930s. Otherwise, the real level of government spending on welfare would rise, in exact contradiction of the objective of smaller government.

17 Quoted by Peter Kellner in *The Sunday Times*, 24 September 1995.

18 Some time ago, I wrote an article reviewing the costs of inflation, 'How Important is it to Defeat Inflation Anyway?', published in the *Three Banks Review*, September 1981. Broadly speaking, I argued that the costs of inflation were seriously overestimated by both the government and the markets and that reducing inflation was not the central requirement for boosting British economic growth. I stand by those arguments and that conclusion. But I do think that in a number of respects, the article underestimated the damage which inflation does, not least its effect on the level of real and nominal interest rates.

There has recently been a survey of the costs of inflation by Clive Briault, 'The Costs of Inflation', in the *Bank of England Quarterly Bulletin*, February 1995, and an excellent attempt to measure the relationship between inflation and economic growth by Robert Barro ('Inflation and Economic Growth', in the *Bank of England Quarterly Bulletin*, May 1995). Barro's conclusion was that the influence of inflation on growth was apparently quite small – an increase in the inflation rate of 10% would reduce the growth rate of real per capita GDP by 0.2–0.3 percentage points – but that compounded over many years this would amount to a very substantial difference in output levels.

19 *The Economist*, 16 September 1995, p. 17.

20 Although the pressure of demand was strong in the post-war world compared with the inter-war experience, the inter-war experience itself was not typical of the old world, indeed quite the opposite. The inter-war depression was more serious than anything previously experienced in the industrial era.

In the US, post-war demand was not particularly strong by pre-depression standards. Unemployment averaged only 4½% in the 1950s and 4¾% in the 1960s, compared with 5½% today. This looks very low compared to the 18% registered in the 1930s. But in the first decade of the century it averaged 4½%. It was 5% between 1910 and 1920 and 4¾% in the 1920s.

The strong demand argument looks more convincing for Britain. In the UK the rate of unemployment for the first 20 years after the war was 1½%, compared with 4¼% for the period 1900–14. Moreover, from 1948 until 1974 GDP fell only once, and then only marginally, in 1958. By contrast, of the 15 years 1900–14, growth was negative in five of them.

21 In the US, only about 16% of the downswing in nominal GDP growth between the second quarter of 1959 and the first quarter of 1961 was absorbed by slower inflation. Similarly, only 20% of the upswing from the beginning of 1961 to the end of 1965 was absorbed by faster inflation. And it was a similar story elsewhere. In the 1965–7 deceleration of GDP growth in Germany, only 26% was absorbed by slower inflation, and in the 1967–9 acceleration only 20% by faster inflation.

22 M.C. Sawyer, *The Economics of Industries and Firms*, second edition, Routledge, 1985.

23 This view of modern business organisations was brilliantly laid out by John Kenneth Galbraith in *The New Industrial State*, Penguin, Harmondsworth, 1969 (first published in the US in 1967).

24 We do not usually think of the US as the home of militant labour, but even there union membership rose from a mere 5% of the workforce in 1900 to a peak of about 27% in the early 1950s, though it fell steadily thereafter. In the UK it rose from nearly 12% in 1900 to more than 50% in the late 1970s.

25 Partly out of a sense of what was proper, influenced by the factors mentioned, partly out of concern that they would lose workers, and partly out of fear that their workers would come to be unionised if they failed to pay up, employers with non-unionised workforces tended to keep pace with the overall level of wage inflation set by the leading unionised sectors.

26 Because state-owned industries were ultimately financed out of public funds, their performance has on many occasions been critical to the level of public sector deficit and the growth of the money supply.

27 This is exactly what happened in late nineteenth-century America. The trend of falling prices between 1865 and 1895 can be thought of as the result of technological progress combined with vigorous competition.

28 What determines how serious this problem of different sectoral productivity growth would be is not solely the extent of the difference between the productivity growth rates in the two sectors. The size of the two sectors is also relevant. When the service sector was comparatively small, the fact that its productivity growth rate was lower than the rate in manufacturing would not exert much upward pressure on inflation.

The situation would be similar if the service sector were very large in relation to manufacturing, for then the manufacturing sector would not exercise such a powerful role as pace setter. Indeed, in economies where manufacturing was a very small part of the economy, settlements in the service sector may set the pace for settlements in manufacturing. The problem is at its most serious at the transition point between a manufacturing and service based economy. The industrial west has been in this transition stage for most of the post-war period.

Chapter 2

1 Edmund Spenser, *The Faerie Queen*, Book VII, 1596.

2 Sir James Goldsmith, *The Trap*, Macmillan, London, 1994, pp. 16–17.

3 This is not to say that there is now an absolute shortage of jobs or that the world, or even the western world, is condemned to large-scale unemployment for ever. This is an age-old

economic fallacy. Granted the continuation of unsatisfied wants, there is always an implicit demand for labour to satisfy them. But the processes of structural change, its nature, and the degree to which the market mechanism is allowed to work, may all mean that technological developments do have a marked impact on both unemployment and inflation.

4   This is a theme developed at length in W.C. Peterson's *Silent Depression*, W.W. Norton, New York, 1994. For a brief discussion of some of the issues see the *Financial Times*, September 6 1995.

5   Central Statistical Office, *United Kingdom National Accounts, The Blue Book*, HMSO, 1995.

6   See Paul Gregg and Jonathan Wadsworth, 'A Short History of Labour Turnover, Job Tenure, and Job Security, 1975–93', *Oxford Review of Economic Policy*, Vol. 11, No. 1, Spring 1995, pp. 73–90.

7   See the report in the *Financial Times*, January 11 1996, p. 2.

8   Figures on the extent of union membership in the UK are taken from *The Employment Gazette*, Department of Education and Employment, May 1995. Figures for other countries are drawn from *OECD Employment Outlook 1994*, Table 5.7.

9   The details about the March 1995 settlement come from *The Wall Street Journal Europe*, October 17 1995, pp. 1 and 12. IG Metall's proposal was made at the union's 18th Conference and reported on Bloomberg on 1 November 1995.

10 See the report in *Business Week*, October 9 1995, pp. 26–9.

11 See the report in *Business Week*, October 2 1995, pp. 21–2.

12 *Financial Times*, October 22/23 1994, p. 9.

13 Quoted in *The Wall Street Journal Europe*, October 20 1995, p. 11.

14 Figures taken from *Economic Trends Annual Supplement 1996*, HMSO, December 1995.

15 I have taken the General Motors and IBM examples from Anthony Sampson, *Company Man*, HarperCollins, London, 1995.

16 *Financial Times*, August 29 1995, p. 1.

17 See the article by Roger Boyes, 'Death of German economic miracle blights town that Volkswagen built', in *The Times*, 11 September 1995.

18 I have drawn on Sampson *op. cit.* for the examples of takeovers in the US and UK.

19 *The Wall Street Journal Europe*, September 21 1995, pp. 1 and 5.

20 *Business Week*, September 18 1995, p. 17.

21 See *Business Week*, September 18 1995, pp. 16–21.

22 *Financial Times*, October 22/23 1994, p. 9.

23 *The Wall Street Journal Europe*, October 19 1995, p. 4.

24 William Overholt's, *China, The Next Economic Superpower*, Weidenfeld and Nicolson, London, 1993, provides a readable account of China's dramatic advances.

25 Figures quoted by J. Sachs and H. Shatz, 'Trade and Jobs in US Manufacturing', *Brookings Papers on Economic Activity*, No. 1, 1994.

26 This information on Hungary is drawn from a report in *Business Week*, October 9 1995, pp. 62–3.

27 This information on Poland is drawn from a report in *Business Week*, November 20 1995, pp. 46–52.

28 The prevailing view among economists is that eastern development has next to no impli-
    cations for inflation in the west. For instance, in his massive, scholarly study of the effects
    of trade between the established and the dynamic countries, *North–South Trade,
    Employment and Inequality* (Oxford, 1994), Adrian Wood makes virtually no mention of the
    impact on inflation. Just about the only time he does refer to the issue is in a negative way.
    In the west (which he calls 'the north'), he says that the effect of trade with the dynamic
    countries may be widespread unemployment, particularly among unskilled workers, which
    does little or nothing to depress rates of pay because the unemployment is 'structural'.
    Accordingly, the trade-off between unemployment and inflation deteriorates.

    Wood nevertheless believes that the impact of trade with 'the east' is significant over-
    all. A different view is to be found in P. Krugman and R. Lawrence, 'Trade, Jobs and Wages',
    Scientific American, April 1994, and also R. Lawrence, 'Trade, Multinationals and Labour',
    NBER Working Paper No. 4836, August 1994.

29 See the article by Tim Burt in the *Financial Times*, September 12 1995, p. 1.

30 Quoted in Burt, *op. cit.*

31 *The Wall Street Journal Europe*, September 14 1995, p. 3.

32 See the report in *Business Week*, December 4 1995, pp. 22–3.

33 *The Wall Street Journal Europe*, October 18 1995, p. 4.

34 *The Wall Street Journal Europe*, October 12 1995, p. 7 and January 4 1996, p. 3.

35 *Financial Times*, September 13 1995, p. 6.

36 Both examples were quoted in a report in *The Wall Street Journal Europe*, October 17 1995, p. 1.

37 *The Wall Street Journal Europe*, October 20 1995, p. 4.

38 *The Sunday Times*, 22 October 1995, Business Section, p. 1.

39 Shortly after Mr Trotman made this announcement, however, came news so redolent of
    1970s Britain that it caused many observers to doubt whether the leopard had really changed
    its spots. Unions at Ford said they would strike in pursuit of a 10% pay claim. Management
    would not concede 10% but it did make a 'final' offer of 4½%, significantly above the infla-
    tion rate. By the end of 1995 it was not clear which way events at Ford would go.

    Even so, despite first impressions, this was *not* a replica of 1970s militancy. In the 'old
    days', Ford workers would claim increases of 30 or 40%. Moreover, if Ford were to concede
    a high increase for 1996, the signs were that other car manufacturers, let alone other
    employers outside the car industry, would ignore it in their own negotiations, leaving Ford
    with a difficult competitive problem. The old 'follow my leader' pay escalator is broken.

40 Modern economic theory has been dominated by the assumption of decreasing returns,
    which implies that, beyond a certain point, costs rise with increasing output. This is impor-
    tant for the issue at hand because it would imply that increased eastern demand for west-
    ern output would increase the costs of production for these goods, some of which would be
    consumed in the west. These increased costs would serve to offset the reductions to the cost
    and price level from lower priced imports of other goods from the east.

    But although this assumption of decreasing returns is widespread now, it is contrary to
    the thrust of classical economic thought and it is highly dubious empirically. See J.M.
    Buchanan and J.J. Yoon (eds), *The Return to Increasing Returns*, University of Michigan
    Press, 1994.

41 Quite apart from monetary mismanagement, rapid growth economies are more prone to bursts
    of excessive demand because once the development process is widely understood, the per-
    ceived stock of wealth and investment opportunities rises dramatically. There is a great temp-

tation to bring as much of this as possible into the present – setting up the new factory, building the new airport, constructing the new housing development. Meanwhile, consumers also may wish to borrow from their future prosperity to subsidise their present standard of living. (In practice, though, Asian savings rates have tended to be very high.)

This tendency may readily be compounded by inadequate monetary control by the authorities. Some of this will relate to the control of private credit, which may be extremely difficult. After all, how do you control private credit in a rapidly developing economy like China whose banking system has no history of capitalist operation and whose private sector is expanding so fast? What is credit in such a situation? What is money?

42 A similar problem also arises from other sources. In fast growing economies, there is intense competition for any particular resource or factor of production which is in short supply. Unless other prices fall to offset the prices that are rising, an overall increase is bound to result. Yet, rather in the way that the oil price rises of the 1970s affected the west, if umpteen prices are being driven up because of rapid development and interaction with the west, it may be difficult for people involved in other sectors to see that their prices should go down.

Moreover, as real income levels rise, the price of land is bid up, even in countries which do not have a significant land shortage. In countries which are acutely short of land, such as Hong Kong and Singapore, the rise in land and physical property prices is substantial, thereby creating a special inflationary difficulty.

For countries moving from an old-style socialist, command economy, like China, Russia and eastern Europe, the process of development is also complicated by problems of transition between systems. In most socialist economies, the prices of staple goods are set way below market levels. When these prices are liberalised, the result is typically a large increase in the price level which may then set off a corresponding increase in wages. (China initially dealt with this problem by liberalising prices slowly, attempting to spread the price rises over a longer period.)

43 Indeed, in theory, they could achieve both rising prices in international markets and falling prices in domestic markets, thereby forestalling the inflationary process which emanates from fast productivity growth in their international sector. In the case of Hong Kong, this is explicitly ruled out by the policy of pegging the currency to the US dollar.

But this is easier said than done. If the demand for imports surges as the development process takes off then the fast developing country may be landed with a balance of payments problem, despite its exports doing well. In these circumstances it will be difficult for the exchange rate to rise. Indeed, if domestic inflation gets out of hand, it may have to fall a good way to offset rapidly rising domestic prices.

Nevertheless, there is an example of development inflation which was successfully contained. Throughout the 1950s and 1960s, Japanese consumer prices rose faster than the OECD average. But the inflation did not render Japan uncompetitive, or require a lower exchange rate. Quite the opposite: the yen became increasingly undervalued. The inflation was being driven by Japan's very success. Without a sharp and continuous appreciation of the yen, however, this process was bound to cause inflation. But although there was always a danger of inflation accelerating, there was no necessary reason for this to happen, and it didn't. Indeed, more recently the pace of Japanese growth has slowed and the yen has appreciated substantially. This combination has transformed Japan from a relatively high inflation country in the 1960s to a very low inflation country in the mid-1990s.

The lesson is clear. If it is only development inflation from which a dynamic country is suffering there need not be a serious problem.

44 All these factors may act to encourage personal savings. In the dynamic countries of the east, people typically devote a very high proportion of their incomes to savings, in contrast to the

meagre levels in the west. (In this instance, Japan is most definitely to be classed with the other eastern countries.) If the west starts to gravitate more towards eastern levels of saving this will itself tend to restrict the growth of aggregate demand and even, on occasion, prompt the process of weak demand which brings about falls in the general level of prices.

45 Mr Jay used this expression in correspondence with me, having coined it earlier for a BBC television broadcast.

Chapter 3

1 Attributed to Sir Winston Churchill, quoted in Fred Metcalf, *The Penguin Dictionary of Modern Humorous Quotations*, Penguin, London, 1987.

2 Quoted in Fred Metcalf, *op. cit.*

3 The source for this data is 'The Housing Market and the Economy' by Joanne Cutler, *Bank of England Quarterly Bulletin*, August 1995. The figures refer to the period 1970–92 except for France (1980–92), Germany (1971–92) and Italy (1970–89).

4 There is an excellent summary of the tax treatment of housing in the leading countries in D. Miles, *Housing, Financial Markets and the Wider Economy*, Wiley, Chichester, 1994.

5 These figures are drawn from Miles, *op.cit.*

6 See article by Lucy Berrington in *The Times*, September 5 1995.

7 See the report in the *Financial Times*, January 20/21 1996, p. 7.

Chapter 4

1 Sidney Homer, *A History of Interest Rates*, Rutgers University Press, 1977.

2 It has to be recognised, however, that these are instruments with peculiar characteristics and due weight must be given to these characteristics in trying to draw any conclusions about real returns more generally. In particular, we must be wary of thinking that the real interest rate on these instruments is 'the' real interest rate which is implicit on all assets, if only these returns were not affected specifically in nominal terms and thereby affected by inflation.

3 See J.M. Keynes, *The General Theory of Employment, Interest and Money*, Macmillan, London, 1936, especially Chapter 12.

4 There is now an extensive literature on the links between commercial property values and inflation. I have benefited from a review of the UK evidence in Martin Hoesli, Bryan MacGregor, Nanda Nanthakumaran, 'The Short-Term Inflation Hedging Characteristics of UK Investments', Department of Land Economy, University of Aberdeen, mimeo. There is also an interesting unpublished paper covering both the US and UK evidence by Randall Zisler of Apogee Associates entitled, 'Property, Inflation, Interest Rates – The Evidence', which was given at the Investment Property Databank Conference in Brighton, England, on November 24 1995.

5 I am grateful to Mr Jim Ward of Savills for making this and other information available to me.

Chapter 5

1 These details about Norwich Union policies and Mr Harvey's remarks were reported in *The Daily Telegraph*, 11 January 1996, p. 22.

2 See *The Economist*, July 13 1974, p. 63.

3 *From Candles and Starch to Camcorders and Cook-in-sauce*, CSO, London, 26 April 1994.

4 CSO, *op.cit.*

5 Quoted in *The Times*, November 14 1995, p. 8.

6 CSO, *op.cit.*

Chapter 6

1 W. D. Slawson, *The New Inflation*, Princeton University Press, Princeton, 1981.

2 See the *Financial Times*, October 6 1993, p. 21, and also *Business Week*, November 15 1993, p. 38.

3 Quoted in *The Investors Chronicle*, November 10 1995, p. 14.

4 Quoted in the *Financial Times*, October 6 1993, p.21.

5 See the report by David Pilling in the *Financial Times*, January 9 1996, p. 5.

6 Somerfield Press Release, 12 September 1995.

7 Quoted in *Business Week*, November 15 1993, p. 40.

8 See the report in *Business Week*, November 6 1995, p. 24.

9 See Martin Feldstein, 'Inflation, Capital Taxation and Monetary Policy', in R.E. Hall (ed.) *Inflation: Causes and Effects*, University of Chicago Press, Chicago, 1982.

10 D.R. Myddleton, *The Power to Destroy*, The Society for Individual Freedom, second edition, London, 1994, p. 67.

11 See Stanley Fischer, 'Adapting to Inflation in the United States Economy', in R.E. Hall (ed.) *Inflation: Causes and Effects*, National Bureau of Economic Research, Chicago, 1982.

Chapter 7

1 J.M. Keynes, *A Tract on Monetary Reform*, Macmillan, London, 1923.

2 Sir Dennis Robertson, *Growth, Wages and Money*, Cambridge, 1961.

3 Penguin Classics edition, translation by David Barrett.

4 J.M. Roberts, *The History of the World*, BCA, second edition, 1993, p. 221–5.

5 Quoted in J.F. Chown, *A History of Money from AD800*, Routledge, London 1994. I have drawn on Chown's book for much of the material about the early history of money.

6 This information on China is taken from F.T. Lui, 'Cagan's Hypothesis and the First Nationwide Inflation of Paper Money in World History', in F. Capie (ed.), *Major Inflations in History*, Edward Elgar, Aldershot, 1991.

7   This is the view taken by R.B. Outhwaite in his *Inflation in Tudor and Stuart England*, Macmillan, London, 1969.

8   These figures and other data on hyperinflation are taken from F. Capie, 'Conditions in Which Very Rapid Inflation Has Appeared', in F. Capie (ed.), *Major Inflations in History*, Edward Elgar, Aldershot, 1991.

9   John Locke, *Further Considerations Concerning Revising the Value of Money*, London 1695, pp. 84–5, reprinted in Patrick Hyde Kelly, *Locke on Money*, 1991, Oxford, Clarendon Press. My attention was first drawn, not only to Locke's writings on economic matters, but also to the history of currency questions in seventeenth-century England, by a fascinating article by Professor Walter Eltis entitled 'John Locke, the quantity theory of money and the establishment of a sound currency' in Mark Blaug (*et al.*), *The Quantity Theory of Money From Locke to Keynes and Friedman*, Edward Elgar, Aldershot, 1995. I have drawn extensively on the material presented by Professor Eltis in his article.

10 The Napoleonic Wars saw substantial rises in prices in all the participating countries, but given the extent of the conflict and the suspension of convertibility of the currency into gold, the rise in the British price level was comparatively small, perhaps only 15–20% more than would have happened if the pound had continued to be pegged to gold. The explanation appears to have been the willingness to levy taxes. Napoleon also relied heavily on taxation, and prices in France seem to have risen less than in England. In the US, however, insufficient taxation saw prices rise about 120% as a result of participation in the wars between 1812 and 1815. See Earl J. Hamilton, 'The Role of War in Modern Inflation', *Journal of Economic History*, 1977, Vol. 37, No. 1, pp. 13–19.

    The operation of the Gold Standard internationally is widely accredited as the foundation for stability and prosperity more generally. In fact in the nineteenth century, monetary arrangements were rather more haphazard, with different countries operating on different systems at various times. Nevertheless, there was a movement towards general acceptance of the Gold Standard in the late nineteenth century. Portugal accepted it in 1854, Canada in 1867, Germany in 1873, the US in 1879, Austria-Hungary in 1892, and Russia and Japan in 1897. And where it was accepted, the Standard did bring some sort of stability.

11 E.H. Phelps-Brown and S.V. Hopkins, 'Seven Centuries of the Prices of Consumables, Compared with Builders' Wage-Rates', *Economica*, Vol. 23, November 1956. Clearly this data cannot be relied on for precise comparison, and it is not intended to be used in this way, but rather to make broad-brush comparisons across periods. Figure 7.1 is intended in the same spirit. I am well aware that professionals will say that in order to bring out detail from the earlier periods the graph should be drawn on a logarithmic scale. But for the purpose at hand, such detail is unnecessary, while the use of a logarithmic scale would baffle many readers.

12 H. McFarlane and P. Mortimer-Lee, 'Inflation Over 300 Years', *Bank of England Quarterly Bulletin*, May 1994.

13 Historical data is drawn from an article in the *Sunday Telegraph*, 15 May 1994, p. 27. Information on taxi fares in 1995 comes from the Public Carriage Office.

14 See P. Cagan, 'The Monetary Dynamics of Hyper-Inflation', in M. Friedman (ed.), *Studies in the Quantity Theory of Money*, University of Chicago Press, Chicago, 1956.

15 See T.J. Sargent, 'The End of Four Big Inflations', in R.E. Hall, (ed.) *Inflation: Causes and Effects*, University of Chicago Press, Chicago, 1982.

16 See R.J. Gordon, 'Why Stopping Inflation May be Costly: Evidence from Fourteen Historical Episodes', in R.E. Hall (ed.) *Inflation: Causes and Effects*, University of Chicago Press, Chicago, 1982. Gordon points out that from the first quarter of 1920 to the third

quarter of 1921, real output fell by about 8% relative to trend, but the inflation rate fell from +20% to –26%.

The historian Peter Temin has compared 1929–33 with the previous period of equivalent monetary contraction, namely 1839–43. Whereas prices fell by 31% in 1929–33, they fell by 42% in 1839–43. But whereas real GDP fell by 30% in 1929–33, it rose by 16% in 1839–43. (See Peter Temin, *The Jacksonian Economy*, W.W. Norton, New York, 1969, 1975.)

The monetarist economist Philip Cagan examined US data from 1890 onwards and concluded that over time, the tendency for prices to fall in depressions had declined so that an increasing proportion of the effect of a given reduction in demand showed up as a fall in real output, and a reducing proportion as a fall in price. And he saw this as foreshadowing post-war inflation. He wrote:

'The startling failure of the 1970 recession to curb the inflation was not a new phenomenon…but simply a further step in a progressive post-war development… The phenomenon of rising prices in slack markets is quite common.' (See Philip Cagan, *Persistent Inflation*, Cambridge University Press, New York, 1979.)

17 Some observers, like Professor Pigou, both lamented the fact and urged efforts to restore flexibility. Others, including most notably John Maynard Keynes, urged acceptance of downward wage and price stickiness or even welcomed it. Yet both groups recognised it for what it was. But a distinction needs to be drawn between wages and prices. Prices did fall substantially in Britain – much more than wages. The fact that wages did not adjust as much as prices, Keynes argued, was at the nub of the unemployment problem.

18 But there were substantial differences between countries in the degree of wage and price rigidity in the 1930s, as evidenced by the size of price falls in relation to output falls. At one extreme, Hungary managed a small rise in GDP while prices fell by more than 30%, contrasted with Austria where production fell by more than 20% and prices fell by only 5%. Italy suffered a drop in production, but did manage to absorb a large proportion of the drop in nominal demand in lower prices, which fell by 25%.

Interestingly, although Germany experienced a far greater decline in prices than Britain, this was a less substantial shock absorber because the decline in demand was so much greater. Downward inflexibility of prices seems to have been particularly serious in Germany, probably because of capital-intensive production (which meant that unit costs rose sharply as output fell), cartelisation, and concentrations of ownership in industry. See H. James, *The German Slump: The Politics and Economics, 1924–1936*, Oxford, 1986.

19 It is widely believed that the strength of demand can be put down to governments following Keynes' teaching. It is certainly true that governments put maintenance of full employment at the top of their priorities and regarded the suppression of inflation as secondary. But this had at most a sustaining and facilitating influence, for in the event it was not government deficit spending which buoyed up demand, but rather spending by companies on plant, machinery and equipment and spending by consumers on the resulting output. The confidence of both industrialists and consumers was buoyed up in a self-sustaining, interactive process. This process produced the goods – both literally and metaphorically. For 25 years, unemployment across the industrial west was sustained at levels which before the war would have seemed unimaginably low, and seem so again now.

20 There is no necessary reason why floating exchange rates should be inflationary. Indeed, it could be argued that if one of the main defects of the Bretton Woods regime was the tendency of the anchor country, the US, to inflate relatively fast, the break-up of the system might be expected to be counter-inflationary. But that is not how things panned out at the time.

21 Germany and Switzerland were exceptions. They managed to contain inflation, but only at the expense of much weaker output, particularly in Switzerland, which was able to avoid

the adverse political consequences by being able to export 'guestworkers' back to Italy and other countries from whence they came.

22 S. Homer, *A History of Interest Rates*, Rutgers University Press, 1977, p. 7. I have drawn on Homer for much of the interest rate history to which I subsequently refer.

23 M. Friedman, 'The Role of Monetary Policy', *American Economic Review*, March 1968. See also E. Phelps, 'Phillips Curves, Expectations of Inflation, and Optimal Unemployment Over Time', *Economica*, August 1967.

24 See J.R. Hicks, 'Economic Foundations of Wage Policy', *The Economic Journal*, September 1955.

Chapter 8

1 Milton Friedman, 'The Counter-Revolution in Monetary Theory', IEA Occasional Paper No. 33, London, 1970, p. 24.

2 This remark is credited to Henry Wallich by Alexandre Lamfalussy in 'Central Banking in Transition', in F. Capie (ed.) *Major Inflations in History*, Edward Elgar, Aldershot, 1991.

3 P. Cagan, 'The Monetary Dynamics of Hyper-Inflation', in M. Friedman (ed.), *Studies in the Quantity Theory of Money*, University of Chicago Press, Chicago, 1956.

4 Economists refer to inflation as a form of tax, imposed on the holders of money. Accordingly, money printing by the central bank is viewed as one among several plausible ways of raising tax revenues for the governments. But for most of the post-war period, western governments did not need revenue from this 'tax', nor were their policies deliberately structured to obtain it. Nor was the burst of high inflation in the 1970s in any sense the result of a deliberate attempt to increase the revenue from the inflation tax.

5 Generations of students have learned that the level of the money supply can be thought of as a simple multiple of the volume of cash (or 'high-powered money' or 'the monetary base') in the system which is directly under the control of the monetary authorities. This of course implies that the money supply is easy both to control and to predict. Accordingly, these same students, unless they have in the meantime unlearned some of this teaching, must therefore be baffled by the apparent difficulty central banks have experienced in controlling the money supply, and the enormous difficulty both they and private sector economists have had in forecasting monetary growth rates.

6 M. Friedman and A. Schwartz, *A Monetary History of the United States*, Princeton University Press, Princeton, 1963, and *Monetary Trends in the US and the UK*, Chicago University Press, Chicago, 1982.

7 T.M. Podolski, *Financial Innovation and the Money Supply*, Blackwell, Oxford, 1986, p. 218.

8 J.A. Schumpeter, *History of Economic Analysis*, George Allen and Unwin, London, 1972, p. 1105.

9 In Britain, Hendry and Ericsson mounted a ferocious attack on the methodology used by Friedman and Schwartz and concluded that their bold assertions were unjustified once the data were analysed using modern econometric techniques. See D. Hendry and N. Ericsson, 'Assertion Without Empirical Basis', Bank of England Panel of Academic Consultants, Paper No. 22.

10 W.E. Mason, 'The Empirical Definition of Money: a Critique', *Economic Enquiry* Vol. 14, No. 4, 1976, p. 532.

11 Paul Volcker, Chairman of the Fed, said in 1984: 'Deposit-like instruments and payments services are springing up in significant volume partially or wholly outside the framework of governmentally protected and supervised institutions.' P.A. Volcker, 'Report to a House of Representatives Committee', *Federal Reserve Bulletin*, 70, 1984, p. 313.

12 Incredibly, this dispute still supplies plenty of fodder for the economic journals. See, for instance, *The Review of Policy Issues*, Vol. 1, No. 5, Autumn 1995.

13 D.N. McCloskey, 'The rhetoric of economics', *Journal of Economic Literature*, Vol. 21, No. 2, 1983, p. 498.

14 Some of Lord Kaldor's most trenchant criticisms of monetarism are contained in his very readable book, *The Scourge of Monetarism*, Oxford University Press, 1982.

15 A.W. Phillips, 'The Relation Between Unemployment and the Rate of Change of Money Wages in the United Kingdom, 1861–1957', *Economica*, 1958.

16 For a defence of the natural rate's record in the US, see S.Weiner, 'Challenges to the Natural Rate Framework', *Federal Reserve Bank of Kansas City Economic Review*, 2nd Quarter, 1995.

   A plausible explanation for the earlier non-acceleration of inflation runs as follows: suppose something occurs to raise the inflation rate and then expectations of inflation set in. Inflation can remain in the system long after the original source of inflation has disappeared. Indeed, at the natural rate of unemployment, inflation will continue at the established level without any tendency to accelerate or decelerate.

   This is an interesting possibility but it should be stressed that it does have an important corollary – there was nothing artificial or unsustainable about the post-war combination of low unemployment and low inflation. And it also begs the question of what it was which caused the inflation in the first place, which brings us to the various shocks and structural factors, both favourable and unfavourable, on which I place such emphasis in the book.

17 This story can be made more powerful by making a further adjustment to reality. Keynes had accepted the classical theory of distribution in its entirety. Industry was organised competitively, labour was paid its marginal product and there was diminishing marginal productivity. This meant that real wages would rise as unemployment rose, but would have to fall as unemployment fell. Now this is not altogether realistic. There are increasing returns in much of industry. This means that as demand contracts, both real wages and employment may fall. Equally, as demand expands, they can both rise.

   The pricing policy employed by firms may reinforce these trends. You might expect that as demand fell, firms would opt to take smaller profit margins in a bid to keep up volume. Quite apart from any assumption of diminishing returns, this would generate lower prices. But in non-competitive conditions there could be a number of reasons for firms not to adopt this approach. They may be operating a full cost pricing strategy, or a strategy designed to deter entry. Or each member of an oligopoly may conclude that there is nothing to be gained by lower prices if other firms follow suit. Depending on the nature of the pricing rule employed, prices may readily be raised in response to reduced demand.

   Increasing returns and non-competitive pricing strategies reinforce the effects of the apparent asymmetry in labour supply. In an inflationary world, they make it more difficult for inflation to fall when demand falls, and make it less likely to rise when demand rises. Indeed, if these were the only factors at work (which, of course, they aren't), the price level would fall with increases in demand.

18 Despite these difficulties with the natural rate approach, for someone used to thinking in its terms, some of the message of this book can be reexpressed within that paradigm. You could say that the thesis is that just at the time when monetary authorities across the world

set about trying to reduce inflation by recession-inducing policies which drove unemployment above its natural rate and thereby set in train the downward interactive movement of
actual inflation and expected inflation, the structural factors to which I have referred in
this book reduced the natural rate of unemployment.

Yet, in many ways, the natural rate framework is unsatisfactory for representing these
forces. In particular, it does not really capture their direct impact on the price level.

It is very similar to the issues surrounding the rise in oil prices in 1973 and 1979. You
could just about describe these as implying an increase in the natural rate of unemployment, but this was hardly satisfactory. Even if there was a new equilibrium 'natural' rate
position after this disturbance, the path to that new equilibrium took the form of sharply
rising prices and it is not possible to argue in any plausible way that prices could have been
prevented from rising. Accordingly, it does not make much sense to describe the oil price
hike as causing a rise in the natural rate of unemployment rather than as causing inflation.

Moreover, the fact that higher prices, rather than an increase in unemployment, must,
in practice, be the transition path to any new equilibrium means that inflationary expectations are raised by the experience. That means that once inflation has been stabilised, it is
nevertheless stabilised at a positive rate, even at the natural rate of unemployment.

19 In a limited and basic sense, there is nothing new in the idea that inflationary pressures will
mount as the economy nears 'full capacity' and that, in general, we can expect inflationary
pressure to be weaker if the economy has lots of spare resources. After all, this was essentially the same view which underlay the full employment philosophy which dominated
macroeconomic policy for the first 30 years after the war. But the output gap approach goes
further than this.

20 The most commonly used procedure for estimating the output gap goes as follows: Take a
base year as your reference point. (This base year should correspond to 'full capacity', or
'normal conditions'.) Then project output forward at the assumed long-term sustainable
growth rate to reach an estimate for this year's 'potential' output; then subtract this year's
actual output from this estimate – the answer is the output gap.

Another variant of this is to try to estimate potential output by reference to the factors
of production – labour, land and capital, given the state of technology. (This is known as
the production function approach.) Again, current actual output is deducted from this
potential output to give a measure of the output gap.

21 There is even a current revival of interest in the idea, once famously proposed by Professor
Hayek, of 'privatising' money, that is to say, taking currency issue out of the hands of central banks altogether and entrusting it to the private sector.

Chapter 9

1 Sir Dennis Robertson, attrib.

2 Bloomberg Business News, October 7 1995.

3 66th Annual Report of the Bank for International Settlements, Basle, Switzerland, June
1996, p. 164.

4 See the report by Robert Chote in *The Financial Times*, 2 September 1996 and the report
by Richard Stevenson in *The New York Times*, 3 September 1996.

5 'How Should Central Banks Reduce Inflation – Conceptual Issues', presented at Jackson
Hole, is published in the *Bank of England Quarterly Bulletin*, November 1996.

6 This speech, entitled 'The Challenge of Central Banking', included a now famous passage on 'irrational exuberance'. It was delivered on 6 December 1996 at an awards dinner sponsored by the American Enterprise Institute for Public Policy Research.

7 'Who's afraid of inflation?', editorial, *The Economist*, September 16 1995, p. 17.

8 Mervyn King, 'Monetary Stability: Rhyme or Reason?", the 7th ERSC Annual Lecture, 17 October 1996.

Index